The Ultimate Wealth Strategy

Your Complete Guide to Buying, Fixing, Refinancing, and Renting Real Estate

The Ultimate Wealth Strategy
Your Complete Guide to Buying, Fixing, Refinancing,
and Renting Real Estate

ISBN: 978-0-9936717-0-8

Publisher: JAQ House Publishing
Copyright Canada, USA & the World 2014

Feedback and Comments:
info@theultimatewealthstrategy.com

A Few of the Rave Reviews from the Real Estate Investing Community

"Finally a real estate book that breaks down exactly what you need to know to invest with confidence. Instructive stories, detailed case studies and real life experiences all rolled into one. We would recommend this book to our family and very closest friends."

– Tom & Nick Karadza,
Founders of *Rock Star Real Estate Inc.*

"Authentic and inspirational, the ultimate wealth strategy is a winning formula for creating wealth through real estate."

– Ian Szabo – Best-Selling Author,
"*From Renos to Riches*" and "*Fix and Flip*"

"As a lawyer and an educator of real estate agents, I have seen several real estate investment strategies. This strategy is unique, delivers fantastic results, easy to implement, and appropriately titled as "The Ultimate Wealth Strategy."

– Brian Greasley, Educator for
Ontario Real Estate Association and Lawyer

"As a real estate investor and an avid reader, this book delivers the biggest bang for buck. The authors have simply explained, and revealed the best investment strategy for maximizing your return on investment and quickly creating wealth. This book is a must read for anyone considering or investing in real estate."

– Mike Schryer, Real Estate Investor and
Marketing Director

"As a realtor that works with many investors as well investing in real estate myself I found this book to be extremely insightful and worth far more than the price reflects. I will be providing a copy of this book to every investor client I have. This book simplifies an amazing wealth building strategy that is used by only the most successful investors."

– Rachel Stempski, Real Estate Investor and Agent

Forward by Richard Dolan

I've met thousands of real estate investors across North America (and the world) over the past decade, from small single-property owners to billion-dollar institutional investors. I'm always impressed by investors' desire to change the world for the better – for themselves, their families, and their communities.

However, there is a special class of investors that I find most inspiring – those who start off as 'regular people' with regular jobs, who (through strong focus and determination) make the leap from amateur to professional investors.

What does it mean to be a professional investor? You might think being a full time investor and quitting your day job is the mark of full time investors, and while this is an option for professional investors, it's not the be all and end all.

What is a professional?

It's having the ability to execute the task at hand efficiently *and still leaving room for creativity*. The top professionals exhibit a kind of creativity that makes us marvel. What kind of a hockey player would Wayne Gretzky have been without creativity? Sure, he understood the necessity to execute the regular jobs of a hockey player, but within the confines of the rules of the game and by using his team in creative ways he made magic on the ice.

The same analogy could be used for any top performer. Elon Musk revolutionizes whole industries. Richard Branson is famous for building businesses creatively. The list could go on and on.

Quentin, Andrew, and Jeff may not be Wayne Gretzky, Elon Musk, or Richard Branson (don't want them to get big heads), but they've used the same principle to revolutionize their own lives, the lives of their families, and now through this book, the lives of other investors. First, they learned the fundamental rules of investment, and from that stable point of knowledge and practice, they each developed their advanced system of Buying, Fixing, Refinancing, and Renting real estate.

The best part is that each of them started as 'regular' guys with regular jobs, but I assure you there is nothing regular about these men. It's uncommon in our world of entitlement mentality for people to take firm control over their lives and create uncommon results.

Each of these men has taken the basic system of real estate investment and turbocharged it with their unique system they collectively call the Buy, Fix, Refinance, and Rent Strategy.

What happens with like-minded investors find each other? They inevitably improve each other's knowledge and execution. The result of Quentin, Andrew, and Jeff meeting each other was an improvement of each other's investment system by sharing secrets.

It didn't take long for them to realize they were doing something unique that could have a massive impact on other investors. They had the dream of helping turn other 'regular' people into power investors.

This book is the result of that vision, and I'm excited because it has the potential to change many lives.

My suggestion to you, the reader, is to read through this book first. Learn the entire system as told here. Next, engage any (or all) of the authors. Quentin, Andrew, and Jeff would love to hear from you, and speaking directly to them will help you get started implementing the strategy. Finally, take massive action.

Turn the next page now and step into your dream. Follow Quentin, Andrew, and Jeff's lead to transform your life.

Richard Dolan

President & Partner The REIN Group

Resident Expert on Performance, Results & Strategy

Miami Heat World Champions Two-Peat, 2012, 2013

"The best way to solve a problem is to – define it, think about it, create a plan, act, and then evaluate the results!"

Quentin D'Souza

Problem Meet Solution

Every Problem has a Solution

Every time period has its own set of problems, and if you have the good fortune to live in Canada, it means a lot of your problems are great problems to have.

Still, we can't help but seek solutions to the problems in front of us. It's human nature, and it's right. Well, it's human nature for action takers, anyway, and if you're reading this book, you're probably an action taker.

Previous generations might have fought grand wars overseas, but we're fighting our own wars. Our wars are to find meaning in our lives and to secure a financial future for our family.

In addition, we find we're battling for our own freedom. We know we want it, but we have the dim sense that we're losing that battle. We don't have freedom as long as we don't have a firm and bright financial future (and present). We don't have freedom if we can't apply our lives to those things that mean the most.

We're doing what we were trained to do. We're ticking boxes, but one question gnaws at us: Did I choose this or did this choose me?

When we finally come to a place of honesty, we almost invariably find that *it* chose us. We got dragged along for the ride, and it's not even leading us where we expected because we find ourselves not trusting our financial future, not finding meaning.

Not being free.

We put in our hours at work, and we wonder if we'll be able to ride it out to our eventual freedom in retirement, but moreover we wonder if *we want to ride it out* even if we could.

Financial insecurity and job dissatisfaction are the twin problems of the modern adult North American. If you're reading this book, it likely means you're already looking for a solution. In fact, there's a good chance that you've already taken steps toward the solution.

You're an action taker. It's why you're reading a book designed to solve the twin problems of our time. Perhaps you've even started investing in real estate.

If so, you deserve hearty congratulations. What you've already learned about real estate investment will serve you well. The *Buy, Fix, Refinance, and Rent* strategy

(BFRR for short) is different from standard real estate investing, but previous knowledge will help you in this new venture, nonetheless.

If on the other hand, you haven't started investing in real estate yet, you're in exactly the right place. This strategy, if applied well, will save you a ton of time and will accelerate your goals beyond anything you've previously experienced. There is no better place to begin than by using this powerful strategy.

What is This Strategy?

Put simply, the BFRR strategy is the solution to the twin problems. It's the path to a secure and prosperous financial future, without sacrificing your financial present.

It's accelerated results combined with proven stability.

It's the most comprehensive, reliable, and trusted strategy for not only getting a strong return over time, but also for building incredible momentum. It's the choice for power investors, yet it continues to be a well-kept secret.

Successful execution of the BFRR strategy produces a prosperous financial future and a world of present day opportunity. It's a path to meaning and freedom, from the trap most of us find ourselves in.

Our Initiation

Those may seem like some bold claims, but they're actually understated compared to the results that each of us has achieved.

We know well how this strategy works. Each of us 'discovered' it on our own before we found each other by chance. This might seem hard to believe, but in spite of the thousands of investors across Canada there are still very few practicing this strategy.

The early days for each of us involved a lot of trial and error, but we found our way over time, and we have shared with each other exactly what works and what doesn't work.

Between the three of us, we've done hundreds of BFRR deals. The common experience between us is that after experiencing the strategy, none of us would consider returning to standard investing strategies.

Nobody does.

Why would they? Every investor that discovers and implements the BFRR strategy has the same experience. It *dramatically* changes the trajectory of their investment careers, and indeed their *lives.* The few others that use the same strategy share the same experience we have had. Namely, which we all liked buy-and-hold investing, but we *loved* BFRR investing.

From being three normal jobholding guys, to becoming full time real estate investors in only a few years, it's safe to say we know the power of this strategy when applied properly.

The knowledge within these pages has the power to change investors' lives. By carefully studying the lessons in this book, then taking targeted, specific, and consistent action, you can secure your financial future *at the bare minimum*. Beyond basic financial freedom, this strategy has much greater power. It can be the vehicle to give you total freedom if you wish.

But, we have to offer you a warning. Even though we've transitioned to full time real estate investing, we're not advocating that you aim for the same goal.

This *might* be your goal, or it might not. That's your decision, and it's a very personal one, but this book won't pretend that real estate success is easy or get-rich-quick. On the contrary, it's a lot of work, and if full time investing is a path you decide to pursue it will take several years of effort.

Don't make that decision rashly! There are more investors who've become full time real estate investors too soon and struggled (or failed) than there are investors who've done it at the right time.

So, while we don't promise it's easy, we do promise that (if properly applied) you will accelerate your financial growth by applying this strategy.

Only fools make specific predictions, so we will refrain from that, but what we can say, without reservation, is that every investor we know that has correctly applied this strategy, has achieved stupendous results.

Nobody goes back to standard buy-and-hold after learning the way.

Taking Action

You just heard about the power of the strategy, but we have to warn you again, this time against the biggest killer of momentum and ambitions.

Procrastination.

It's the cruelest of obstacles. You see, when you gain life-changing knowledge, you (simultaneously) acquire a sacred duty to apply that knowledge immediately.

It's commonly believed that knowledge is power, but it's not. Action with the correct knowledge is power.

The steps in this book are actionable. They can and will change your life if you begin implementing them immediately. However, if you wait, the chances of taking action drop dramatically.

Just as solving our problems is hardwired into us, so is procrastination. We're in a battle against it every single day of our lives. We would venture to guess that you might have missed out on other opportunities in the past by procrastinating.

So have we. Everyone has.

But, we don't want that to happen here, so take the first step right now by diving into this book. Grab a pen and take notes while you're at it. The more you actively you read, the more you will learn, and don't forget to visit us at our virtual home www.theultimatewealthstrategy.com.

There, you will find a ton of tools to kick your BFRR investing career into high gear. It's also where we're available to answer questions and provide additional support and insight.

You didn't think we'd let you take this journey alone did you? We want to help. It's why we wrote this book, but we can't help you unless you take action so get at it now, and join the select company of real estate investors who know how to apply this life changing strategy.

Acknowledgments – Quentin D'Souza

First off, I'd like to thank my incredible wife, Laura, for putting up with all of my ideas. Without her support, I would not have been able to attempt this book or build our portfolio of properties. I'd also like to thank and send big hugs to my boys, Darcy and Lucas, who make me laugh and smile every day.

There are so many contributions from people that I have encountered over the years. Thank you to the thousands of real estate investors, landlords, and real estate business owners that I have met at the Durham Real Estate Investment Club (DurhamREI.ca) meetings, events, seminars, and courses.

There are a few people that I need to specifically thank with regards to the implementation and execution of this strategy. I want to thank Ian Szabo who has always helped me to think differently about renovations. I want to thank Kevin Boughen and Georgel Miloje for the help and support around financing. I want to thank my joint venture partners; I do cherish your trust in me.

I also want to thank my co-author's Jeff Woods and Andrew Brennan. I'm grateful and appreciative to you both. It has been a blessing to write this book together with you.

When I started writing this book, I was working full-time, running a real estate investment club, and building a portfolio of properties. Most people were amazed at what I was able to accomplish. There are so many people (too many to name individually) that I leaned on at different times who've helped and supported me, and I want to thank each of them for their advice and support.

Dedication – Quentin D'Souza

To my mummy – who was always proud of my accomplishments both big and small. I love you and miss you.

Acknowledgements –
Jeff Woods

"You can have everything in life you want, if you will just help other people get what they want."

Zig Ziglar

No one ever achieves great success on their own, and the creation of this book is no exception. This book represents a masterful compilation of many great minds and a life time of real world experience. I would like to use this space to thank and acknowledge my amazing team because without them this book would have never been brought to life.

Dino Mazzulla and Kevin Fraser, my friends and business partners. Thanks for standing by my side and giving me the creative freedom, and inspiration to achieve my goals. You two are the reason Woods & Mazzulla Properties has enjoyed many years of continued growth and success. I look forward to a lifetime of building our company so that it transforms and positively impacts the lives of millions of people throughout the world. www. wamproperties.com

Marcel Lacroix my friend and brilliant Property Manager for all your support through the growing pains, and handling the sometimes daunting issues; freeing my time to focus on helping others. You make wamproperties. com a better place.

Dana Woods my amazing sister for her unwavering love, support and devotion. You are a blessing in my life and a great asset to Woods & Mazzulla Properties.

James Altmann, my friend and realtor. Thank you for believing in me at a time when many others did not. You have been a huge contribution to the success of my company. I look forward to a lifetime of lucrative real estate transactions and a ton of fun along the way!

Rachel Stempski, it has been a privilege and an honour working with you. Your professionalism and devotion have been a tremendous value to me and my real estate investment company! You are an amazing person and an even better real estate agent.

James Rocca, your valuable legal advice has been instrumental in the growth of Woods & Mazzulla Properties. You are a great lawyer and we are privilege to have you on our team.

Mike Schryer , it has been said that "when the student is ready the teacher shall appear." Thank you for encouraging me to overcome my fear and share my message with the world.

Darren Chapelle, simply a tax and accounting genius. Woods & Mazzulla properties is grateful to have you overseeing our accounting. You have been an important member of our real estate team.

Amanda Vollmer, your knowledge in mortgages and financing is second to no one. That combined with your kind heart and relentless desire to serve your clients is why I am glad you are a vital part of my real estate team.

Peter Maiuri, you have been an asset to Woods & Mazzulla properties from the very moment I met you. We are grateful to have a man of your knowledge and commitment over seeing our insurance needs, coverage, and asset protection.

Andrew Brennan and Quentin D'Souza, I could not have asked for better co-authors then the two of you. I am grateful and blessed to have the opportunity to work with both of you and proud to call you guys my friends!

My parents Carson and Marilyn, thanks for bringing me into this amazing world and providing for me when I was not able to do it myself. I know that you both did the best you could with what you had; and for that I am eternally grateful.

Last but certainly not least; if you are reading this I want to thank you for the opportunity because without you this book would not be possible. It is my hope that you discover within these chapters the strategy that will change your financial future forever. Implement what you read and wealth is just around the corner.

Dedication – Jeff Woods

I would like to dedicate this book to the amazing group of people around me, including my business partners, joint venture partners, employees, my real estate power team, and my family and friends.

It's been through your courage, commitment, and belief that I've been able to pursue my dreams with passion and perseverance. It was through you that I've been able to show the world that whatever you desire, believe in, and pursue with consistent determination can be achieved. For you, I am eternally grateful and abundantly blessed!

Jeff Woods,

President of Woods & Mazzulla Properties

www.wamproperties.com

Acknowledgements – Andrew Brennan

To my wife Sheryl – without your encouragement, support and help I would have never made the journey to where my career is today. I owe it all to you.

To our children, Cassie, Ainsleigh, Leah, Shane and Tyler, you motivate me to be successful in both business and personal life.

I met Bob McGugan when he became my big brother in the Big Brother program. To this day, I consider myself lucky to have had him in my life. As a kid growing up in government housing, he kept me out of trouble, provided guidance to help me grow, and he remains a great friend today. He is a true example of a great person.

To be successful in business you need a team that understands your business. Andrew McKay is a realtor who understands the needs of a real estate investor. He has proven several times his commitment to me as his client and friend. I thank you for all your advice and service.

I would like to thank my joint venture partners for helping me grow my portfolio, especially Tony Markic who showed faith and trust in me early in my investing career.

Bruce Johnson put aside his best interest of collecting a commission on the sale of our personal home and convinced us to convert the property to our first rental. Thank you for starting me on the path to success.

To Jeff Woods and Quentin D'Souza, it has been an honour to create this book with you. I believe we share a synergy that will lead to many more great things together.

Of course there are others that have helped me along the way. To my parents John and Cindy, Bryan White, Marcel Greaux, Georgel Miloje, Brian Greasley and David Cook, thank you for helping me get to this point.

Dedication – Andrew Brennan

This book is dedicated to our children Cassie, Ainsleigh, Leah, Shane and Tyler. I hope this book is an example that you can achieve your dreams no matter how big or small.

Table of Contents

"You have two choices; you can either move forward into growth and greatness or you can retreat backward into the mediocrity of your comfort zone. Success lies in moving forward even though it is often very uncomfortable."

Jeff Woods

CHAPTER 1

Coaching Call

The Cure

Have you ever worried or been concerned about your financial future, the stability of your job, or your job satisfaction? If so, you're not alone. In fact, most people have the same concern. We live in a time when the traditional paths to retirement and financial security are eroding. Mutual funds are a joke, and the job market is rapidly transforming.

These are all serious problems, but perhaps even worse, most people aren't happy in their jobs. It's so bad that in a recent North American survey, only 19% of respondents said they were satisfied with their job. Consider that for a moment – a large majority of people spend most of their waking hours doing something they hate. This is a societal concern.

These twin problems of financial insecurity and job dissatisfaction affect everyone, but this doesn't mean people aren't doing something about it. Simply put: we're looking for change, and the good news is that others have gone before and are ready to show the way forward.

This book demonstrates and teaches one (proven) path out of the financial and labour quagmire. In these pages you will see not only how to profit from real estate, but also how to maximize real estate investing using the Ultimate Wealth Strategy.

The first chapter of the book is dedicated to the problem of job instability, financial uncertainty, and job dissatisfaction. Here, you'll see the link between taking control of your future and the mindset required to do it. You'll also see how applying the right real estate investment strategy can accelerate personal and financial growth.

The (Soon to be) Famous Equity Café

"It feels like I'll never get ahead. I've always worked like a dog, yet here I am in the same position I was 10 years ago," John complained.

The two men have been friends for 20 years. It started when John saved Bill from the wrath of a bully at their junior high graduation dance. The jokes and banter had never stopped since then.

John was the more serious of the two, but Bill could always make him feel better since he never took life too seriously. John worried a lot about the future, but Bill could snap him out of a state of anxiety after 5 minutes – usually.

They'd shared in many triumphs together. Along the way they both married the women they loved and each had two kids. John had two girls and Bill had two boys, a coincidence that was an endless source of amusement and speculation for the friends.

Their families had shared good times over the years, and they'd celebrated career successes together – starting in their early twenties when they landed 'good jobs' with stable companies. Promotions and raises in the coming years led to homes and cars, which laid the financial foundations for them to start families in their late twenties.

They were very much normal guys but they – John especially – longed to escape the normal trappings of society. He entertained fantasies about getting out of the rat race. He knew he'd barely be able to retire comfortably if he continued on the same path he was on, and that he had many years of unfulfilling work ahead of him even to achieve that (undesirable goal)

Life was breezy in the early days of their working lives. They were accustomed to clinking champagne glasses to toast another step upward on the career ladder.

They'd done it several times over the years, but a new feeling had settled over them recently. They found themselves commiserating about the unmistakable feeling of 'stuckness', rather than celebrating. It felt awkward and unnatural, but they had made it a habit nonetheless.

Those glasses of champagne had come at a cost. Both men had fallen into an all too common trap that had them wondering if the ladder they were climbing was against the wrong wall.

They made more and more money as they climbed the ladder, but with each higher income bracket their expenses *always* matched income growth – and in many cases outpaced it.

The back and forth between income and expenses was like a great hockey game where one team takes the lead, only to see the other team catch up immediately. It sounds exciting, but as a financial fact of life it was stressful for the men and had landed them firmly in the rat race. They both had nice cars, nice houses, and nice stuff, but daily feeling was unease.

The 5-dollar lattes they were sipping while complaining about life together had become staples of their diet. They often joked that they could feed the entire North Korean military for a year on their combined latte budget.

Over the years, spending had become habit for them. It was out of control for a time, but both men had become aware of it and each had taken measures to get their spending under control.

Kids' baseball games, dance recitals, and trips to the local water park became entertainment norms instead of trips to the movie theatre and Las Vegas.

They both improved spending habits, but it wasn't as though they lived as monks, and let's be honest, there was no way savings alone would ever create the retirement they desired.

Life had changed by default, and both men were focused on getting ahead now rather than living paycheck to paycheck, but whereas they once felt they had unlimited time to achieve dreams, they were now concerned about whether or not they'd make it to the finish line.

Would they have enough cash, investments, and energy to retire in comfort and happiness? Or, would theirs be tales of sadness, despair, and discomfort?

The once quick climb up the ladder of success had slowed. Bill noticed that each step upwards seemed harder to achieve. There was more competition for fewer spots on the next rung of the ladder. Younger, more qualified, and more ambitious people were jumping the queue on Bill's road to success.

John had experienced the same phenomenon. He worked on a large sales force at a major power company, and while he'd always loved the hustle and grind of his job (and had been successful), it had become apparent to him that he wasn't sure he wanted another promotion *even if he could get one*. This fact scared him.

He felt like an aging professional athlete. They always say they know it's time to retire when they no longer love the competition. They disconnect from the process, and their game slides. The self-aware athletes decide it's time to quit at that moment. Others hang on until someone else tells them what they should have been able to figure out on their own. Quitting wasn't a luxury John had, and he didn't want to be told it was time to go – although that possibility was always in the back of his head.

In the early days, John loved the game. He loved working with a team to expand his company's reach to new markets and deepen the grip on existing markets. He loved the internal tension of cooperation and competition that pushed everyone in the office to give their best effort and perform better week after week. Most of all, he loved it when the team would crush the external competition. This feeling also reminded him of sports, but it was fading fast.

John always thought he was born for the battle, but it had occurred to him over the past 5 years that he was investing a mighty effort to make the shareholders and CEO of his company mighty rich.

He didn't have a problem with helping make others rich; it was the correlation between others getting rich and him remaining stuck (there's the word again) that he didn't like. John wanted to reap more reward for the effort he put in.

Only half-jokingly, John would say that it was like he was doing push-ups while someone else got in shape. He laughed a little less every time the company took new liberties with the pension or made another slew of his colleagues 'redundant', and this thought was on his mind the day he and Bill were commiserating over a latte.

"I'm sick of working so hard without seeing results. I don't even know if I'll have a job in 2 years let alone financial stability. *Financial freedom* isn't even a dream I can consider," John continued.

"What about your investments?" asked Bill.

"You mean those worthless pieces of paper called mutual funds I've owned for the past 8 years without so much as a penny in return? I'd have been better flying to Vegas and putting it all on a single hand of blackjack. At least I'd have gotten a cheap thrill," said John.

"I know. I have the same worthless paper. I'm talking about your real estate. I thought your houses were doing great. I hope you weren't pulling my leg about that. I was thinking about getting into an investment property," said Bill.

"Oh, those investments. Yeah, they're working well. I've made a solid return on my investment over the past couple years, but I'm out of cash and credit to buy more properties. But listen, it's not like my two properties produce much extra cash for today. In fact, it will probably be several years of just barely getting by before I can take a return on those," said John.

"Oh? I thought real estate produced cash flow on top of appreciation. Isn't that true?" asked Bill

"Well, they do and they don't. There's cash left over at the end of every month, but it doesn't make sense to use that cash for anything other than putting back into the property. There are always repairs to make on houses, especially rental properties, and even though the future is looking fairly stable, you always have to be prepared for the worst. The extra 'cash flow' doesn't flow into my pocket. It just allows me to keep the property in good shape for the long haul. Appreciation and mortgage pay down are the long term bread and butter." said John

"I guess that means we'll both be working harder than we probably should for the next couple of decades while our kids grow up. I always hear people talk about working smarter, not harder, but that doesn't seem to apply in my life. Hard work doesn't bother me. Everyone has to work. I'm just concerned about retirement. I keep hearing stories about people retiring and expecting to be taken care of by their pensions, only to find out their pension wasn't enough," said Bill.

"I've heard some horror stories, too. Pensions are a problem, but with my real estate investments I'm less concerned about my pension than I used to be. It's being 'downsized' that really worries me. It's a lot harder to start all over at 35 than 25. Being on the ground floor at a different job doesn't appeal to me now," said John.

With those words, a silence fell between friends as they both turned to their coffees. Bill was staring off into the distance, and John's brain went into overdrive.

He knew this kind of negative talk wasn't helping either of them, nor was it helping his family. He wanted to do his best, and there was a time when he didn't doubt himself, but these days he was full of doubt.

John reflected that he'd never heard his dad complain or worry. Then again, his dad didn't drink $5 lattes, either. They were different in many ways, but they were the same in their in their desire to love, protect, and care for their families.

John fidgeted and ran his fingers through his hair. "What's wrong with me?" he thought to himself. He'd noticed this feeling of dread creeping over him a few times in the past few months, and he didn't like it. He felt tight in his shoulders and neck, and he felt strain in his face. This wasn't how he pictured himself growing older.

John continued to fiddle. He picked up his smart phone, and noticed 8 new emails. "I just left work a half hour ago, how is that possible?" he thought.

It was then he saw a man slightly older than himself sitting a couple tables behind Bill. "That's it. That's how I pictured myself growing older," he thought. The man looked relaxed and happy as he browsed his newspaper. There was something different about this man than the tightly wound characters he usually hung around with.

John did what he'd done too often lately, he compared himself to the man, "How is this guy so relaxed and happy? Doesn't he work? Doesn't he have a family? How does he have time to sit around reading newspapers? He must be filthy rich. He probably inherited it," thought John.

These questions came to John's mind whenever he encountered someone who appeared to be 'winning' at life. He couldn't help comparing himself, and in his comparisons he always came out on the bottom. The mystery man's relaxed and happy energy was a stark contrast to what he'd been feeling for the past several months – in fact the past couple of years. "What can I do? I have to change something," thought John

"Okay, I'd love to sit and chat about how horrible our lives are, but I have to pick up groceries, go watch my son's baseball game, and mow the lawn. I'm out of here. Are you and Nancy still coming to our place for that BBQ on Saturday?" asked Bill

"Huh?" said John. Bill's question jolted him out of his thoughts.

"Did you forget already? Come on man, you're not that old are you?" Bill said.

"Oh, umm, yeah we'll be there. We're bringing a salad, right?" asked John.

"Yes, salad and beer. If I want to retire before 100, I can't be supplying beer for the likes of you," Bill joked.

They said goodbye, and Bill headed for front door. John was distracted and fidgety again before Bill reached his car, "I hate this constant worry," thought John.

He leaned back in the comfortable café chair and closed his eyes, trying to breathe through the stress, "In with the good energy, out with the bad," he thought, trying to recall a breathing technique he'd learned somewhere.

In the past couple of years he'd tried meditation, yoga, weightlifting, running, walking, and pretty much anything that might help reduce stress. Each of them had a temporary effect, but it was apparent he needed a structural change in his life rather than just a stress reducing habit or two.

"Excuse me, do you have a minute?" John was jolted out of his thoughts for the second time in minutes. It was the 'happy and fulfilled guy'. John's thoughts started racing again, "What does this guy want with me? I must have scratched his car in the parking lot or something. Great. Just what I need."

"Um, yeah sure. I have a couple minutes. What's up?" John answered.

"I couldn't help overhearing the conversation you were having with your friend. Your conversation was interesting. I couldn't help listening in. I apologize. You and your friend were talking about real life and real problems. It piqued my attention because it sounded a lot like the problems I had 5 years ago," said the stranger.

"Really? I mean, sorry where are my manners? I'm John. Please sit down. Can I get you a coffee? I really like the lattes in this place," John said.

Just a Regular Guy

"Thanks. I'm Jaq. It's a pleasure to meet you John. I've probably had one too many lattes already, so I'll decline. I had a couple of meetings in this café earlier today. My last meeting ended just before you and your pal so rudely interrupted me with your real life talk," said Jaq.

"What? Sorry about that. I didn't realize we were so loud," said John.

"I'm joking, John. You weren't rude. What's rude about two friends having a real chat? I'd never hold that against anyone. You're pretty serious. That's another thing that reminds me of myself 5 years ago – no enjoyment of life. I was stressed all the time. I just felt heavy and unhappy. Forgive me if I'm misreading you, but based on what you were saying to your friend along with your body language, it seems like you're a bit stressed out yourself. Am I right about that?" said Jaq.

"Am I that obvious? I mean... I can't figure it out. On one hand I don't have any right to worry. I have it all – a great wife, wonderful kids, a beautiful home, and a good job. On the other hand, I wonder if I'm doing enough for the future. I worry about my pension, about getting downsized, and about whether or not my kids will have the opportunity I had," John said.

Jaq replied, "It's interesting you say your wife is great and your kids are wonderful, but that your job is merely 'good'. To be frank you didn't say it with much belief or enthusiasm, either. I know what you mean about the pension, being downsized, and worrying about your kids' future. Five years ago I was downsized from a company I'd served for 15 years."

"What? That's terrible. I'm so sorry for your misfortune," said John.

"Don't be. It was the best thing that ever happened to me. Of course, it was devastating at the time. I was stricken with fear and worry. Actually, I had seen the writing on the wall. It had happened to so many of my colleagues and friends that I had suspicions. Worry, and a general feeling of 'stuckness' had crept into my life beforehand, but being 'downsized' pushed me deeper into the pit. There were a few months where I wasn't sure if I'd pull through, but in the end it was the best thing that happened to me," said Jaq.

John chuckled for what felt like the first time in years.

"I'm happy to see my pain and suffering brings you joy and laughter!" said Jaq.

"No, no, it's not that. I'm sorry, that was inappropriate. I'm laughing because you used that word 'stuckness'. Is that even a word? It's the exact word on my mind these days. I just finished telling Bill about the same feeling. I'm okay in life, but I feel somewhat stuck. I don't know what I expected out of life, but I sure didn't think I'd be this full of worry and dread. I mean, it seemed like my dad had everything figured out by the time he was 35," said John.

"I highly doubt he did, but let's be honest here: we were raised with higher expectations than our parents. The idea of drinking a $5 latte would be ridiculous to our parents. They'd be at home drinking drip coffee and probably working in the backyard garden right now. They also knew hard work would lead to a safe and stable retirement. We don't have that luxury. We have to do a little extra to achieve the same security and the lifestyle on top of it, which is why I got into real estate," said Jaq.

"You're into real estate investments? So am I," said John. He was happy to have more in common with Jaq that he'd thought. Perhaps he wasn't as far off the path as he thought.

"I know. I was eavesdropping. That's what piqued my interest. Everyone has doubts, and many people complain, but very few are proactive about change. It sounds like you are. When I heard you mention real estate I knew you were miles ahead of the game. That's what prompted me to approach you. I wanted to tell you you're on the right path. That might sound a bit condescending, but it's not meant to be. I'm just speaking from experience. When I was downsized, it was real estate that pulled me out of my funk and got me started on a new career path that was ten times more fulfilling and profitable than my previous career," said Jaq.

"Okay, now you have my attention. The two investment houses I own are far and away my best investments, but there's no way I'll be retiring from them any time soon. In fact they take a lot of time for the return they bring. Owning them makes me feel I'll likely have a stable retirement, but I don't see them reducing stress or making me wealthy enough to make any significant changes in life," said John

"I agree. Standard real estate investments are stable, create long-term wealth, and take more effort to maintain than those worthless paper investments. Heck, the extra work is the reason so many people buy the paper in the first place, but if properly leveraged, real estate can help you create wealth a lot faster than you think," said Jaq.

"Whoa, you must be rich! Unfortunately, I'm stuck with the two properties I own, but I can't get any more. I don't have the cash for more down payments, and the banks wouldn't give me more money even if I did," John interjected.

"Whoa, whoa, slow down John. You're making a lot of assumptions. First of all, I sure as heck didn't have much money when I started five years ago. Second, it's not necessarily about having more properties; it's about having excellent properties. Yes, more properties will accelerate the growth of wealth, but all things being equal you'd be better off having 5 excellent properties than 10 average ones. Third, you don't need much money to be successful in real estate. You just have to learn how to leverage other people's money and provide them with an outstanding return," Jaq said.

"Sorry, I guess I did jump to a few conclusions there. So wait, you're telling me I can make a lot of money in real estate without having a lot of money to begin with? That's news to me. I thought I'd be stuck grinding it out in my job forever," said John.

"That's exactly what I'm telling you. In fact, I wouldn't be here if I didn't think you could. I don't like to invest my time in people unless they're ready to make a change. Forgive me for being presumptuous, but it seems like you're ready for change. Am I right about that?" said Jaq.

"Yes. You're right. It's exactly what I was saying to myself before you so rudely interrupted," said John.

Both men laughed out loud.

Mindset

"It sounds like you're doing well. Now it's my turn to apologize for being presumptuous. You may not have been rich before, but you must be rich now. I mean, you look so relaxed and happy, and you seem confident. That's another one of my problems. I'm not confident enough to do something like that. It's all I can do to handle the two properties I have, hold down my job, and spend a bit of time with my family. I know you said losing your job was the best thing that had ever happened to you, but I don't have the guts to quit my job. How did you get so confident?" said John.

"Those are more assumptions. First of all, nobody is asking you to quit your job. I was forced out of my job. This event made me wake up, give my head a good shake, and seriously think about what I wanted in life. It would have been nice to have the stability of a good job while I got rolling in real estate. That's not the way it worked for me, but if I had to choose between doing it with a good job or no job, I'd say having a good job is far better. Second, confidence doesn't grow in a vacuum. To build confidence you have to take slow and steady action. Once you experience success, your confidence grows, which leads to taking more right action, which leads to more success, which leads to more confidence. Confidence is no secret formula. Some people get too hung up on building confidence before being successful. The two come hand-in-hand. They key is to know the right thing to do and get started," said Jaq.

"But how do you know the right thing to do? I already told you I don't have any more money to invest in real estate. How much real estate do you own anyways?" said John.

"I have enough, but it won't do you any good to get hung up on that. I started with less than you have now. The thing to remember is that you don't need much money to be successful in real estate. You need the right knowledge. Then you must apply the right actions based on that knowledge. It's as simple as that," said Jaq.

"Simple? This is starting to sound too good to be true," said John.

"Hold on. It's simple, but notice I didn't say it was easy. It takes a lot of work, persistence, patience, and learning," said Jaq.

"Great. Persistence is my strong suit," said John.

"That's a great asset, but listen I forgot to mention one key thing about confidence. To develop confidence you need the right influences in life. I'm sure Bill would support you no matter what, but our existing friends don't always have the right knowledge to help us. How can we grow, learn, or be inspired to action without a model to follow? It's vital to have a community of people to learn from along the way. If all the people we hang out with have the same level of knowledge as us, we're bound to remain stuck," said Jaq.

"There's that word again. That's a good point. I've never thought of it that way before. Talking to you definitely has a different feel than talking to most people in my circle," said John.

"That's because I've been through the battles, and I'm certain there's a simple and repeatable path you can follow. The really cool thing is that after you walk this path, your presence will inspire others. That's when life gets fun," said Jaq. "Okay, what's this really about? You keep talking about 'the path' and 'real estate' abstractly. What's so different about the way you do real estate than the way I do real estate?" said John.

Jaq laughed out loud.

"Easy partner, I want to tell you one more thing about mindset first," said Jaq.

"Fair enough," said John.

"The successful people who've gone before you are no better than you. They only *seem* different because they've walked 'the path', but there I go talking abstractly again. Let's talk about what this is really about," said Jaq.

The Strategy

"It all started about five years ago, and there are so many parallels between what you're feeling right now and what I was back then. Just like you, I felt stuck – even before I was downsized. Like you, I'd started investing in real estate, and like you I knew there was long-term potential in real estate. I'd also assumed that I had maxed out my opportunity to grow or expand. It wasn't until I was downsized that I started to think about real estate differently," said Jaq.

"How did that happen?" said John.

"Well, just like you now, I didn't have much of a community of people around me to learn how to take the right action. Still, I did have one friend named Tim that was doing well in real estate. I told him I was newly unemployed and he asked me if I wanted to work with him," said Jaq.

"I wish I had that," said John.

"It was handy for me. I've since learned that there are three ways to learn new things. You can work for free, pay someone to teach it, or you can make the mistakes yourself. Working with Tim gave me the knowledge I needed to move forward," said Jaq.

"Sounds like a great situation," said John.

"It didn't seem that way at first. In truth, I just needed to get out of the house, so I said 'yes' before I even knew what he was asking. It turned out he needed help renovating a property, and it felt great to get my hands dirty after years of working in the office. I'd already enjoyed doing hands-on work around my own home. After being downsized it was perfect work, but it was so much more than that. As we renovated his rental townhouse together, I learned about the investing strategy that would eventually change my life," said Jaq.

"You got into flipping houses? I don't know. I've heard that's really hard and risky. I'm not handy like you, and my wife, Nancy, would never approve of that," John replied.

"Easy Captain Presumptuous. I didn't say that. Listen, house flipping can work. I know several people who make great money from it. You're right that it requires a specialized set of skills, but that's not what I'm talking about," said Jaq.

"But you said you did renovations with a friend and he taught you everything about the business," said John.

"Right, but you're assuming the only way to make money in renovations is by flipping. This isn't the case. I'm talking about a strategy that allows you to earn money in the short term by adding value to the property through renovations but still keep the property and capitalize on the long-term wealth-building benefits of real estate. What if you could have the best of both worlds?" asked Jaq.

"It sounds great, but I can't do renovations. It's totally not my thing. I struggle changing light bulbs at home," said John.

"Well, some people who use the *Buy, Fix, Refinance, and Rent* (BFRR) strategy do all their own renovations, but many of them hire others to do all the work. It's your choice how you approach it. You don't have to do the renovations yourself. I sure don't," said Jaq.

"I'm a great team-member, but not such a great manager. In fact, that's why I'm stuck in my current job. I was given the chance to lead a team a once and dropped the ball. Ever since then I've been stuck firmly in the middle of the pack. I don't think I could manage a team of contractors. That's scary to me," said John.

"I totally understand your fear, but I'm here to tell you that you can do it. It's about choices. Do you want to live with that feeling of 'stuckness' for the rest of your life? Doing something new takes a lot of courage, but it's the only chance to overcome the general malaise so many people suffer with. That feeling doesn't go away without taking action. In the end it's about making a choice," said Jaq.

The conversation was interrupted by a buzzing sound coming from Jaq's phone. It was a text message that Jaq took a quick look at.

"Shoot! I was enjoying our conversation so much I forgot about picking my daughter up from her friend's house. That was her reminding me. I have to go, but listen, I'm going to be here tomorrow between 4 and 5 pm. I'd love to continue this chat if you're interested," Jaq said.

He grabbed his phone, said goodbye, and bounced out the door. Jaq was as happy and energetic as he'd been the entire time. John was still confused, tired, and slightly depressed. In his brief conversation with Jaq, he got excited many times, but in the end he was still certain he couldn't do what Jaq was suggesting. This 'strategy'

Jaq was talking about sounded too good to be true, like a network-marketing thing or winning the lottery. Then again, Jaq did say it took a lot work and a ton of patience to be successful. It wasn't as though he was selling the 'strategy' as being easy.

John chuckled at the memory of Jaq distinguishing between simple and easy.

John was intrigued, but as he gathered his belongings to leave, he was certain he wouldn't come back the next day to finish the chat. Anyways, he wasn't finished work until five o'clock, so it would be impossible. It was a nice daydream while it lasted, but there was no way it would happen. "Back to the grind," John thought to himself as he walked out the door.

Mindset is Great, Knowledge is Too

You've just learned about the importance of mindset and how utilizing the BFRR (Buy, Fix, Refinance, and Rent) real estate investing strategy can help create wealth.

You've learned that confidence grows along with success and that one success builds on the next. You've seen how the BFRR strategy combines the best of traditional buy-and-hold real estate and flipping.

What you just read and learned is valuable, but just knowing it isn't enough to reach success. There are millions of people across North America that have good information but don't take action. The next chapter is dedicated to showing you how to move from good information to action. As you'll see it all starts with a decision.

"Charlie and I only find 3 or 4 deals per year that we really like, and when we do our ears perk up."

Warren Buffett

CHAPTER 2

It Takes a Decision

Digging Deeper

Have you ever felt like you had come upon a great idea, yet for some reason you weren't able to put it into practice? This is a common problem – especially in the information age. We have all the information, but we lack the ability know-how to apply the information.

In this chapter, we'll show you how to ask and answer the key questions to enable you to execute, which is exactly what you'll need to succeed using the BFRR strategy.

Mindset without execution is useless.

Strap yourself in – you're about to learn about the importance of making decisions, the 4 phases of the BFRR strategy, risk mitigation, and how value is created when using the BFRR strategy. Understanding each of these is required to move forward using the BFRR strategy.

Making Decisions

John fidgeted at his office cubicle the next day. After reviewing the sales numbers for the morning, John had spent the rest of the day doodling and mindlessly checking Facebook.

He couldn't sleep the night before, either.

He'd decided he wasn't going to meet Jaq, but for some reason he couldn't shake the image of Jaq from his mind. He'd seen others with this 'relaxed and successful' look before, but he always assumed they were somehow different than him. He imagined they were born into wealth. Who wouldn't seem successful, relaxed, and happy after enjoying a lifetime of luxury? John never imagined someone could create so much success in five short years as Jaq did – especially after losing his job.

Jaq challenged his notion of success. It was uncomfortable. How many other people like Jaq had picked themselves up after setbacks and created financial freedom? Jaq's existence (and his success) undermined John. The obstacles he assumed were holding him back now felt like feeble excuses. This didn't fit with the story John told about himself.

His mind was unsettled, and he couldn't work. The thought that he was making excuses dogged him, and he kept thinking about inventing a reason to leave the office, and then running for the door.

In his entire working life, he'd never done this before and the thought made him uneasy. He was a good worker and a good team member, but lately he'd been questioning the value of these traits. Sure, it was good to work hard, but he was starting to think the deal was a bit unfair.

It occurred to him that he'd been a 'good worker' for years and it wasn't leading him anywhere he wanted to go. He knew he'd need to make a change (even if it was just a small change) to improve. Was ditching work the kind of small change he needed to make?

He'd helped his company make a lot of profit over the years, yet there he was, still grinding it out with no end in sight. One (half) an afternoon of hooky wouldn't hurt the company, and it might change everything for him.

Still, he was unsure.

The clock kept ticking – all afternoon. By 3:45pm, John knew he had to make a decision, fast. The Equity Café was a 45-minute drive away, and he knew Jaq was leaving by 5pm. This meant he had to leave within the next 5 minutes.

Decision time.

"Why am I so bad at making important decisions?" John thought. He was thinking of his past leadership failure again.

Tick. Tick. Tick.

"It's now or never. I have to give it a try," he thought.

John knew he'd regret not going if he chose to stay in his cubicle rather than run out the door.

Without thought, he snatched up his briefcase, put on his coat, and headed for the door – thinking he could sneak out early on a Friday afternoon without anyone noticing. After all, he hadn't done it once in 13 years. Quite the opposite – John often worked past the normal quitting time.

His dream of sneaking out unnoticed was shattered when he saw Karl, a sales team member (and company lifer), "Where the heck are you going? Everyone's heading down to *O'Flanagan's* for a couple of pints. It's beer o'clock in approximately... 75 minutes," Karl said, before laughing hysterically as though he was the first person in the history of cubicles to say 'beer o'clock.

"Sorry Karl, I ummmm, I have to go. I have to meet a client. Sorry, gotta go," John mumbled, rushing away without giving Karl a chance to reply.

Catching Jaq

Traffic was hideous that day, and as John sat in the crush of nice cars, choking fumes, and unhappy people he reflected on the insanity of it all. He was surrounded by millions of people just like him – everyone working too hard, spending too much, making someone else rich, and nobody happy. He couldn't wait to meet Jaq.

Something had to change. He hoped he wasn't too late.

As he pulled into the Equity Café parking lot he continued to be amazed. *Escalade, Lexus, Grand Cherokee, BMW...* John drove a $50,000 Volvo. It wasn't the flashiest by any means, but it was probably twice the car he really needed, "How many of these people can really afford these cars?" he thought to himself.

As he pulled into his parking stall he glanced down and saw it was exactly 5 o'clock. Then he glanced up and saw Jaq walking out of the café. John quickly shut down the engine and walked across the parking lot to catch Jaq before he got into his... *Toyota Corolla!*

"What?" John thought to himself. I thought this guy was a high roller. Here is he driving a practical car." The thought of the car threw him off so much that he forgot what he was doing.

"I thought you were a no show," Jaq said.

"Oh, um, ah, yeah. Sorry, I just pulled in and it looks like you're leaving. Sorry about that. I guess I missed you today. I won't bother you. Have a good day," said John. He was secretly relieved. This silly dream was over and he could go back real life.

"No problem. I have lots of time. I was only leaving because I thought you were a no show. My other meeting ended, so I was about to leave. I wasn't sure if you'd ditch out on work to meet me," said Jaq.

"You knew I had to work? Then why did you ask me to come between 4 and 5?" said John.

"I asked because I wanted to see if you would make a decision. This might seem insignificant, but trust me when I say it was a big move. You just chose yourself and your family ahead of corporate interests. Your company will be fine without you for one hour, but choosing to take control of your own future can be life-altering for you. Anyways, enough small talk, let's head back inside," said Jaq.

Everything felt different when he sat down in the Equity Café. He transformed from sweaty commuter to relaxed entrepreneur immediately. As he looked out the window to the street with piled-up traffic, everyone nudging each other, and saw the unhappy scowls on all the faces he was again struck by the insanity of it all. Only now he felt separate from it.

He took off his suit jacket, untied his tie, unbuttoned his shirt, pulled out a notebook, took a sip of his coffee, and said, "I could get used to this."

The Strategy

"So, tell me about this strategy. I'm thoroughly intrigued, but I'm a concrete thinker. I need to hear about the specifics and the details before I can grasp it," said John.

"I understand. I'm the same way. I had the benefit of working alongside Tim and seeing the strategy in action as I learned. I recommend you come check out my current projects as soon as you have a chance. When you see the property, along with the numbers, it'll all make more sense," said Jaq.

"I'd like that, but for now, can you tell me more about how it works?" said John.

"Absolutely. We'll dive in soon, but before that, I have a question for you," said Jaq.

"What is it?" asked John.

"Today I'll lay out the strategy in broad strokes, but to properly execute the strategy you'll need a lot more guidance. My greatest joy is helping new BFRR (Buy, Fix, Refinance, and Rent) investors get started, but it's also a business for me. Are you ready to invest in coaching with me?" said Jaq.

"I have no problem with that. If this strategy is as great as you say, it should be well worth the investment, but I do have to talk to Nancy about it first," said John.

"No problem. Of course you need to speak with your wife first. I hope she's on board because there's no better investment than your own education. I've spent tens of thousands of dollars on education and coaching over the years. You can let me know if Nancy agrees later, but for today let's discuss the broad strokes," said Jaq.

4 Phases

"The BFRR community is rather small, which is part of the reason we call it 'the ultimate wealth strategy' amongst ourselves. However, it might properly be called the 'Buy, Fix, Refinance and Rent' strategy. Others call it the 'flip and hold' or the 'long-term flip' strategy. There might be more names for it, and people looking in from the outside call us 'renovators' or 'flippers'. There are components of all these things in the strategy," said Jaq.

"It's not flipping, though, right? Nancy would not go for that," said John.

"No, but there are several different ways the strategy can be executed, which can make it confusing. To identify the strategy, we look for some basic principles that each deal shares. I will start by explaining these basics. Once you understand them, you will be able to grasp the various derivations," Jaq began.

"That sounds like a plan. I like to build slowly from the bottom up," said John.

"Great. For starters, there are 4 distinct phases of the strategy. First you 1) buy the property, then you 2) fix the property, next you 3) refinance the property, and finally you 4) rent the property," said Jaq.

Buy

"The buying phase is perhaps the most important. Saying that doesn't lessen the importance of the other phases, but without buying correctly the other phases are much more difficult to execute. It's the master key to a successful BFRR deal. There's a famous saying in real estate, 'you make your money when you buy'. While most investors know this expression, very few of them practice it. Most investors are content to just buy at market value, get a tiny bit of cash-flow, and wait while the mortgage is paid down and market appreciation work their magic over 20-25 years time," said Jaq.

"Yeah, that pretty much explains my real estate investment strategy. My properties are looking good for the long haul, but in the short term they're a lot of work for a small return," said John.

"That's how it works. It's rare enough that people invest in real estate at all, and it's even rarer that people buy more than one or two properties. Interestingly, I find that the rare ones that buy more than two usually employ some form of the strategy," said Jaq.

"Really? Why do you think that is?" said John.

"The BFRR strategy lets investors build momentum faster, and the significantly higher cash flow lets us buy more properties. Overall, BFRR investors just make more money and have more capacity to grow, but we'll talk more about that later," said Jaq.

"I didn't know it was so common to get stuck on two properties," said John.

"Yep, it's a common problem, but let's focus our discussion on the buying process for now. During this phase it's vital that investors buy *below market value*. Actually, this term is a bit of a misnomer. Still, it's commonly used, so let's stick with that term. All it means is that you don't buy a property for the same price that a similar property would sell for in the same area. You're seeking to buy below that price. Please note: It's not the case that you get the same property for cheaper. The property you buy is cheaper because you will have to repair it. Another way to look at it is you're solving a problem that the seller has. In return for solving that problem they sell for a lower price. When a seller is motivated, the lower price is the right price," said Jaq.

Normal Property Value of a Similar Property: $250,000

BFRR Property Purchase Price: $220,000

This makes a Difference of: $30,000

"Once you get accustomed to applying the strategy you'll find that the hardest part to repeat on every deal is buying right. This is because the strategy doesn't work with every property. When you do a straight buy-and-hold real estate investment there is a bigger pool of properties to choose from," said Jaq.

"Yeah, I just called a local realtor when I bought my investment properties and he found a bunch right away," said John.

"Exactly. That's the easiest way for most investors to buy, which is why it's the most common path to investment. However, if you want mind-blowing results you have to be more selective when you buy," said Jaq.

"It's important, but with the right knowledge, it is repeatable and most importantly effective. When you're ready to make the leap, we will talk about buying in more depth. For now, let's move onto the next distinct phase of the BFRR strategy – fixing," said Jaq.

Fix

"I still don't think I'll be able to pull off the renovation. It's rather scary to me," said John.

"Okay, I'm going to ask that you just pretend you're not scared for now. We will demystify the whole process in more depth when it comes time to do the renovation later. The purpose of our conversation today is to share with you the purpose and strategy of the fixing component," said Jaq.

"Okay, I can do that," said John.

"Great. Remember how we have to buy a property that costs less than the average in order to be successful with the BFRR strategy?" said Jaq.

"Of course," said John.

"Well, the trade-off for that lower price is a property that will require renovations," said Jaq.

"Right, but what's an average property versus one that a BFRR investor would target?" said John.

"Well, an 'average property' has to be in at least average condition. Since properties deteriorate over time, there will always be a couple of things needing sprucing up. An average property will always have a few things needing attention but be generally well kept," said Jaq.

"You just described my rental properties, and my home for that matter," said John.

Jaq chuckled and said, "Yes, and let me guess, you did those few little fix-ups when you bought the property thinking you were done with repairs for a while, but then a few months later something small came up and you've been fixing small things since then?" said Jaq.

"It's like you've been watching me," said John.

"Ha! Not at all, this is a normal with buy-and-hold investing. The couple hundred bucks a month of 'cash flow' you earn isn't yours. It's the property's money, and if you steal it from the property, you'll be stuck paying out of pocket later," said Jaq.

"Yep, that only happened once. It was the best trip to Vegas I've ever had, but I'll never do that again," said John.

Jaq laughed again.

"When you use the BFRR strategy, you will have fewer repairs over the long haul. Don't get me wrong, I'm not suggesting you'll never do a repair again, but since we renovate the property as soon as we buy there are less renovations overall," said Jaq.

"I like the sound of that," responded John.

Jaq grinned, "We all do. It's one of the reasons those of us who use the ultimate strategy love it so much, but the real benefit of the fix is the *value we create*. Purchasing the property correctly and then renovating correctly leaves us with a property that's typically worth the same or more than an average property. As long as we spend less on the renos than the value lift, we've created value. This created value is the master component of the BFRR strategy," said Jaq.

"Okay buddy, back the truck up. You just finished saying to be successful in the strategy you had to buy for less, which means the property is *worth less* than the 'average property'. Now you're saying it will be worth more. It sounds too good to be true," said John.

"I know it sounds amazing, but this is exactly how it works. By renovating correctly, you're able to lift the value to the same as the 'average property' and often higher. At the end of the fix, which is only a couple of months after you're left with a bunch of equity," said Jaq.

"Slow down Jaq. Again, it all sounds hunky dory, but how do you pay for the renovations? They don't happen for free. Whenever I renovate my properties it's expensive. Don't you just spend all the savings from buying cheap on the renovation?" said John.

"Good work John. As long as you continue to question everything, you will do well, but you're misunderstanding this component. It happens all the time. I take a lot of' time explaining this to new joint venture partners," said Jaq.

"Glad to know I'm not alone," said John.

"Not at all. Most people don't understand how the property value can be lifted more than the amount of money invested in renovations, but we do it all the time, which is what makes the strategy so powerful. We'll discuss this in more detail later, but for now just remember that $1 spent on fixing the property should always equal significantly more than $1 in value lift. We do this is by being strategic with our renovations. Materials, tradespeople, and planning are meticulous. *How you fix the property* is the second key component. Can you guess the first?" said Jaq.

"You already mentioned buying right," said John.

"Right. Buying for the right price enables you to add value easier. When a good buy is combined with a good fix, the results can seem magical, but they're not, it's actually the application of a universal principle of real estate value creation – improvements. Improving a property to the same level as the market will ensure the value is lifted to the same or higher, so the trick is in adding more value than is spent on renovations. There's a formula to this that we'll discuss later," said Jaq.

> **Average Property Value:** $250,000
>
> **Purchase Price:** $220,000
>
> **Difference:** $30,000
>
> **Closing/Holding/Renovations:** $10,000
>
> **After Repaired Value (ARV):** $255,000
>
> **Value Lift:** $25,000 ($255,000 – [$220,000 + $10,000])

"There's a lot involved in executing the fix phase of the strategy properly and we'll discuss it in detail when the time is right, but the main thing to note here is that you have to spend less than the value will go up. Doing that right is a bit of a challenge, but when you know the recipe, it's not that hard, especially when the property was bought for the right price, which is why we say buying is the most important phase," said Jaq.

"So, what do you do then?" said John

"Great question. The third basic component of the strategy is refinancing the property. Remember, we will ultimately rent this property, so we now need the right financing in place for the holding period," said Jaq.

Refinance

"I don't want to say this phase is easy because executing it properly involves its own set of skills and knowledge, but if you've already bought the property at the right price and then fixed it correctly, the refinance should be easier to execute. It's not always, but it's usually easier. Having the right team of finance professionals in place is key. Actually, relationships are important at all phases of the strategy, and we'll talk about each kind of relationship more later," said Jaq.

"That makes sense to me. Relationships are key to any professional or business success," said John.

"And never more so than when executing the refinance phase of the strategy, but what I want to stress now is how much momentum is built during this phase. Think of it like this – the goal is to refinance the property *at a higher value* than the total you've put into the property (purchase price + closing costs + holding costs +improvements)," said Jaq.

"Sounds great, more mortgage debt, just what everyone wants," said John.

"I understand your sarcasm. More debt is usually considered worse than less debt, but we're talking about good debt here versus bad debt. This isn't like the debt you have on that depreciating asset in the parking lot. Banks loan up to a maximum of 80% of the value of the property," said Jaq.

"So, we want the entire loan? Why not less if possible? Then we'll have less debt," said John.

"We want the entire 80% because our goal is to minimize or eliminate the actual amount of cash remaining in the property. The BFRR investor's goal is to make the total of the money you've invested into the property (purchase price + renovations/finance expense) less than 80% of the end property value if possible. On the remarkable deals, it's not unheard of that the refinance mortgage amount is *greater* than the total amount of money invested into the property," said Jaq.

"What happens then?" said John.

"Well, you get all the money back that you used to purchase and improve the property, and what's left over goes into your pocket. To top it off, you will then have 20% equity in the property as you would a normal rental property, but here you'd have zero dollars invested. It's an infinite return," said Jaq.

"That sounds remarkable. How often does it happen that way?" said John.

"Full disclosure – that's not every deal. You will hit homeruns once in a while, but the singles win the game. What I just described is the best-case scenario, and most people who practice the BFRR strategy get the odd homerun, but I want to stress that you don't need to do this every time to be successful. A 'normal' deal using the BFRR strategy results in *some* cash remaining in the property, but not nearly as much as with a traditional buy-and-hold deal," said Jaq.

Average Property Value: $250,000

Purchase Price: $220,000

Difference: $30,000

Down Payment: $44,000

Closing/Holding/Renovations: $10,000

Cash Required for Purchase and Renovation: $54,000

Refinanced Value: $255,000

Net Value Created: $25,000 ($255,000 − [$220,000 + $10,000])

Refinance Amount: $204,000 (80% of $255,000)

Cash Returned: $28,000 (($204,000 New Mortgage)– (176,000 Old Mortgage))

Money Left in Property with Refinance: $26,000 ($54,000-$28,000)

Equity Return on Cash Remaining (EROCR): 96% (Net Value Created/Money Left in Property with Refinance)

> **Total Investment Left in 'Average Property' not Using the Strategy:** $54,000 ([220,000 x 20% = 44,000] +$10,000)

"I can see how it would be powerful to pull all or at least a big chunk of the initially invested money out, but I'm still stuck on the money thing. Where do you expect me to get so much money to begin with? How does this work if there's nothing for me to invest with in the first place?" said John.

"Listen, not many people have that kind of money laying around on any given day. Like most BFRR investors you'll have to leverage other people's money to achieve lasting success. You gain momentum that way because when you give investors an amazing return on their investment they tend to tell their friends. We'll talk about money partners later. For now, let's move onto the next distinct phase – renting," said Jaq.

Rent

"Buy-and-hold investing isn't flashy, but I'm not here to belittle it. Most investors stick with buy-and-hold because it works and it's simple. The key to buy-and-hold is in that word – hold. The longer you own real estate the more powerful it becomes. Equity is created by mortgage pay down alone – even if there is no appreciation, but you have to hold the property to make that happen. If you hold the property long enough there's usually market appreciation, too," said Jaq.

"This is why I'm holding onto my two properties," said John.

"Right, and this value of long term holding is exactly why BFRR investors also hold properties long term. Using the BFRR strategy we benefit over time like buy-and-hold real estate investors, but we also like to benefit from the creation of value on the front end, too," said Jaq.

"So, on the back-end it looks just like a normal buy-and-hold investment?" said John.

"Yes indeed, and it is pretty much a normal buy-and-hold investment at that point. What makes it different is what you do on the front end," said Jaq.

"Right. Those difference are that a) there's a lot less of the investor's cash remaining in the property, and b) it's already been renovated, and c) there's created value," said John.

"You've got it right, but I want to point out one more thing – the power of not selling. Many investors' goal is to raise the value of a property and then make money by selling the property – in other words flipping. To the untrained eye, it looks like we're doing a flip on the front end of the strategy. Other investors raise value by holding for a long time, then and selling when the value appreciates. This is a standard buy-and-hold. Our BFRR deals look like this on the back end – to the untrained eye. However, as we know it's not the same because we've already added value through our buy and fix phases," said Jaq.

"Right, so by using the strategy we're combining the best of flipping and buy-and-hold," said John.

"Right, and there's one big problem that's not discussed by flippers or buy-and-holders. The problem is selling because profit is eroded by the cost of selling. By the time you pay legal fees, realtor fees, staging fees, and sometimes mortgage breaking fees 10% of the total value is usually gone," Said Jaq.

"That's a lot," said John.

"I know. It's not much better than mutual funds at that point, and to make matters worse, it's easy to get a big tax bill if you haven't structured your business right. When you consider these costs, it makes more sense to hold and refinance. This is why flipping is costly and buy-and-hold is stable," said Jaq.

"I hadn't thought of it like that before. The same thing happens on my mutual funds. I mean, the statement they send me looks good (although it doesn't always), but the management expense ratio fees I pay always erode the real return. When I bought them I wasn't aware. It was my fault since I didn't read the fine print. I'd hate to think that's what might happen with my real estate," said John.

"Well, if your investment strategy involves lots of selling, then you're guaranteed to be paying a lot of fees and withering away returns, but the longer you hold the property, the less money you waste on fees. Cash flows go up over time as well," said Jaq.

"Right, so holding is important. Well, the good news is that I can tell Nancy I won't be flipping," said John.

"Definitely not. The BFRR strategy derives its power from the rare combination of immediate money and long-term wealth. With only money now (like on a flip), you're always looking for another deal – in essence real estate is like a job. On the other hand, if you do buy-and-hold, you're only making money later, which means it's an awful lot like any other long term investment play. In the future you'll feel wealthy, but it will be several years until that day arrives. The BFRR strategy makes you money now and makes you wealthy in the long term," said Jaq.

"Sounds like a killer combo," said John.

"It is, and people who discover the BFRR strategy never go back. Listen John, it's been a great time chatting with you, but I do have to go soon. Before I do I want to discuss risk mitigation," said Jaq.

Risk Mitigation

"I'm looking forward to this. I have to admit, the whole time we've been talking I've had an uneasy feeling like this is somehow riskier than a normal buy-and-hold investment. It's a bunch of things I'm not familiar with. The biggest question in my mind this whole time has been, 'what if you get stuck with a bad property?' There has to be some risk that the value lift won't be high enough and that you end up owning a property that doesn't refinance like you described, right?" said John.

"Great question. This strategy wouldn't be so powerful if risk mitigation wasn't built in. It comes down to two things: 1) built in equity, and 2) multiple exit strategies," said Jaq.

"Okay, I think I understand the built-in equity part. You're referring to the fact that on each BFRR deal you buy below market value and then add value through strategic renovations, right?" said John.

"Yep. I've also called it *created value.* Having equity is the best risk mitigation you can ever have in real estate. The more equity, the more likely you can attract money and get it refinanced. Refinancing is difficult if there's not enough equity," said Jaq.

"What happens if we can't refinance," said John.

"Without a refinance you may not be able to recover the cash input of the renovation. However, that should never happen as long as you remain obsessed with equity. Buy right, renovate right, raise value," said Jaq

"Okay, I understand the built-in equity side of risk mitigation, but what's the multiple exit strategies part about?" said John

"This means you'll never be 'stuck' with a property. The great fear with real estate is that you end up holding a property that costs you more for mortgage, property tax, and other expenses than it earns in rent. Using BFRR we always make sure that *even in a worst-case scenario* we could still rent the property without losing money monthly," said Jaq.

"So you just keep the initial financing on the property, consider the renovation costs to be sunk and rent it out?" said John.

"That's right, and we also have the option to sell since the property is already renovated. This isn't our goal in the BFRR strategy, but it's always nice to know we could sell and walk away without losing money," said Jaq.

"No doubt! Nancy would kill me if I did. She's has a sharp business mind and won't let a bad idea get past her," said John.

"That's a good thing. It forces you to refine your thinking. If it's not a good idea, she'll catch it before you try. Just like you had to make a decision to come here today, you'll have to make another commitment to showing her the power of the strategy if you choose to give it a try," said Jaq.

"I get a bit nervous with tests. I feel like if I dive into this I'm going to be asking you a lot of questions. I'm ready to hire you as my coach, but I just need to get Nancy on board first," said John.

"Absolutely. I'll be ready when you are. Nothing makes me happier than to see someone else take control of his or her financial future. It's why I coach BFRR investors. I hired my friend Tim to coach me when I started, and I never would have made it without his help. It's critical to find others who've done the same thing you're trying to do," said Jaq.

"I can see that. There is a lot to consider here," said John.

"There certainly is. One more thing I wanted to mention was that it helps to surround yourself with the right people. Hiring me to coach you will be helpful, but it's also important to regularly discuss progress with your peers, too. I recommend you join the local Cashflowsville Real Estate Investment Club. I'm a member and there are others in the club doing the BFRR strategy," said Jaq.

"That would be great. It's nice to have some support," said John.

"It's the best. Listen, I have to run now but I want you to remember one thing. Knowledge is power, but a little knowledge is dangerous. Today I've only shared the 10,000-foot view of the strategy. Don't rush into anything. Go home, share this idea with your wife, and think seriously about it. Call me if you're ready to make an investment in yourself and your family's financial future. Here's my number, call me if and when you're ready for the next step," said Jaq.

Jaq passed his business card to John and made his way for the door. For the second day in a row he experienced a wide range of emotions as he sat alone. On one hand he was excited by the possibilities, but on the other hand he was paralyzed with fear. Would Nancy support this venture? How was he going to manage a renovation?

John sat for a few more minutes before heading home. He had a big conversation ahead of him, and he didn't know what the outcome would be.

Building the Support Team

John rehearsed his 'pitch' all the way home. He and Nancy had discussed their financial picture several times in the past, and they were always trying to find ways to improve. Together they'd gotten their spending (mostly) under control, which was good, but they needed to do more.

They'd worked together on improving their investment picture, and it was Nancy who'd first introduced the idea of real estate investing to John. She had a good business mind and was as focused or perhaps more focused than John on making things better.

The two had different approaches and bridging the gap between their different thinking could be difficult at times. John had been known to rush off on tangents, but Nancy was more methodical. He was nervous that Nancy would think him hasty, so he made an effort to present the strategy simply.

He pulled his car into the driveway and saw that Nancy had just arrived home with their two girls. John got out of his car and his two daughters ran to him for a hug. After a happy greeting, the girls ran off to play in the backyard, leaving John some time to chat with Nancy.

He walked in the front door, gave Nancy a kiss, and decided to get right into it, "Nancy, I learned about a unique real estate investment strategy today. Do you want to hear about it?"

"Ummm, yeah sure. I need a drink of water, though. Want to wait a minute and join me in the living room after I grab some water?" said Nancy.

"You go to the living room, and I'll bring us both a glass," said John.

A minute later he settled into his comfortable chair in the living room, "Well, you know how real estate is the best investment we've made, right? Today I learned about a way to profit from the long-term benefits of real estate while still creating wealth in the short term. How does that sound to you?" said John.

"It sounds incredible, but most things that sound too good to be true are too good to be true. What's the catch?" said Nancy.

"There's no catch. It's called the Buy, Fix, Refinance, and Rent strategy, and it uses the time-tested principles of value investing, built-in equity, and risk mitigation to maximize return on investment," said John.

"Fix? You mean like a flip? I've heard of people doing well in flipping, but I've also heard it's a difficult strategy that takes a lot of effort to pull off. How are you and I going to pull that off? Quitting our jobs isn't an option," said Nancy.

"No, we don't have to quit our jobs. It's not the same as flipping. Yes, we have to do some renovating, but we can hire others to do the work, and the turnaround time isn't too drastic. From the time we buy the property until the time we refinance it and rent it should only take a couple of months. Listen, I have a lot to learn still," said John.

He continued to explain everything he could remember about the strategy that he'd discussed with Jaq. He mixed in his own healthy dose of skepticism and explained to Nancy about meeting Jaq and the fact that Jaq was willing to coach them through the strategy.

"Well, I like that we'd have help pulling it off, but I need to meet Jaq and ask him several questions. I need to see real deals he's done before I'd believe it. It sounds a little too good to be true, but I'm impressed with you. You seem cautious and level-headed about this," said Nancy.

"Well, I need to make change, but I'm aware of the difference between a get rich quick scheme and a real path to wealth. You know how work is and you know the risks we run by just staying on the same path we've always been on. I'm ready to try this and see if it works," said John.

"Okay, let's meet with Jaq and learn about the next phase," said Nancy.

John had to admit something felt different about this. He was cautiously optimistic that he could make it work, and he had a good feel for Jaq. The strategy seemed legitimate, and he was excited to learn more. He picked up his phone and called Jaq.

"Nancy wants to meet you and move forward. Of course, she has a lot of questions. Do you have time to meet this weekend?" said John.

"Thrilled to hear it John. I'm excited to meet your better half," Jaq chuckled.

"I'd protest, but you're 100% right. Nancy is a gem, and I'm excited to introduce the two of you. How does Sunday morning at the Equity Café sound? My in-laws will take care of my girls for the morning, and Nancy and I will have time to chat," said John.

"Sounds great. See you then," said Jaq.

They hung up the phone and John enjoyed his Friday and Saturday thrilled that he was finally moving forward out of the fear and uncertainty that his life had been filled with over the past several years.

The Grand Scheme

In this chapter you learned about the power of making a decision to better your future. Financial improvement starts with a decision, just as John decided to skip an hour of work and meet Jaq.

You also learned about the 4 phases of the Buy, Fix, Refinance and Rent strategy, how value is created using the BFRR strategy, and about risk mitigation. These together acted as a broad overview of the strategy.

In addition, you learned about the importance of surrounding yourself with the right kind of people.

This chapter helped move you from an initial understanding to the beginnings of taking action. However, executing the BFRR strategy requires a thorough preparation.

Too many real estate investors jump into a new strategy without taking the preparation steps. These naïve investors end up like pigs at the slaughter. It's not a pretty sight, and it happens most often with some kind of renovations, whether it's unprepared flippers or normal renovators.

So, while the last chapter was a good introduction to the strategy, it won't be very useful without the next step – preparation. The next chapter discusses this vital step. Read on to learn.

"The meeting of preparation with opportunity generates the offspring we call luck."

Tony Robbins

CHAPTER 3

Preparation

Failing to Prepare is Preparing to Fail

Have you ever felt unprepared for a big task or job? Of course you have, we all have at one point. Some people learn, while others continue to struggle. Most of us desperately want to be prepared in our work, business, or life, but often we just don't know how to prepare, so we end up scrambling through.

Scrambling once or twice isn't so bad as long as we learn from the experience and develop systems to be prepared for the next time. Still, many never develop a repeatable system, especially in real estate investing, which explains why most investors stop growing their business after 1 or 2 properties.

Still, it's necessary to scramble even the first time. Others have gone before you, and they can teach you the system for proper BFRR pre-investment preparation. Learning from others' mistakes is a master step to success in real estate investment.

The last chapter helped you get a better understanding of the key points of the BFRR strategy, but just knowing isn't enough. This chapter will help take you from a simple understanding into skillful preparation, which is the first major step to BFRR success.

Sunday Meeting

John and Nancy walked into the Equity Café, which was already familiar to John. It was impossible to miss the sight of Jaq eagerly waiting for them. They were right on time, but it looked like Jaq had already been there for a while. He looked up and greeted John and Nancy with a smile when they walked in.

"Hi guys. Nancy, I'm Jaq. Nice to meet you," said Jaq.

"Nice to meet you, too," said Nancy. She warmed to his earnest personality immediately. He was a nice surprise as she was expecting more of a 'shark' than a good guy. Jaq didn't fit her stereotype.

"Listen guys, I hope you don't mind my abruptness, but I think we all know why we're here, so is it okay if we jump right into it?" said Jaq.

"Absolutely," John and Nancy said in unison.

They all chuckled and Jaq got started, "John, I know you've already explained everything we discussed the other day to Nancy. That was just an overview, but if you plan to move forward you'll have to learn the details from start to finish. Like any good process, the BFRR strategy requires a preparation phase. Have either of you ever worked in or seen a busy restaurant kitchen at work?" asked Jaq.

"I worked in a kitchen like that during college," said John.

"Cool, so you'll know that most of the work in a busy restaurant is done during the prep phase. There's no way a busy restaurant could deliver so many meals without an enormous amount of prep done in advance," said Jaq.

"That's true," said John.

"Well, the same could be said about executing the BFRR strategy. Preparation is vital. At first, it might sound like a lot of work when you just want to jump into action, but it will get easier after the first deal. The BFRR strategy is all about momentum. The more of it you have, the better it gets, " said Jaq.

"That makes sense, so what's involved in the preparation phase?" asked Nancy.

Initial Financing

"Nancy, you read my mind. Remember that every BFRR deal will need to be financed twice. We'll talk about initial financing first – there are several ways to go about it, and you'll feel more comfortable financing creatively as you get more advanced," said Jaq.

Jaq showed John and Nancy a page with some basic forms of initial financing listed:

1. Bank Mortgage
2. Private Money
3. Cash
4. Line of Credit
5. Vendor Take Back (VTB)
6. Self Directed RRSP Mortgages

"*Bank mortgages* are the most basic and traditional way to finance the up-front portion of the deal," said Jaq.

"But how many mortgages can one person get before the bank rejects your application? I've heard banks will only approve a few mortgages before they shut off the money tap," said Nancy.

"Well, if you're aligned with the right mortgage professional, you'll be able to hold more than just a few mortgages under your own name, but you're right in principle. There's only so much bank financing a person can hold at any given time, which is why BFRR investors rely on joint venture relationships where the 'money partner' supplies the down payment and puts the mortgage in their name," said Jaq.

"How does that work?" said John.

"Well, with joint ventures you can hold an unlimited number of mortgages because they're in your partner's name. We'll discuss joint ventures in detail later. For now we're talking about the initial financing, and a straight up bank mortgage is often the best way to finance the front end of the deal. There are other, more creative, riskier, and more advanced strategies, but boring is often best," said Jaq.

"There's a philosophy I can get behind. I like to invest in things I understand," said Nancy.

"Where have I heard that before? Oh yeah, Warren Buffett, the Oracle of Omaha, also known as the greatest value investor who's ever lived, says the exact same thing. Anyways, bank mortgages are often the best way to finance on the front end. To prepare you'll need 1) the right mortgage broker in place – they will be able to tell you quickly if you or your partner can qualify, 2) down payment money, and 3) the ability to qualify – it could be a joint venture partner or yourself," said Jaq.

Tips When Using Bank Financing

1. **Mortgage + Improvements –** Not many people are aware of this type of mortgage, which works exactly as it sounds. The bank lends money for the purchase as well as for improving the property. The key to using this type of mortgage is to 'bump' the value of the property up more than the amount lent for improvements. The bank lends a maximum of 10% of the value of the property for this.

Please also note that mortgage + improvements mortgages can only be used for your primary residence or an investment property that is also your primary residence.

2. **Open Mortgage –** Always get an open mortgage rather than a closed mortgage on initial financing. Why?

An open mortgage allows you to pay out the entire amount of the mortgage at any time without penalty. They have higher interest rates than closed mortgages (often by a lot), but you'll save money because they don't charge mortgage-breaking fees.

On the other hand, closed mortgage breaking fees are the equivalent of 3 months interest (or more). Paying a higher mortgage payment (for a couple months) instead of the big breaking fee will save about $1000 on every BFRR deal you do.

3. **Blend and Extend –** This is a mortgage option where you take an existing mortgage and blend it with a new mortgage, thereby extending the length of the mortgage and also blending the two different mortgage rates together.

This enables you to take advantage of a preferential interest rate if one comes available.

> **4. Add a HELOC Behind the First** – One option
>   for additional financing is to put a Home Equity
>   Line of Credit on the property behind the initial
>   mortgage financing.
>
>   Banks register a collateral charge in this
>   scenario, which allows them to advance more
>   money on a property without having to do a
>   full refinance.[1]

"Right now we could probably qualify for one more mortgage, but we'd have to talk to a mortgage broker to make sure. I'm sure we won't be able to do too many more like that, though, so why don't you tell us about the other ways to finance on the front end?" said John.

"Good idea. First, there is *private money*, which is a mortgage you take from an individual or a group of investors. Private lenders do three things. First, they'll often lend when banks won't. Second, they make the money available super-fast once they approve the borrower (and more importantly the deal). Third, they charge a much higher interest rate than the banks and usually have up-front fees. Borrowing private money is more costly than traditional bank financing, but it has its advantages in terms of speed and flexibility. It's a viable option. I use it regularly, but I'd only recommend doing it once you've got a bit of experience under your belt, since

---

1   Go to www.theultimatewealthstrategy.com for more tools, information, resources, and tips for financing options.

it's riskier. You can be stuck with high interest costs if anything goes wrong," said Jaq.

"Okay, private money is an option for later, but it's probably not best at the start. *Cash* is easy to understand, and I could see why it would be nice to do this, but we don't have enough cash on hand to purchase a whole property," said Nancy.

"Again, you might not have it, but you'd be surprised how many joint venture partners do. In truth, you probably won't purchase many properties with all cash, but it's more common than you think. Using a *line of credit* is much more common, and it's a fantastic option for purchasing the property up front. Many investors have access to a line of credit and are willing to use it for the initial purchase. Lines of credit often have favorable interest rates, which makes them an attractive option. It's like a combination of *bank financing* and *private money* – it's available quick and it's relatively cheap. Many people lend out their line of credit as a private loan and make money on the spread between the interest rate they pay the bank and the interest rate they pay," said Jaq.

"Hmm, that might be an option for us. We've been getting letters from the bank inviting us to apply for a line of credit. With market appreciation and our mortgage pay down over the years we have a fair bit of equity built up and would likely qualify for a line of credit," said Nancy.

"Fantastic, it's great to have options. Just remember that if you do use a line of credit it will have to be a secured as opposed to an unsecured line of credit. This just means the line of credit is secured against an asset such as your primary residence," said Jaq.

"Right. Ours would be secured against our primary residence. Now, I'm interested in hearing about these VTB mortgages you mentioned," said Nancy.

"Bingo. This is one of the best-kept secrets of residential real estate investing. People usually only associate the VTB with commercial investing, but it's common enough in residential real estate. It's just when the seller of a property agrees to finance the purchase directly to the buyer. You enter into a legal mortgage agreement as you would with a bank mortgage, but rather than payments going to the bank they go to the seller directly. The great thing about the VTB is that you sidestep the bank's qualifying process, and depending on the seller you might even be able to finance the entire purchase amount in this way," said Jaq.

"That does sound good, but I imagine you have to pay high interest on a VTB," said John.

"Not necessarily. It's entirely dependent upon what you negotiate with the seller. A lot of sellers will be scared to do a VTB, but when you do find one it's not uncommon to have similar terms as a normal bank mortgage," said Jaq.

"That's great, then! We'll definitely keep our eyes out for VTB deals. Now what about RRSP money? You mentioned that, but I thought it was impossible to use RRSP money for real estate investing," said Nancy.

"That's what the banks want us to believe, but it's not true. Investors are allowed to convert their RRSP funds into a self-directed account and then lend them out as a mortgage – to you for example – for a much better rate of return than they normally would achieve within their

RRSP by sticking with a standard mutual fund," said Jaq.

"It would be hard to do any worse!" said John.

"That's right, which is why this strategy is such a win-win. It allows investors like you to purchase a wonderful property and it provides the RRSP holder to actually make some money in their RRSP – for many it might be the first time they've ever done so," said Jaq.

Steps to RRSP Mortgage Success

1. **Find a Lender –** This can be anyone holding an RRSP except immediate family members.

   There are so many people with RRSPs[1], which is to investors' benefit because most RRSP holders are unhappy with the returns inside their registered plans.

   Once you find your lender, you can negotiate the terms of the mortgage. Anything goes here, so long as both borrower and lender agree it to, although keep in mind that it has to be worth the lender's time.

2. **Choose a Trustee –** The industry standard is *Olympia Trust*, which is generally regarded as the best trustee for RRSP mortgages.

---

2   Please note that this strategy is applicable to any registered plan such as TFSA, RESP, LIRA, etc.,

3. **Lender Opens and Funds a Self-Directed RRSP Account with Trustee –** Your lender will not be able to advance the funds to you unless they are first transferred to the trust account. To be able to do that, the lender must have an account with the trustee first.

   Once the lender has opened an account they are able to transfer the funds into the trust account. Remember that there are no tax implications from this since the lender never removes the funds from their RRSP.

4. **Execute Mortgage and Receive Funds –** The funds from the lender will be advanced to you as an official mortgage, which means a legal mortgage agreement must be in place and properly carried out.

   You will be advanced the funds once the agreement is in effect.

"Is an RRSP mortgage only provided for a down payment, or is it used to finance the entire purchase price?" said Nancy.

"It all depends what you negotiate with the RRSP lender, but it's more common to borrow only the amount of the down payment as there aren't as many people with 2 or 3 hundred thousand dollars (or more) in their RRSP as there are people with 50 or 60 thousand," said Jaq.

"Right. That doesn't sound too difficult," said Nancy.

"There are a couple more things to consider. First, most often when using an RRSP mortgage you have to put it against another property in order to access the cash," said Jaq.

"Why is that?" said John.

"Well, banks don't want you to be financed above 80% on a property, and if you're using the RRSP mortgage as a down payment it means you'll be financed 100%. To mitigate this, they ask you to put the RRSP mortgage against another property. If you refuse, they refuse you the loan," said Jaq.

"That makes sense. You said there was one more point?" said Nancy.

"One more strategy for RRSP mortgage is to put it against the property after closing as a way of kicking back the renovation costs. This makes sense if the added expense of the RRSP second mortgage doesn't eat up too much of the monthly cash flow. You have to maintain strong cash flow," said Jaq.

"Right. Anything else?" said John.

"We'll talk more about financing later when you're ready to buy, but for now we're still talking about preparation. Getting your initial financing in place is a big piece of the preparation puzzle," said Jaq.

"What are the other ways we need to prepare?" said John

"Let's talk about the cash requirements for purchasing a BFRR deal, as getting the money in place is often the trickiest part for new BFRR investors," said Jaq.

Other Costs – Down Payment, Closing Costs, Carrying Costs, Emergency Funds, and Renovation Money

"The biggest cash requirement is the down payment. Banks require 20% on investment properties. In preparation you need to know exactly where this is going to come from. 20% is no small bit of cash considering the price of real estate, so many people use other sources of funds such as a line of credit, an RRSP mortgage, or a VTB to fund the down payment. Still, cash is usually the best source of down payment money," said Jaq.

"I guess a lot of BFRR investors use joint venture money for the down payment?" asked John.

"Absolutely. It's no different than doing a joint venture on a standard buy-and-hold investment. The money partner brings the money and qualifies on the mortgage, but with a standard buy-and-hold all of the investor's money remains in the property. This is the big difference between a BFRR deal and a standard buy-and-hold. You get money back! Rather than putting 20% down for the duration of the hold (which can last several years), JV partners get a big chunk (and sometimes all) of that money back while retaining ownership. This makes the JV partner's return better and puts more money back in their hands to reinvest – hopefully with you," said Jaq.

Front End Expense Estimates

When preparing prior to making a purchase it's important to have cost certainty. Below is an estimate of the cash requirements for purchasing a BFRR deal:

1. **Down Payment** – 20% of purchase price

2. **Closing Costs** – Approximately 3% of purchase price

3. **Carrying Costs** – This expense will depend on the terms of your initial financing and how long it takes before you refinance and rent the property. Typically, it's wise to prepare 2 months worth of mortgage payments as carrying cost.

4. **Reserve Fund** – One model is to prepare whichever is greater between3 months rent and $5000.

   Another model is to prepare the equivalence of 3 months expenses/carrying costs. Whichever you choose, ensure your reserve fund is well endowed.

5. **Renovation Cost** – This will vary greatly depending on the scope of renovations. We will discuss renovation types below.

"Right, and I guess the other costs can be paid for with cash out of pocket, money partner's cash, or a line of credit?" said John.

"Absolutely, the important thing to remember here is that you'll need a source of money available to pay for the renovations and closing costs (land transfer fee and lawyer fees), carrying costs, and an emergency fund along with the down payment. The strategy doesn't work unless the property can be renovated and rented!" said Jaq.

"Right. When we talk about needing cash we need to consider all of these costs, not just the down payment," said Nancy.

"That's right, but the biggest one is the down payment," said Jaq

"I'm still left thinking about how we're going to come up with this cash. I don't know how we'll get very far with what we have," said John.

"That's where joint ventures comes in. Most of us need them to grow beyond a certain point. For investors only wanting to do 1 or 2 deals, joint ventures aren't necessary. However, joint venture money seems to become more available once you've done one or two successful deals. When you prove you can make money, more seems to appear," said Jaq.

"Money attracts money," said John.

"That's right. People are used to minimal return. You've mentioned that you have mutual funds through your RRSP. Correct me if I'm wrong, but you'd probably be ecstatic with a 5% real return on those mutual funds, am I right?" said Jaq.

"Yeah, we'd be thrilled. As of today, we're still about $10,000 in the hole on the 'investment' we made 8 years ago. I use that term loosely, as my understanding of an investment is that you make a return," said Nancy.

"You're not alone, and as bad as the RRSP industry is for investors, it's actually a boon for BFRR investors because we stand apart from the crowd. Your investors will tell their friends when they see the results," said Jaq.

"So, how do we land joint venture partners[3]?" said John.

"Well, it has to be someone with enough funds from cash or a line of credit to fund all the costs we discussed above, and they must be able to qualify for a mortgage, too. You have to meet with prospective investors to show them you have a plan, a property, a budget, and proof that it's worked before. If you haven't done a deal before, you can borrow proof from others who have," said Jaq.

"Right, but first we have to identify prospective investors," said John.

"Yes, but eventually your track record will solve the problem of where to find money partners. Each success will cause your partners to tell their friends," said Jaq.

"Sounds like a catch 22. You need a track record to bring the money, but you need the money to build the track record," said Nancy.

"It's a bit of a catch 22, and the tried and true way around this problem is to fund the first deal yourself, document every step of the way, kick butt on your first deal, and then sell others using the proof of that first

---

3   Go to www.theultimatewealthstrategy.com to find out more about attracting and qualifying joint venture partners.

deal. Some BFRR investors do their first deal as a joint venture, but it's more common to do the first (and often second) deal with your own money. Success on the first one is critical to build momentum," said Jaq.

"I like the sounds of that. I don't like the idea of using other people's money until I'm confident that I can make it work. Luckily, I think we'll be able to do our first deal with our own money," said John.

"That's great, but please remember. If for any reason it's not a possibility, you don't need to give up. Joint venture money is available for a first timer. Anyways, you two aren't exactly first timers. You've done buy-and-hold deals already," said Jaq.

"That's true. We will cross that bridge when we can't finance a deal ourselves. So, what else is important during the preparation phase?" said Nancy.

Contractor Relationships

"Developing relationships with a contractor is another vital piece of the preparation phase. Some BFRR specialists do the renovations themselves, and this can be a fantastic way to execute the fix phase of the strategy, but there are plenty of BFRR investors who don't want to, can't, and never will do the renovations on their own," said Jaq.

The Value of Your Time

A common problem that some flippers, renovators, and BFRR investors have is that they don't value their own time. They end up doing the work themselves and rather than being paid on the merits of their real estate investment skills, they pay themselves (poorly) for their labour.

There is nothing wrong doing the work yourself. Some people enjoy it. Some are experts at it. It doesn't matter why you do it, so long as you're valuing your time. The guideline is this: Would the property make money if you weren't doing the work yourself?

Is it worth it if you have to work at the property 12 hours per day, 7 days per week, for 4 months, to earn $30,000? This is the equivalent of $22 per hour. It might be worth it if your normal job pays you $12 per hour, but for many investors the payback of being at the job site all day isn't worth it.

You must calculate what your time is worth and find out if working in the property is worth it. If the property can't be profitable without lifting a hammer, then look for another property.

"That's us," Nancy and John said in unison.

They all chuckled.

"Yeah, I've gotten that sense from John in our previous conversations. John has also mentioned his fear of managing a small team of contractors. What's that about?" asked Jaq.

"Well, as has been proven at my company, I'm not really management material. I'm a great team member, and I'll always do whatever it takes to make the deal work or benefit the team, but I'm not good at making difficult decisions under pressure," said John.

"It sounds like there's more to the story than you're letting on. Did something specific happen that makes you say that?" Jaq said.

"About 5 years ago I was fully engaged at climbing the corporate ladder at my company. I'd been getting a promotion and raise every couple of years, and the next logical step was for me to move into a leadership role where I'd have my own team. Things seemed to be going well for the first month until I lost one of my company's biggest accounts. I was demoted back to my previous position, and I've never moved up again, which I think is a good thing. I don't think I could handle that pressure again," said John.

"You're not alone. It was exactly this kind of event that ultimately put me first in line for being downsized at my old job. I wasn't considered a rising star of the organization after that, so when cuts happened I was on the chopping block before anyone else. Let me ask you this – knowing what you know about me and the success I've had using the strategy, would you say I'm 'leadership material'?" asked Jaq.

"Yes, obviously. You're already a leader to me, and I just met you a couple days ago," said John.

"I'm no different than you. I had my doubts before I started. I still have my doubts, but these disappear quickly when you start stacking one success upon the other. The truth is you'll likely be nervous about managing a small team of tradespeople until you do the first one and find out how easy it is. It will be easier and easier every time you do it after that. Sometimes when we have doubts, we simply have to do the thing we fear and trust it will work out. Just because you perceive you failed once before doesn't mean you're 'not management material'," said Jaq.

"You're right about one thing. I'm definitely nervous about it! I'll guess I'll just have to trust that I can do it and focus on doing it as well as I can," said John.

"Building relationships with contractors isn't hard, but it's vital. Having your team in place in advance allows you to finish your renovation quicker and therefore get the property refinanced and rented quicker. Failing to have workers ready to go can cost you money," said Jaq.

"How do you find them and have them ready? We've always found contractors to be expensive and busy – they always cost more than we expect and take longer to get started and finished than we would like," said Nancy.

"Remember how I suggested you find a mortgage broker from within the existing community of other real estate investors? The same goes with contractors. Getting a referral from the people who are already doing it is your best bet for finding contractors who 'get it'. The right contractor won't put up roadblocks, and they will help you execute your renovation plan on time and on budget. This makes the difference between a successful BFRR deal and an unsuccessful one," said Jaq.

"Is it as simple as that?" asked John.

"Not exactly. You also need to know what kinds of renovations to do and have a clear plan. You also need to budget well, which means you need to understand the cost of materials and what kinds of renovations you need to do, but we'll talk about that in detail later when it comes time to buy. For now I want to stress that it's important to start building relationships in preparation," said Jaq.

"Any other tricks for managing these relationships?" said John.

"Always make sure to get things in writing and get multiple quotes on work required. Once you find a great contractor, pay them well and treat them well, as they are valuable members of your investment team. Oh, and one more thing. Make sure your insurance covers you in case of accidental damage by the contractor," said Jaq

"Okay, I'll probably ask more questions later when we get to this stage of the game, but for now we'll start developing those relationships in preparation. How about budgeting?" said John.

Budgeting

"You have to know what repairs the property needs in order to do an accurate budget. Knowing what repairs are needed is about knowing what kind of project you're going to do. Some BFRR specialists do big renovations, and they can be very profitable, but it's generally considered a good idea to only take on a 'lipstick' type of renovation at the beginning," said Jaq.

"What do you mean by that?" asked Nancy.

"Some properties are in good shape, and they only require cosmetic upgrades. These are colloquially referred to as 'lipstick' renovations. They usually involve new flooring, repairing walls, painting, re-facing cabinets, updating lighting and faucets, and improving curb appeal. These kinds of renovations aren't as expensive as bigger renovations that include rewiring, re-roofing, replacing furnaces, or structural work. Don't get me wrong; there will be plenty of times when one of those 'bigger jobs' is required. I wouldn't suggest you avoid them entirely, but a good principle on your first deal is to do a 'lipstick' renovation deal," said Jaq.

"I think that would make sense for me. I'm a bit freaked out by renovations to begin with, so I can't imagine myself wanting to take on a big expensive renovation job," said John.

"Good idea. You can make plenty of money banging out smaller 'lipstick' jobs. Plenty of BFRR investors focus only on small jobs. They buy properties for between 75% and 80% of the After Repaired Value (ARV), and then they spend less than 10% of the total value on the renovation before refinancing and renting the property. If you're keeping score that means they've created 10% of the properties value in equity," said Jaq.

Sample Lipstick Deal

Purchase Price: $177,500

Down Payment: $35,500

Closing/Holding/Renovations: $15,000

Cash Required for Purchase and Renovation: $50,500

Refinanced Value: $230,000

Net Created Value: $37,500

Cash Returned: $42,000 (Difference between original mortgage $142,000 and new mortgage of $184,000)

Money Left in Property with Refinance - $13, 000

Equity Return on Cash Remaining (EROCR): 289% (Net Value Created/Money Left in Property with Refinance)

Yearly Cash Flow – $8,328

Yearly Mortgage Reduction - $5,460

Yearly Profit before Appreciation: $13,788

First Year Equity Growth at 3% Appreciation: $6,900

Total Annual Equity Growth and Profit: $20,688

Annual ROI Assuming 3% Appreciation: 159%

If this property had been purchased as a normal buy-and-and-hold, the money partner would have left $46,000 invested in the property rather than $13,000. Returning this money to the investor provides an outstanding immediate return and sets the property up for long-term success.

"Jaq, I've never seen you get so far off topic. You were going to talk about budgeting, but instead you went on a rant about doing 'lipstick' renovations," said John.

"Right. Budgeting. Well, I guess it wasn't that far off track because what I meant to say was that your budget will be determined by how much work is required during your fix phase. What I meant to say was that you can't budget accurately until you know what work needs to be done on the property. Once you know that, it's a simple matter of pricing materials and labour, and then adding the carrying cost," said Jaq.

"Right, but it's the labour part that I'm not sure about," said John.

"I know that can be intimidating, but you can budget it once you have a list of excellent contractors ready. It's just a matter of bringing them to your job site and having them give you quotes for the work required. You choose the best quotes based on price, contractor availability, and referrals. Better yet, you choose them because you've worked with them in the past and they've delivered results. You pay them promptly and treat them with respect, and there you have the basis for a great working relationship. Price certainty isn't hard to achieve with good relationships," said Jaq.

"Right, I think I understand all of that, but isn't it too late to get a budget and price certainty in place when buying the property? I won't know the renovations + purchase price are too high until after I've purchased it," said John.

"I understand your fear, but why would you buy the property unless you're fairly certain that the purchase price + renovation expense is considerably less than the after repaired value? After all, that's our business model. We want to create outstanding results and set it up so that we (and our investors) are given back a big chunk (if not all) the money invested at the time of refinance," said Jaq.

"I don't want to, but how will I know before hand?" said John.

"Well, your level of certainty will rise drastically after doing a couple of deals, but don't forget that you can do a detailed analysis of the work required on the property *before* you buy it. When you're not certain about the numbers, simply don't close on the property. To get price certainty on the numbers, just bring along your contractors during the inspection – before you remove your purchase offer conditions and before you have a legal obligation to buy the property," said Jaq.

"You can do that?" said John.

"Of course. I'd never advocate you take such a big risk as buying a property without having a high level of certainty about the numbers. It's not difficult to be certain about the numbers. Experience helps. Most BFRR investors find a specific property type and a couple neighbourhoods that work. Then they keep doing slight variations on the same deal over and over again. They know their basic numbers before they even look at the property. After a quick walk through they roughly know the renovation expenses. Once they have these numbers in mind, it's just a matter of doing the due diligence to ensure there are no big surprises. Having an excellent property inspector on your team who will alert you to any of these big expenses is an absolute must," said Jaq.

"Right, we used a property inspector for our other investment property purchases," said Nancy.

"It's a must. My inspector has saved me his fee many times over. In fact, I know some investors who even make it their mission to save *at least* more than the amount they pay for the inspector each and every time they hire an inspector," said Jaq

"Okay, so budgeting and risk mitigation is about due diligence. That's right up my alley. Now, what kind ratio of purchase price to ARV should we be considering when buying?" said Nancy.

"The most you can pay for a property is what we call the MAO, which is short for Maximum Allowable Offer," said Jaq.

"Right, that makes sense, so what is the MAO as a percentage of the ARV?" said John.

"Unfortunately, it's not that clear cut. To know the MAO you have to consider the ARV as well as the cost of renovations. To calculate, you start from the end and work your way backwards," said Jaq.

"What does that mean?" said John.

"First, you get clear on the ARV. Next, you subtract the cost of repairs and holding. Finally, you subtract the amount of profit you want to make," said Jaq.

"Which is?" said Nancy.

"Well, each deal is different, but wouldn't you agree that a simple lipstick renovation would be a success if you could create 10-15% of value through your efforts?" said Jaq.

"It sounds like a pretty good deal," said John.

"This is the definition of a BFRR single. Homeruns are great, but singles get the job done. Yes, it's possible to get 25% or more value on a property, but the fact is, it would be rare to do this on a lipstick deal. On a much bigger project, this is more possible. Not only is it possible, it's even required since you'll be taking a bigger risk on the bigger renovation," said Jaq.

"Okay, but since we've already agreed to focus on lipstick jobs at the beginning, we should probably aim for 10-15%. So what does that look like in MAO terms?" said Nancy.

"Well, if you know the ARV on a property will be $200,000, and you're certain the renovation and holding expense will be $5,000, then your MAO would be $175,000 if you're aiming for 10%," said Jaq.

"Right because you have to calculate 10% back from the ARV minus expenses," said John.

"Yep, and so long as you're doing a 'lipstick' job and you've done your due diligence, you should be able to predict your budget with relative certainty. Going a little bit over budget won't kill you so long as you've followed the buying and renovation guidelines of the 'lipstick' job," said Jaq.

"I'm kind of impatient, so I want to get moving. Assuming we take all these preparation steps you're talking about, can we please buy a property now?" said John.

"In theory of course, but don't skip these steps. Don't linger on them either. Take action immediately. Give me a call once the prep is in place, and then it'll be time to talk about my favourite subject – buying BFRR deals," said Jaq.

Jaq stood up, gathered his things with his normal efficiency, said his goodbyes, and waltzed out the door. John and Nancy mumbled goodbyes in return. Again, John was left sitting with a million thoughts, but this time he wasn't alone.

"Okay, I'm on board. I still advocate caution, but as long as we can understand our budget and mitigate risk in the ways Jaq talked about, I think we can do this. I didn't want to discuss our personal finance while Jaq was here, but I'm 99% sure we can pull off our first deal without a joint venture partner. I'm more comfortable doing our first one like that," said Nancy.

"I agree, but looking into the future, I'm sure I know a few people who might like to invest. Everyone at the office is stuck with the same worthless paper we have, paying for the Bay Street bums' yachts. If we can pull off one or two BFRR deals on our own dime, I'm sure we'd have a never-ending supply of money partners available," said John.

"It's the same at my office, but let's not get too far ahead of ourselves. Shall we go? Mom and dad are probably ready for a break from the kids, and we have a lot of preparation work to do before our first BFRR deal," said Nancy.

The both held their heads higher than normal as they strode out the door to resume their Sunday activities.

Preparation Action Steps

1. **Budgeting** – To properly budget, investors need to know the 'average property'. This average price is what their end value will be (or hopefully a little above). Once this baseline is established, investors can seek out undervalued properties that require cosmetic renovations.

2. **Down Payment, Closing Costs, Renovation Costs, Carrying Costs, and Emergency Fund** – Many investors like to fund their first deal themselves. Playing with one's own money the first time is a great way to build credibility before asking others to invest. However, some investors use others' money on the first time.

3. **Investor Presentation** – In advance, prepare a presentation for your future investors. Borrow numbers and materials from more experienced BFRR investors if you don't have your own deal models yet. Seeing concrete examples of other deals and others' presentations will help you develop your own. Plug your own numbers and photos into the presentation when you complete your first deal.

4. **Contractor Relationships** – Contact, communicate, and share plans and mutual goals with contractors long before needing them to work at your deal. Once the relationship is established and it's clear it will be beneficial for both parties, then prepare them to start. The wrong time to be scrambling to find contractors is on the day you close on a property purchase.

5. **Mortgage Broker** – Not every mortgage broker is right for BFRR investors. Most mortgage brokers will not understand the strategy or needs of a BFRR investor since they focus on homeowners. The best way to find an excellent BFRR specialist mortgage broker is to get a recommendation from another BFRR investor. Go to investor groups and meetings to locate BFRR investors.

6. **Other Relationships** – Just as contractor and mortgage broker relationships are important, so are relationships with other professionals. These include real estate agents, property managers, and lawyers. Always seek investor specialists. Look for referrals within the real estate investor community.

7. **Line of Credit** – Many homeowners have (significant) money available through a home equity line of credit (HELOC). Unfortunately, many decide to spend this money on an expensive vacation or a depreciating asset, such as a boat or motorcycle. Using it (for the short term) to purchase a fantastic investment can be an excellent use of the available money. Prepare by speaking to your bank about your own HELOC, and speak to investors about theirs.[4]

From Prep to Purchase

You've just learned about the key preparation steps required for success n the later phases of the strategy. You learned about the importance of developing contractor relationships, budgeting, getting initial financing ready, and calculating other costs.

Would you believe that many investors go through these stages of preparation only to abandon the process before ever purchasing a property? The abandonment is often caused by 'analysis paralysis', which is a common problem with new investors.

To overcome this problem investors must implement a clear plan and take decisive action. Too many real estate

---

4   Go to www.theultimatewealthstrategy.com to learn more about preparation steps.

investors' only plan is to 'buy real estate'. This vague notion isn't conducive to taking action and building a well-constructed portfolio.

In the next chapter you'll see what it takes to move from a prepared wannabe to a prepared BFRR investor buying the right properties in the right neighbourhoods. You'll see what it takes to be able to move from preparation to pulling the trigger.

"It's tangible, it's solid, and it's beautiful. It's artistic from my standpoint, and I just love real estate."

Donald Trump

CHAPTER 4

Buy

Buyers are Winners

Have you ever noticed that a select few real estate investors always end up owning the best deals? When the same few people always achieve the same results, it can make you wonder what special knowledge these people have.

What if I told you that knowledge is available to all? Would you like to learn, practice, and apply the same knowledge? Of course you would, and that knowledge is exactly what this chapter is all about. Only, you'll learn that it's not too difficult or special after all.

You see, these power investors know that success in real estate investing is largely the result of how you buy the property. They understand that 1 excellent property is more valuable than 3 average properties, and they have the patience to only buy excellent properties.

Power investors know that a lot of activity doesn't mean success, so they carefully select excellent properties that will move them closer to their goals. This chapter will move you from excellent preparation to excellent purchases. Read on to learn how to buy 1 excellent property at a time.

Dealing With Adversity

After their Sunday meeting Nancy and John got to work on the preparation for their first BFRR deal. The couple's plan was to buy the property with bank financing, using cash they'd saved for the down payment. They had about $55,000 put aside, which they assumed would be enough in their local market.

They found out through research that the average well-maintained single-family property in their target neighbourhood sold for about $250,000. This meant Nancy and John would be looking to buy a property for around $200,000 and lift the property value by about $50,000.

With 80% bank financing on the initial purchase, they'd be required to bring 20% cash for a down payment of $40,000. This would leave them with about $15,000 cash remaining for renovations and carrying costs. They believed this would be sufficient as long as they selected a property that only required lipstick renovations.

After refinancing, the couple expected to get $40,000 back, so they'd only be left with $15,000 of their initial cash outlay returned to them.

John and Nancy had spoken to an excellent mortgage broker named Diane (who came recommended by several members of the Cashflowsville Real Estate Investment Club[5]) in preparation for their first BFRR deal. Diane got John and Nancy pre-approved, they supplied documentation, and financing was ready.

They'd also spoken to several contractors recommended by Jaq and other members of the club. After discussing the types of renovations they'd be doing, John and Nancy were confident they could pull off the renovation in less than two months using a team of professionals and very little of their own time.

It was decided that John would drop by the job site regularly after work but that John and Nancy wouldn't take any days off work for the project. After developing a few solid relationships they were confident the contractors could do the job without any handholding.

Everything was in order, and John and Nancy were about to start searching for a property. That was when catastrophe struck.

It started with a phone call at 11:30 pm one Monday evening – a couple of weeks after they'd last spoken to

---

5   Go to www.theultimatewealthstrategy.com/reiclubs to find a complete list of real estate investing clubs near you.

Jaq. Nancy glanced worriedly at John when the phone rang, as they didn't usually get calls this late.

Nancy picked up, "Hello."

"Nancy, it's Erica. We need your help," said the voice. Erica and her husband Chris were tenants in one of Nancy and John's rental properties.

"What is it Erica? Is everything okay?" asked Nancy.

"Not really, something happened over here. The basement is under about a foot of water," said Erica.

"What?" said Nancy.

There had been heavy rain over the previous 3 days, and as the image of a flooded basement settled in, Nancy's stomach dropped. She liked investing, but she hated the real world problems sometimes associated with real estate.

"What is it?" John asked. He knew something serious had happened by the tone of Nancy's voice.

"Okay, we'll be over there soon," Nancy said to Erica.

"Erica and Chris's basement flooded. I guess from all the rain, but I don't understand why this would happen. Our house is fine. Damn. What are we thinking? Why would we buy more real estate? We don't have time for this. What do you want to do?" said Nancy.

"Ugh, you go to bed, I'll head over there and see what needs to be done. Tomorrow is going to be a long day," said John.

John stopped getting ready for bed. He reached for his rarely used physical labour clothes. He quickly put them on and headed for the door.

He was awash in powerful emotions.

On one hand he hated the situation, yet the thought of doing the right thing gave him a kind of satisfaction, "This time feels different," he thought. In the past he might have run from adversity or gotten scared by it, but now he was facing it head-on.

He knew that more real estate would bring more challenge, but at that moment he knew he'd be able to get through anything. It was different, and he liked it. He felt alive and in control as he walked through his house and out the door.

The Fallout

"Never, never, never give up."

Winston Churchill

The damage was a lot worse than Nancy and John had imagined. They learned that there was a crack in the foundation, which wouldn't have been so bad if the drainage around the property was better. They found out that the soil around the foundation had been sinking. The big rainstorm caused a pool of water to form, which then started leaking into the house.

The cleanup was costly, but the biggest expense came from the post-flood renovations. In addition to dry walling most of the basement, John and Nancy were forced to update some of the electrical components of the property.

The disaster set them back several weeks, and when all the numbers were crunched, they'd spent over $30,000 on repairs.

It was strange that John had such a feeling of taking charge as he walked out of his house to handle the problem because it was through the process that he learned how little responsibility he had actually been taking.

None of the expense would have fallen on his shoulders if he'd spent the time and effort to properly insure the property. He thought back on the day he purchased insurance. He remembered that he had chosen an old friend to be his insurance agent. This friend wasn't a real estate investment specialist, and as a result John didn't get the best coverage possible.

As confident and businesslike as John felt the evening of the flood, he was feeling equally as unconfident after writing what seemed like an endless number of cheques to repair the house. It was more proof of his poor management skills.

The process drained him, and he and Nancy both forgot about BFRR investing. Once everything was done, John needed a night out to forget about everything.

As he'd done several hundred times in his life, he called his good friend Bill. Again, it wasn't for a celebration. John just wanted to take his mind off the problem, have a bit of fun, and forget about real estate investment altogether.

The two decided to meet at a local watering hole for a beer and a chat. John poured his heart out as he poured beer down his throat.

Bill, as always, was ever ready with a quip, "You don't need to 'flood' me with the details, John. I get it; you're just 'swimming' in problems aren't you? Things could be worse. I mean, you could be 'awash' in debt," Bill joked.

"Seriously man, that's not funny. I'm trying to tell you about a serious problem here," John began.

Then they both burst out laughing. "Thank goodness for good friends to keep things in perspective for me," he thought. It wasn't so bad after all. He'd been (literally) saving for a rainy day, so at least he was able to pay for the flood related problems.

The friends ordered beers and dinner. John relaxed, and with lighter hearts the men talked bigger picture.

"Of course it's annoying, and it'll minimize the returns on that property, but that's not the worst of it. In the process, we blew through the cash we were going to use to buy a much better deal," said John.

"Oh really? I thought you'd never consider real estate again after this," said Bill.

"Well, for sure I'd do it differently. For one thing I'd make sure to inspect foundations and gradients better! For another thing, I will be properly insured, but I'm talking about a far superior way to do real estate. We were ready to do a different kind of deal until this happened," said John.

"What do you mean?" said Bill.

"Remember that chat about 'stuckness' we had at the Equity Café a couple months back?" said John.

"I've been trying to forget. You wouldn't stop complaining," said Bill.

"Right, that's the day. The strangest thing happened after you left. This guy had overheard us talking, so he came over to talk to me. He's been successful in real estate using a strategy he calls the buy, fix, refinance, and rent strategy," said John.

"That's a tongue twister," said Bill.

"Right. It's BFRR for short. Anyways, he and I started talking about this strategy. Essentially, you create value by purchasing a property under market value and then renovating. It's based on sound fundamental real estate investing principles, and we did our homework on it. Since you create value during the renovation, the returns are far better than normal buy-and-hold real estate investing," said John

"That's exciting considering buy-and-hold works well as is," said Bill.

"Definitely. We did a bunch of preparation and were a couple of days away from starting to search for our first property when we got flooded, but the 30 grand we spent repairing pretty much means we won't be doing a deal now. Back to being stuck," said John.

"I could lend you the cash," said Bill.

At first, John thought it was another of Bill's jokes, but as he scanned Bill's face he could see no sign of a smile.

"What?" said John.

"Yeah. It sounds like a winning investment strategy. Listen, you've been more active with real estate than me but don't think I haven't been paying attention. I've read a lot about investing, but I'm just trying to get my head around the time it would take to invest in real estate. I've come to the conclusion I don't want to invest the time, but what you're describing sounds an awful lot like value investing, which I understand and like," said Bill.

John couldn't believe what he was hearing. Jaq had told him that people were attracted to the strategy, but he assumed it would only happen after he'd done it a few times.

"I don't have a track record," said John.

"Not with this strategy, but with your buy-and-hold investments you do, and more importantly to me, you have a track record in life. You've never done anything untrustworthy in all the time I've known you, and as much as you don't believe in yourself sometimes, you've done a lot of great things. Just like you buckled down and took care of the flooded property, I know you'll take care of my money. Go ahead and get started," said Bill

John's head was spinning. His mind flooded back to all Jaq told him about joint ventures. He wasn't expecting to do one until he'd proven himself a few times. He didn't realize his character, focus, and determination would be enough to convince Bill.

"I'm flattered and honoured by your confidence in me, but I have a different idea – a better idea," said John.

"I'm all ears," said Bill.

"Okay, you said you're looking to get into a hands-free investment right? What if we partnered on the property rather than doing a loan? Then we could both benefit over the long-term. I'll take care of the active work of buying, renovating, refinancing, and renting, while you put up the money and qualify for financing?" said John.

"I'm still listening," said Bill.

"Okay, we'll need about $55,000 to pull off the strategy, but the good thing is you should have over half of that money back in your pocket after the refinance, and we'll be left with a top-performing property that hopefully won't flood," said John.

"Don't start 'watering' down your plans!" Bill joked.

"Come on man," said John.

"Okay, okay, I'm sorry. I can't help myself. How does it work? I like the result you described, but how do we get there?" said Bill.

"Well. As mentioned, I will do the work, but you'll bring the cash and qualify on the mortgage. The property will be in both of our names. When we refinance the property, you will get back most of your cash. Later, when the property makes more money, all of the cash will go to you until you've received your entire investment back," said John.

"That makes sense. What else?" said Bill.

"After that, any profit we earn will be split 50/50. All expenses will also be split 50/50, but we should never have to come out of pocket since the property will produce cash flow, which will pay for all property expenses, including renovations over the long term," said John.

"How long of a time horizon are we talking about?" said Bill.

"I suggest we have a 5 year term with the option of continuing to hold the property longer if we both agree, although if we do decide to keep it, we can refinance after 5 years to pull some of our profit out," said John.

"I'm in. I would have been happy to lend you the money but your suggestion is even better," said Bill.

John was sitting on the edge of his seat with excitement, ready to explain, convince, and discuss every component of the strategy. He was shocked when Bill was convinced and seemed ready to change the subject.

His initial instinct was to keep talking and closing, but he was suddenly overcome with a feeling of confidence and calmness. He's said enough, and it was time to enjoy the evening.

The old friends continued their evening together with several more bad jokes, a lot of happy memories, and a newfound excitement about the future.

The Inactive Joint Venture Partner

The BFRR investment strategy might not be right for some readers. It's a powerful strategy, but it's certainly not a hands free method of investing. Like Bill, many investors don't want to do the legwork necessary to execute a BFRR (or even a buy-and-hold) deal.

The desire to invest hands free is the reason investors keep plugging cash into mutual funds through their RRSP, despite their dismal performance. Many are unaware of a better kind of hands free investing.

If you're reading this and you know you don't want to undertake the job of actively investing with the BFRR strategy, we urge you to find a successful BFRR investor and invest your money *as the inactive partner in* a solid BFRR.

The results are remarkable. Take a look at this example from earlier in the book:

Average Property Value: $250,000

Purchase Price: $220,000

Difference: $30,000

Down Payment: $44,000

Closing/Holding/Renovations: $10,000

Cash Required for Purchase and Renovation: $54,000

Refinanced Value: $255,000

Net Value Created: $25,000 ($255,000 – [$220,000 + $10,000])

Refinance Amount: $204,000 (80% of $255,000)

Cash Returned: $28,000 (($204,000 NEW Mortgage)– (176,000 Old Mortgage))

Money Left in Property with Refinance: $26,000 ($54,000-$28,000)

Equity Return on Cash Remaining (EROCR): 96% (Net Value Created/Money Left in Property with Refinance)

Yearly Cash Flow: $2,700

Yearly Mortgage Reduction: $3,934

Yearly Profit before Appreciation: $6,634

First Year Equity Growth at 3% Appreciation: $7,650

Total Annual Equity Growth and Profit: $14,284

Annual ROI Assuming 3% Appreciation: 55%

Even with this *average* example of a BFRR deal, you can see the power of the strategy for both partners.

Leverage in Real Estate

The back end of a BFRR deal is the holding phase, and it's (in essence) the same as any normal buy-and-hold investment.

Remember that any real estate investment purchased with 80% of the bank's money and 20% cash still benefits from the *power of leverage*. This means that even a small appreciation in the market leads to an impressive return on cash invested.

For example, 4% appreciation means a 20% ROI for the investor when leveraged 80%. The reason for this is based on the definition of a *return on investment*. ROI is calculated based on the cash invested, not the total value of the asset.

If you purchase a property for $200,000 with 20% down payment, it means the total investment is $40,000, not $200,000 (20% of $200,000). So, if the property value increases by 10% (which often happens quickly in real estate) the total asset value would then be $220,000. Since the value of the asset has gone up by $20,000, it means there is a 50% return (50% of $40,000 = $20,000).

When this fact, which is shared by all long-term hold real estate, is combined with the benefits of BFRR (getting cash back right away), you can see that no other kind of investment gives the bang for your buck like the BFRR strategy.

If passive BFRR investing is a better fit for you than active investing, we urge you to read the rest of this book, and get educated on the strategy. Then take steps to find and qualify an excellent active partner.

Use the knowledge you gain in this book (and elsewhere) to choose an investor to work with and to do due diligence on individual deals.

Getting Ready to Buy

"We're ready to buy," John announced to Jaq at their next Equity Café meeting, only a couple days after Bill verbally committed to joint venturing their first BFRR deal.

"I hadn't heard from you guys in a while. I wasn't sure if you were going to take the next step or not. Many people get sidetracked along the way, and I wasn't sure whether or not you were going to go for it or not," said Jaq.

Nancy and John both laughed a little too hard.

"We had every reason not to take the next step. Wow, a lot has changed since we last saw you. After our previous meeting, we left our last meeting to do pre-purchase preparation. We identified that we had enough cash to purchase our first property, and our new mortgage broker, Diane, assured us we'd be able to qualify. We were going to call to talk to you several weeks ago, then we experienced a flood at one of our buy-and-hold properties," said Nancy.

"Ouch. So, I guess you were busy cleaning up that mess. I hope it wasn't too costly or stressful," said Jaq.

"Oh, it was plenty of both! In fact, we had to spend most of our savings to get the property back in shape. In fact, I gave up on the BFRR strategy," said John.

"Yet, you're here. What got you back on track?" asked Jaq.

"Remember my friend, Bill? He was sitting with me here in this café the day you and I met. Well, I told him about the flood. I also told him about the BFRR strategy and that we wouldn't be able to do a deal now. I didn't ask him to joint venture. He offered to fund it. I didn't sell him at all," said John.

"Oh really?" said Jaq

"Yeah, in fact he was willing to lend it directly to us based on my description of the strategy and his trust in me, but I offered to joint venture instead and he jumped on the opportunity," said John.

"That's incredible! Although, I can't say I'm surprised. You have a strong character, and the strategy attracts money. Regardless of where the money is coming from, you've now done the preparation and are ready to roll. Am I right about that?" asked Jaq.

"Yes, now spill the beans. We're ready to buy, but we need to know how to find these great deals we've heard so much about," said Nancy.

"Great. I love talking about buying. It's a beautiful thing when done correctly," said Jaq.

"I wish we had this conversation a few years ago, before we bought the flood house," said John.

"The buying formula is certainly powerful. Like most aspects of the BFRR strategy it's simply but not easy," said Jaq.

"That's my new mantra. Where do we start?" said John.

"Well, one component trumps all else for finding great deals. Like most things, you have to know what you're looking for before you'll find it. In other words, you have to know what a great deal looks like before you can find one," said Jaq.

"I thought I knew a great deal already," said John.

"Many think they do, but very few actually do. Have you ever heard that the most important principle of negotiations is to be able to walk away from any deal?" said Jaq.

"That sound familiar," said John.

"It's a vital principle, and it just means that you know your top price. Let me rephrase that: it means you're laser-focused on your top price. It also means you refuse to go beyond your top price, but if you think about it for a minute you will always refuse to go beyond your top price if you're hyper-aware about what makes a great deal," said Jaq.

"Let me guess, figuring out the top price for a BFRR deal is simple but not easy," said Nancy.

"Yep. Although it gets easier as you see results," said Jaq.

"What do you mean by that?" said Nancy.

"Being patient is only hard at the beginning when you don't have any deals under your belt. Once you understand that patience wins, and that excellent deals eventually come along, you will never jump at a bad deal again," said Jaq.

"So, how do you calculate that top price, then?" said John.

"It comes down to understanding values on a particular type of property in a particular neighbourhood. The best BFRR investors know whether or not a deal will work just by seeing the address and the price," said Jaq.

"Wouldn't it be rash to buy without doing more research?" said Nancy.

"It definitely would. I'm not saying you buy on that initial estimate. I'm just saying true geographic specialists know their top price inside out. After a quick glance, we're usually accurate in our ARV[6] calculation within a couple thousand dollars," said Jaq.

"So knowing how much to pay is a matter of knowing how much the end value is? It sounds simple. What else comes into play?" asked Nancy.

"Well, the other big piece of the equation is knowing how much the renovations will cost. This is why we do excellent due diligence, no matter how well we know the property and neighbourhood. Once you know the

_____

6   After Repair Value

renovation expense and ARV, you're well on your way to knowing your MAO[7]," said Jaq.

"So what percentage of the ARV are we allowed to pay for a property?" asked Nancy.

"It depends on the scope of renovations. If the renovation expense will be tiny, you can have a higher MAO. If the renovation expense will be high, you will have a lower MAO," said Jaq.

"Makes sense. So, to know how to buy, we also need to know how to fix," said John.

"Well, you need to know how to calculate renovation expenses in order to buy well. The principle behind it is this: there's no better way to exceed expectations and minimize risk than by *starting the holding period with created equity*," said Jaq.

"Who wouldn't want that?" said Nancy.

"It's the best, and the best way to create this is by ensuring MAO and renovation expense is a bunch lower than ARV. This created equity is the famous ROI rocket fuel formula that BFRR investors are so fond of," said Jaq.

"Once we know the average ARV and renovation expense we can calculate the MAO, but it still doesn't explain how we find these deals. I mean, why would anyone sell for that much of a discount anyway? And where do you find these people?" asked Nancy.

"Don't underestimate the power of clarity. Being clear on the MAO is fundamental because you can to speak about *your property type* to everyone in your network.

---

7   Maximum Allowable Offer

Clarity enables positioning, which brings referrals," said Jaq.

"Why would others bring us a great deal when they could buy it themselves?" asked John.

"Most people don't know about or practice BFRR deals. Many buy-and-hold investors don't want to do renovations, and a lot of flippers want bigger renovation jobs. There's a lot of opportunity taking the middle ground, but I don't want you to get the impression these deals are easy to find. You don't come across them every day, which is why it's all the more important you make quick decisions when they come up," said Jaq.

"So people just bring us deals? What's our next action step, then? Do we call our realtor?" asked John.

"That's a decent start, but I want to impress upon you that this process is like casting a net, which you will use to catch every deal in your target neighbourhood," said Jaq.

"So, the deals are like fish," said Nancy.

"Right, but remember you can't put a net across the entire ocean. Rather than trying, it's better to have one excellent net in one excellent location," said Jaq.

"That analogy works for me, so how small of a net are we talking about?" said John.

"Well, I'm an expert on 30 different streets spread out over two small cities in one region. Within those realms, everyone knows I'm a buyer. I mean everyone, and if I find people that don't know, I tell them," said Jaq.

"Right, because only the right people can give the right referrals," said Nancy.

"Exactly. The right people need to know you're looking for a specific property type on a few specific streets. They need to know that you'll buy if the deal is right. By the way, the right people includes sellers, but I will get specific about how to net deals once you have clarity," said Jaq.

"Please do," said John

"Work with a few excellent realtors. Please note the word 'specific'. Not every realtor will work. They must understand the BFRR strategy and be able to identify the right properties before they hit the open market. Most properties aren't suitable for a BFRR investor. It's enough as long as one or two deals hit every couple of months," said Jaq.

"That's not many," said Nancy.

"Nope, but you don't need many. Using excellent realtors is a great strategy when you first get started. It's the first effective net as you build the other nets," said Jaq.

"Other nets?" said John.

"Yes, we'll talk about those in a bit, but the reason you want to start with realtors is that they're often well connected. Not only will they find you deals themselves, but they'll also know people who will find you deals. By building solid relationships with a few key realtors you'll be pleasantly surprised by who else you can meet," continued Jaq.

"And those others become other nets," said John.

"Yep. So, you have realtors and their networks working for you. Next, *call all the FSBO (for sale by owner) signs and online ads that fit your target neighbourhood.* I find the less professional the FSBO, the better chance there is for a deal. Most of the discount real estate company listings are overpriced for my goals, but old faded FSBO signs and simple online ads are often a rich source of solid leads," said Jaq.

"Why the discrepancy between different types of FSBO?" said Nancy.

"It's curious. I can't say exactly, but it seems that the discount real estate listing types don't have run down properties. If it's not run down, there's no deal to be had. We have to add value somewhere," said Jaq.

"Right, what's next?" said Nancy.

"*Print and distribute flyers to target streets.* New BFRR investors often spend too much unfocused effort on this kind of 'shotgun' marketing. Focus is everything, here. Doing a widespread mail drop, hoping to find a gem or two is okay, but 99 out of 100 leads generated in that way turn out to be a wild goose chase," said Jaq.

"That's too time consuming," said Nancy.

"Yep. You're better off to target the exact properties you want. In my ads I simply say I'm looking to buy a property, that I'm not a realtor, and that if I buy their property they won't have to pay any fees. I don't use any tricks or gimmicks. Often people won't call right away, but I'm the first one they call when they're ready to sell later. This gives me a jump on any other investor, and by saving them realtor fees and closing quickly, I'm able to put together a good deal for all involved," continued Jaq.

"So, you just drop mail on your 30 streets?" said John.

"Exactly. Those are the properties I want anyway, why not target them immediately?" said Jaq.

"That's true. What else do you do to find deals?" said John.

"Next, maintain a simple website8 that says you buy houses. If people are searching Google to sell a house in your area, there's a good chance they'll find your website. This is relatively cheap and it will get you a couple of qualified leads every year," said Jaq.

"That's easy enough. It' another small net, I guess. What else?" said Nancy

"Pay wholesalers to bring you deals," said Jaq.

"Wholesalers? Like Costco?" said John.

"Not quite. A wholesaler is an individual who knows how to find BFRR type deals but doesn't carry out the entire strategy. There aren't a lot of these people out there, but when you find a good wholesaler it can make your life a lot easier," said Jaq.

"So, you pay them to find you deals?" said Nancy.

"Yep, and compared to what you get in return, it's cheap. Typically, I pay the wholesaler between $5,000 and $10,000 depending on how much I will make. That's sounds like a lot, but when the deal brings between

---

8 Go   to   www.theultimatewealthstrategy.com/websites/   for examples of house buying websites.

$25,000 and $60,000 worth of created equity, it's well worth it," Jaq went on.

"I'd say. This is starting to sound like a solid net," said John.

"Yes, and it's not complete yet. *You can also send emails directly to people having garage sales and to certain landlords that post rent ads,9"* said Jaq.

"Cold emails? That doesn't sound as targeted as some of the other methods you've shared," said Nancy.

"It sounds random, but once you get good at knowing who to email, you'll find this is an indirect method that works over time. If you think about it, a garage sale is a good indication that a person is getting ready for change, which often means selling their home. Often these deals won't come immediately, but when the seller is ready to sell, they will often call you first if you've made an inquiry via email," said Jaq.

"Seriously?" said John.

"Yep. I guess out fishing analogy runs dry here. This is a bit more like farming. You have to nurture some leads," said Jaq.

"Right. You also mentioned landlords," said Nancy.

"Yeah, I don't recommend you email every landlord that puts up an ad, just the ones that appear to be tired. If the ad is sloppy or unsophisticated, it's often a sign of a landlord getting tired of the job. These landlords have a tendency to let their properties get run down, which

---

9   Go to www.theultimatewealthstrategy.com/tools/ for sample emails and ads.

makes them perfect candidates for a BFRR deal. Just as with garage sales these deals often take a bit of time," Jaq said.

"Wow. I never would have imagined. I guess this will give us the jump on realtors and other investors," said Nancy.

"That's right. Moving on. The old school, tried and true BFRR deal finding method is, *door-knocking and driving around neighbourhoods looking for properties.* I don't often do this anymore, but if I happen upon a property with a big bin parked on the front lawn, I'll still knock on the door. This method can be time consuming, but I've found deals this way," said Jaq.

"Is it wise to do this in the beginning?" said Nancy.

"Yes, it's the best time to do it because it helps you shore up your net, but moreover it helps you get to know your target neighbourhood," said Jaq.

"Okay. The net is getting foolproof. Anything else?" said John.

"There are endless ways to find deals, and I urge you to use more than just the ones we're discussing here. These are simply the tried and true methods. One more I will mention now, is to *have every property that fits on the MLS emailed to you*," said Jaq.

"Are there many good deals through the MLS?" said Nancy.

"Most BFRR investors buy more deals off the MLS than on, but it's still worthwhile to scan targeted listings," said Jaq.

"Targeted meaning our 30 streets, or however large our area is?" said John.

"Right, but also look on the listing for information about who is selling the property. If it's bank owned or an estate sale, you can get an idea of the seller's motivation. Don't neglect the MLS. It's a source for significant deals. In my case, it probably accounts for 25%," said Jaq.

"That's significant," said Nancy.

"Indeed. As mentioned, there are probably a lot more. Don't limit yourself, and remain true to the principle that everyone connected to real estate in your target neighbourhood should know you're a buyer. Over time, leads come to you more easily, but early on you have to hustle more," said Jaq.

"That makes sense. A rocket ship always burns the most fuel on takeoff," said John.

"Yes. The same principle is at play here. Just remember that a rocket ship always has a specific destination in space. It's not just headed to any old place in space, and you're not just buying any old house. You have to niche down to a specific set of neighbourhoods and even specific streets in specific neighbourhoods. Your target area has to be big enough so you can find deals, but it also has to small enough to focus," finished Jaq.

"I guess we have some work to do to find a good deal," said Nancy.

"Yeah. Remember the most important principle of the entire strategy is to *buy for the right price*. It's better to wait a month or two (or more) to find the right deal than it is to pay too much for a property just to get into something. Momentum comes, and good things come to those who have patience but at the same time get out and look. The reward is well worth the patience," said Jaq.

"I'm good at pounding the pavement. It's what I've done my whole career, but what about once we've located a deal? Are there any special ways to negotiate a BFRR deal? I've been known to be too eager in the past and end up with a less than perfect deal. I'd love to hear about how you negotiate a great deal," said John.

"That's a great question John. Locating a property is only one part of buying a great BFRR deal. Exercising skill as a negotiator is every bit as important as finding the deal. If you find a great deal but can't negotiate the price you need, then you haven't found a deal after all," said Jaq.

"It's happened to me a few times. In fact, I think it happened to me on our rental properties," said John.

"Let me guess, you had a realtor who was telling you someone else would scoop up the property if you didn't?" said Jaq.

"How did you know?" said John.

"That's most realtors' job. Don't feel bad. It's happened to all of us, but it doesn't have to happen. Negotiation is a skill, starting with the attitude you bring into the negotiation," said Jaq.

"Attitude?" said Nancy.

"Yeah. It all starts with knowing that negotiation isn't about 'winning'. It's not about some epic battle to the end. The buyer and seller both need to win in order for a deal to be done," said Jaq.

"I've never thought of it like that before," said Nancy.

"I'm glad I'm not telling you a bunch of stuff you already know! Win-win is the only way to put together deals, but believe it or not the same underlying principle that lets you identify a good deal is the same underlying principle that allows you to negotiate well," said Jaq.

"That's handy. What do you mean?" said John.

"It sure is, and once you've mastered it you'll no longer have that feeling of desperation that leads to overpaying. Remember how you told me a few moments ago you've thought you had a good deal to start with and later you realized it was nothing special? That happens because we want the deal so badly that we bend on price. We get attached to the deal. Sellers can sense when a buyer is desperate, so *being clear on your MAO will keep you from taking a bad deal*," said Jaq.

"The same thing that helps locate great properties – like you spoke of earlier," said Nancy.

"Exactly. You're not buying 'real estate'. You're buying a specific property for a specific MAO that will be renovated for a specific amount, which will lead to a specific ARV," said Jaq.

"There's that formula again," said John.

"Yes, but it's one thing to know it when locating a property. It's another thing to stick with your guns, no matter what, when negotiation. Too many investors fall in love with a property and delude themselves into thinking they can make up for a bad buy with another part of the process. Don't fall for this delusion," said Jaq.

"What parts of the process do you mean?" said Nancy.

"People think they will add more value through renovations or will get an above market refinance, but if they were honest with themselves, they'd realize they were just talking themselves into paying too much," said Jaq.

"Yeah. That happened to me. I wanted the property bad, and I told myself it would appreciate so fast it would make up for it," said John.

"That's what happens, and there are even more chances for self-delusion when dong a BFRR deal because there are more components. Remember that just as a seller can sense desperation when you're not clear, they can sense your staunchness when you are clear," said Jaq.

"What do you mean?" said Nancy.

"Your certainty eventually helps convince the seller. Many of my deals appear to be dead before they get done because I will tell a seller I'm walking away. It's not an act or a ploy. I intend to walk away because I know I can't do the deal at the price they're offering. Often they'll consider their options, which will involve several more weeks of advertising, showing, and perhaps engaging an agent. Once they consider all these things they end up calling me back, suddenly willing to accept my price," said Jaq.

"That's what you mean by being willing to walk away," said John.

"Exactly, and you can tilt the balance in your favour. Remember that I said every deal has to be win-win? Well, the thing that will most likely make it a win for you is getting the price you need," said Jaq.

"Okay, I follow you so far," said Nancy.

"Money is main *our concern* because we're dealing with an investment, but we often falsely assume money is the seller's main concern, too. It's not always. The seller is often looking for minimal time and effort when selling. After knowing your top line price and being willing to walk away from the deal, *dealing only with motivated sellers* is the next important negotiating principle," said Jaq.

"Motivated seller?" asked Nancy.[10]

"A motivated seller is someone who has a good reason to sell the property with minimal hassle. A lot of sellers are stuck with a property that for some reason is a hassle to them. The last thing they want to do is worry about renovating, renting, or even sprucing the place up for sale. They just want to sell, fast. After finding a property the next thing is to identify if the seller is motivated," said Jaq.

"How do we do that?" asked John.

"There are a few types of situations associated with seller motivation. *Bankruptcy and foreclosure* are big reasons. People lose jobs. They have financial difficulty for all kinds of reasons. In such cases, people have two immediate needs. First, they need to stop spending monthly money on a mortgage. In fact, they often don't

---

10   Go to www.theultimatewealthstrategy.com/tools/ to get your free motivated seller checklist.

have the money to pay mortgage, and that's why they end up in foreclosure. Second, they need to raise extra money. If there's any cash left in the property, they need to access it. I keep a close eye on *power of sale* deals in my target neighbourhood," said Jaq.

"Are there any more circumstances that cause sellers to be motivated?" asked Nancy.

"*Divorce* is another big one. Each half of the divorcing couple often moves into separate, smaller homes. Neither of them is planning on keeping the home they lived in together, and they need to dispose of it. The last thing they want is to go through a lengthy sales process. In other words, they're textbook *motivated sellers.* In divorce cases, what you can offer is a quick and painless sale," said Jaq.

"And if we provide that they will trade a good deal. Got it. Any other kinds of motivated sellers?" said John.

"*Tired landlords* are great because they're realistic. Many properties you see listed with a realtor or a self-listing service are overpriced because the seller thinks her property is special. We even see this when the property needs repairs and should be priced 15-20% below market," said Jaq.

"I guess tired landlords are different?" said Nancy.

"Yes, they are realistic. They're well aware of the cost and time involved in renovating a property – it's why they didn't do it themselves. Often the landlord has extracted value out of the place for several years and in the process has let the property get run down. They know it's run down, so they know the price will be lower than the 'average property'. They know they won't get top dollar for the property, but they also know they can save $10,000 or more on fees by selling privately[11] rather than using a realtor. Tired landlords are often motivated," said Jaq.

"Is that it?" said Nancy.

"Well, each property that looks like a fixer upper in your target market is a potential motivated seller. It might not be one of the kinds of motivated sellers just mentioned, yet might still be willing to sell for the right price. A run down property is always worth a try. Identifying types is just helpful so you know where to look," said Jaq.

"So that's all the categories?" said John.

"Well, there is one more category that I can think of – *estate sales* often have motivated sellers. This is because every estate has an executor, and most executors are children of the deceased," said Jaq.

"Yep. I was executor when my mom passed away," said Nancy.

"Right, so you know what an immense job it is. In fact, it's practically a full time job for many people – a full-time and often unpaid job. Since most executors are also people with full-time jobs they just want the disposal of assets to happen quickly. As a buyer, you can often take their biggest problem off their hands. If you can do it quickly and painlessly for them you will often get a good price in exchange," said Jaq.

---

11   Please visit www.theultimatewealthstrategy.com to learn more about private deals.

"Okay. Is that it?" said Nancy.

"That's the basics of it. Remember, both finding deals and negotiating well start from knowing your market, which enables you to pass up on bad deals and put laser focus on excellent deals. Knowledge combined with firmness and patience will ensure you also negotiate momentum building deals," said Jaq.

"You can't manage what you can't measure."

W. Edwards Deming

Tracking Leads for Marketing Success

One of the biggest mistakes new BFRR investors make is to not track leads. Over time this mistake will slow down progress and lead to more work with worse results. Why?

Tracking leads gives you data, which can tell you where to put lead generation focus. It gives you that edge that leads to stunning instead of mediocre results.

Successful investors apply the 80/20 rule (also called Pareto's Principle), which states that 20% of activity will provide 80% of the result. This means the other 80% of all activity leads to a paltry 20% of the result.

In practical terms this means that if an investors has 5 different ways to find leads, then 1 of those ways will likely produce in the range of 80% of the results.

Burnout is one of the biggest problems real estate investors face. It's easy to lose track of the long-term vision. This is why we need a strong 'why' in this business, as it brings us back to our vision when we'd otherwise forget.

The devil is in the details, and we're forced to put much of our energy into those details. Applying the 80/20 rule helps minimize the burnout associated with the day-to-day activities.

This is why tracking seller leads is important. You may use several methods to attract motivated sellers – especially at the beginning when you're finding what works. Undoubtedly, some of the methods of marketing will be more successful than others, *but each investor will find success using different methods.* This is why it's important to try each of them and find out which ones work.

As you develop and systematize the BFRR business you'll want to cut out all or most of the 80% of activity that leads to little result (20%). Cutting these activities out will simplify the business so you can develop momentum and maintain energy.

Just paying attention to the more effective methods of lead generation is good, but there is a more accurate method of tracking leads. Let's look at this system step-by-step.

> First, set up an account with the *Grasshopper* system. It can be found at www.grasshopper.com and costs very little (starting at $12 per month). With this system you can set up multiple VOIP lines. Use a different number for each lead source. Every time a call comes in you'll know which source it came from.
>
> Next, you set up a simple tracking chart that shows the source of each lead.
>
> Finally, you record all leads and soon you'll know what are your best sources of leads. If you notice an 80/20 pattern has formed, you will want to spend less energy chasing the 20% and focus more on the 80% lead sources.

Due Diligence

John and Nancy were eager to get started applying the strategy after their long chat. Jaq taught them much, and their heads were swimming. They wanted to get going since they knew that immediate action would cement all the lessons already learned.

"Well Jaq, it's been a slice, but I think we have to get going. We have a lot of work to do. Time to start tracking down some deals and get this strategy into gear," said John.

"Hang on a second. There's one more topic we have to cover before you go. Nancy, I know you'll love this topic," said Jaq.

"I will?" said Nancy.

"Yes, in real estate we call it due diligence. We've already spoken in general terms about this topic, but what are the exact guidelines we use to ensure each property works? That's what we need to discuss now," said Jaq.

"John and I have already discussed risk mitigation. Nancy, has John shared that with you?" said Jaq.

"He has, but I'm sure there's more to learn," said Nancy.

"You're right about that. We do risk mitigation at every phase, but much risk mitigation is done *during the condition period*. During this time we take a series of steps known as *due diligence* to ensure we're buying the right property at the right price. It's risk mitigation in practice," said Jaq.

"Great. I like sleeping well," said Nancy

"This will help provide that. Now, at this point we should be almost certain we've got the right property, but due diligence gives us greater certainty. We wouldn't have made an offer on it unless it fit our criterion for MAO, ARV, repairs needed, neighbourhood, and cash flow. Still, there are always unknowns, which is why we take this series of due diligence steps," said Jaq.

"Sing it," said Nancy.

"For sure. Now, there will be times, hopefully when you're more experienced, when you don't even have a condition period. This happens when the deal is so good we have to have it, and the seller won't allow conditions. In these cases, the deal you're getting acts as an insurance policy against being surprised by major expenses. However, it's probably not a good idea to write a condition free offer unless you have the cash available to close on the deal if financing doesn't materialize," said Jaq.

"Yeah, we won't be doing that at first," said Nancy.

"Good idea, so let's discuss a small renovation, normal deal, with some basic conditions. Due diligence comes after a) finding the deal, and b) negotiating the deal," said Jaq.

Total Due Diligence

We tend to think of the condition period as due diligence time, however there is diligence to do during the finding and negotiating phases, too.

Due diligence is simply being thorough in your process, which is necessary at all stages, although the condition period is the most important period of due diligence.

One example of due diligence during the finding phase is to never accept comps provided by others. You need to do them yourself and/or have your own realtor provide them to you. Remember that comps can be subjective. The person presenting them will always present the ones best for his or her purposes.

Another example of due diligence is getting referrals about any wholesaler that might bring you a deal. If the wholesaler has a great track record of finding and wholesaling great deals you can have more confidence that you will get a great deal.

> The purpose of due diligence is to move you to action-taking when you don't have enough information, and on the other side it's to stop you from moving forward when the information learned demands it.
>
> Excellent BFRR investors learn to apply total due diligence in every stage of the process.

"Got it. So, what do we need to know?" said John.

"The first part of condition period due diligence is *doing a cash flow analysis,* which is an interesting topic. On one hand it's simple, but many investors don't calculate cash flow accurately. They cut corners because they want to make a deal work even when it doesn't work," said Jaq.

"More of that self-delusion we spoke of earlier," said John.

"Exactly, and the most common way investors delude themselves is by not calculating certain expenses when calculating cash flow. The rule is simple and unbreakable: every expense required to maintain the property must be covered by the property's income. Increasing cash flow can be done in two ways. You can raise income, or you can lower expenses," said Jaq.

"The two sides of the ledger," said Nancy.

"Correct. First, you need to know your total income; therefore it's vital to have solid evidence when projecting rental income. This is one reason we become geographic experts when investing in real estate. The more we know our target area, the more certain we can be about rental income – because we've freshly renovated, we always shoot for the high end of comparable rents," said Jaq.

"There's a benefit we don't have with our normal buy-and-hold properties," said John.

"Not usually. Now, rental income is the main source of income, but we should seek other types of income wherever possible. Parking, coin operated laundry (in multi-family buildings), and storage rental are all common ways to obtain additional income. There are others, and some investors get creative about this. What's important to note here is that you take all of the sources of income, and then add them together to get your income numbers. This is the first component of cash flow analysis," said Jaq.

"What about the other side of the ledger?" said Nancy.

"Next, it's a simple matter of forecasting our total expenses and subtracting that number from the income numbers. I say it's a 'simple matter', and it is, but as mentioned, investors delude themselves about the real expenses generated by a property," said Jaq

"We won't do that," said John.

"Great. Now, mortgage is the biggest expense. By working with an excellent mortgage broker in advance of the refinancing phase, you can ensure you will know what your post-refinance mortgage expense will be during the due diligence phase. It makes sense to start a new mortgage application for the refinance the day after closing on the property. This allows you to reserve the interest rate for 90 to 120 days without having to worry that the mortgage rate will go up," said Jaq.

"Right. We need this for expense calculation. What else?" said Nancy.

"*Property tax* is a big expense. Get a copy of the tax bill from the seller during the due diligence phase to make sure you have accurate property tax numbers," said Jaq.

"Right, what else?" said John.

"Another important one is *insurance*. In order to be properly educated on this, add a real estate investment specialist insurance agent to your team. Get educated on the right kinds of insurance policy for rental properties, and get exact quotes from your agent to ensure you know your insurance expense in advance. Being cheap with insurance is not a good idea on a rental property. Make sure you're covered for the specific issues encountered by real estate investors such as rental loss protection and tenant vandalism," said Jaq.

"Yeah. We just learned that from our flood. What else?" said Nancy.

"It's better with a BFRR deal than a normal buy-and-hold deal, but we still have to account for a *maintenance* expense during the due diligence phase. Set aside 4% of total monthly income for maintenance," said Jaq.

"That would be nice rather than coming out of pocket for maintenance during the holding period. Tell me, though, what would that expense be on a normal buy-and-hold deal?" said John.

"8% is pretty common, although this number will vary depending on the property," said Jaq.

"That's a significant difference," said Nancy.

"Indeed. The next expense is *property management.* Even if you're managing the property yourself, you must calculate an expense for property management in the expense numbers. This will ensure you're prepared when the day comes to hire a professional property manager. You can also pay yourself this property management fee, which is important for putting a value on your time. Don't forget to calculate this important expense! You can expect to pay as much as 10% of gross rent collected for property management," said Jaq.

"We never thought of that on our other properties," said Nancy

"Most investors don't. The next expense to prepare for is *advertising.* With online advertising services available these days the expense required to advertise a property is minimal. However, some of the bigger online classified websites are now charging if you post multiple ads. Ensure that you calculate this expense during the due diligence period," said Jaq.

"I guess advertising becomes more expensive as you grow?" said John.

"Yes, with the classified sites now charging, it seems that way. The next expense to consider is *utilities.* Now, it's always a good idea to have your tenants pay for the utilities, but if having utilities in tenants' names is impossible for any reason, the cost of utilities *must* be built into the rent. There have been many landlord horror stories over the years about tenants using the oven to heat the home, leaving windows open in winter, and any other unimaginable wastes of energy," said Jaq.

"Yikes," said John.

"I know. The thing to remember is to always get the utilities in your tenant's name, but if this isn't possible, you must account for it in your expenses *and* charge higher rents," said Jaq.

"Got it. Anything else?" said Nancy.

"The last main expense to calculate during due diligence is a *vacancy allowance.* Just as you put aside money every month for future maintenance expenses, you must also put aside money every month for the eventuality of vacancy. A good rule of thumb is to take your region's published current vacancy rate and put aside double that percent each month. So, if your region has a 4% vacancy rate, you should put aside 8% of the total rent for vacancy allowance. This, along with the maintenance allowance builds up your reserve fund over time," said Jaq.

"How do we know our local vacancy rate?" said Nancy.

"CMHC publishes the industry standard reports on the topic," said Jaq.

"Great. Is that the whole cash flow analysis part of condition period due diligence?" said Nancy.

"That's it unless there is other income or expenses that are unique to your property," said Jaq.

"Okay, so what's the next component of due diligence?" said John.

"You must prepare a detailed *renovation plan.* If you're making an offer on the property it means you already expect the renovations to fit into your strategy, but during condition period you need to think about the details, since your strategy depends on costs remaining within the pre-specified range," said Jaq.

"I hate surprises," said Nancy.

"Unfortunately, they happen, but they can also be mitigated. A furnace replacement, roofing, or foundation work can quickly blow a budget. During the due diligence period the investor has a responsibility to get answers to every question about a property's upcoming renovations expenses. Knowing before closing the deal is essential," said Jaq.

"I wouldn't feel comfortable without knowing," said Nancy.

"Right. So we need a great renovation plan. This must: *include a clear scope of work, consider adding value, calculate material costs, calculate permit costs,* and *calculate labour costs,*" said Jaq.

"That sound like a thorough renovation plan," said John.

"It has to be. This is our business. The first step of the renovation plan that will allow us to complete the rest of the plan is to develop a *clear and thorough scope of work*, which is simply a complete list of all the work to be done and the specifications of how it will be done. Once this is done you can put together the rest of your renovation plan," said Jaq.

"The scope will make my life a lot easier," said John.

"It's a must. You need it in order to get multiple contractors to provide quotes and to get contractor referrals, both of which help plan renovations and develop strong relationships with contractors," said Jaq.

"On what basis do we develop the scope of work?" said Nancy.

"Every scope of work starts with the end in mind, which in this case is to *add value* to the property. It sounds crazy, but it's possible to renovate a property without adding any value. People over-renovate all the time. The main goal of the renovation phase is to bring the property value in line with the 'average property' in the area, and this means improving the surface. You have to raise the value significantly more than the amount of money you spend on the property," said Jaq.

"Is it possible to raise the value above the average?" said Nancy.

"It is possible with some more advanced strategies. This might involve adding an extra suite or bedroom to a property. We'll talk about that later, but for now let's say the main goal is to purchase the property below average and bring it up to the neighbourhood average with renovations," said Jaq.

"Right, so we have to know exactly what needs to be renovated," said John

"Correct. Once you're certain you can bring the value up to the average, then the next part of the renovation plan is budgeting *material costs*. The art of keeping material costs low is a learned art – one that a great BFRR investor must master. The best way to do this is to implement a repeatable system for renovations. This allows the BFRR investor to buy in bulk and streamline the process for maximum efficiency. By doing this a BFRR investor can usually estimate material costs within a few hundred dollars per deal," said Jaq.

"Any other pieces of the renovation plan we should know about?" said John.

"Depending on the kind of renovation you do, you might have to pay for development permits. On a basic lipstick renovation we try to avoid the need for permits as it adds a level of complexity that isn't always worth the effort and cost. With that being said, there are many occasions when permits are well worth the effort and cost," said Jaq.

"Okay, we'll have to cross that bridge when we come to it, although I'd like to do at least the first one without having to take out any permits," said John.

"Absolutely. A basic lipstick renovation doesn't usually require permits," said Jaq.

"Cool. What else is involved in the renovation planning?" said John.

"Well, we've already discussed material costs, but we haven't mentioned *labour cost certainty*. This is important, as labour can add up quickly if it's not tightly controlled.

"That's one of my fears," said John.

"Yes, you've mentioned that. Fortunately, price certainty is achievable. All you have to do is secure firm quotes from contractors before starting the work. To get firm quotes, just bring all of the necessary contractors along to prepare quotes at the property during the due diligence period," said Jaq.

"Is it that easy?" said Nancy.

"Well, it can be tricky to organize. I tend to not let a whole gang of contractors into the property at once. A little competition is great, but you don't want to humiliate anyone. I only allow 1 or 2 in at a time, but I definitely schedule them back-to-back so that they know they're not the only one bidding on the job," said Jaq.

"That makes sense," said John.

"That's just a tactic, though. The real trick is having a flawless scope of work, but almost as important for price certainty is to *never pay contractors until work has been done.* This keeps them from walking away from unfinished work, or if they do walk, at least you still have the money available to bring in a new contractor to complete what the first didn't. With excellent relationships this is usually avoidable, but we'll discuss that in more detail later," said Jaq.

"Is that it for renovation planning?" said Nancy.

"Yes, but we will speak about this in more depth later. Due diligence is like a bridge between buying and fixing. You need to be aware of it now, but these components of due diligence will require a bigger conversation after you get a property under contract but before you remove conditions," said Jaq.

"I look forward to it. So, renovation planning is a big part of condition period due diligence. What else is involved in this due diligence process?" said John.

"You also need to do a *property inspection.* This is important for a few reasons. First, it ensures there aren't any expensive surprises after you make the purchase. To do it right, hire a professional property inspector to go through the property with a fine-toothed comb," said Jaq.

"I thought that was the only reason for an inspection," said Nancy.

"There's another great reason. It also provides proof to renegotiate the price. In fact, it's the best renegotiation tool there is. Often you're getting at least the cost of the inspection as discount off the purchase price, often more. "said Jaq.

"Cool. We definitely won't skip that step of condition period due diligence, and we'll use the inspection to renegotiate, but is that it for now? With all the information you've shared with us, I think we're ready to get out there and buy a property now, as long as we take all the necessary steps. What do you think?" asked John.

"Only the two of you know for sure, but based on what we've learned thus far you're ready for the next step. We'll need to discuss the renovation in more detail before you start it, but you should know enough to start looking for a property. You have to jump in eventually. Just make sure you jump in with your eyes wide open," said Jaq.

"We will. Thanks Jaq. We'll let you know about our progress during our next weekly meeting. How does that sound?" said Nancy.

"Perfect plan. Move swiftly, but with purpose and remain loyal to the system. Don't cut any corners and be patient. Good deals are out there, you just need to be ready when they come available," said Jaq.

"We'll make sure of that. Take care and talk soon," said Nancy.

They all said their goodbyes and Jaq sat back with a wry smile on his face. He knew they were in for an adventure. It's one thing to understand how to do a BFRR deal in theory, but executing is another matter.

As Jaq sipped on his latte, he was confident they'd pull it off, but he was also aware they'd have a few hitches along the way. He was interested to see how the couple would handle the challenges ahead.

Condition Period Due Diligence Action Steps

- **Develop Renovation Plan**
    - Clearly Define Scope of Work
    - Consider Adding Value
    - Calculate Material Costs
    - Calculate Permit Costs
    - Calculate Labour Costs
- **Cash Flow Analysis**
    - Income
        - Rent
        - Other (Parking, Coin Laundry, Storage, etc.,)

- **Expenses**
  - Mortgage
  - Property Tax
  - Insurance
  - Maintenance
  - Property Management
  - Advertising
  - Utilities
  - Vacancy Allowance
- **Property Inspection**

Buyer Beware

In this chapter you learned about the importance of dealing with adversity, as well as the method of buying BFRR deals to create outstanding results – from finding to negotiating to carrying our condition period due diligence.

It's commonly believed in real estate that most of the money is made on the buy. This is a true statement, and this chapter is designed to teach you every component of ensuring you buy right.

However, knowing the theory behind buying BFRR deals and actually pulling off a deal are two different things. In the next chapter, you will see an example of how to land a great deal.

The next chapter will drive home all of the lessons learned in this chapter, as you'll learn through the experiences of John and Nancy how to find and negotiate an excellent BFRR deal.

"Unless the deal is a win-win for everyone involved, it's not a deal at all and I want no part of it."

_____

Jeff Woods

CHAPTER 5

Getting the Deal

Translating Theory to Practice

Have you ever had a hard time moving from knowing how to do something to actually doing it? The truth is that we've all experienced this problem. It's not always that big of a deal, but when the topic matters most, implementation is top priority.

Much of what we learn isn't the right fit for us, but if you've come this far in this book, there's a good chance you want to implement the BFRR strategy in your life.

In the previous chapter you learned how-to properly execute the BFRR buying strategy, but this chapter will demonstrate the results of patiently carrying through the buying process. We'll also see how old fears can arise when trying to do something new, and how moving through that fear is crucial to success.

Ready to Make a Difference

Nancy and John were brimming with useful information after their latest conversation with their coach, Jaq. After several years of feeling somewhat the victim of their own circumstance they were now taking control of the hero role in the adventure of their own life.

They were ready to take the next step, which in this case meant purchasing a property, rather than learning more. With their confidence (as a result of Jaq's coaching), they were ready.

John got busy placing ads, knocking on doors, building the "We Buy Houses" website, and ordering the bandit signs. It was a perfect fit, as John was an old school hustler. This kind of work resonated with him. He knew if he put in the work that the leads would come pouring in.

Nancy was more methodical. Building relationships to find leads resonated more with her, and she made it her job to let everyone know that she and John were now in the business of buying great deals in their target neighbourhood. John saw the value of this approach and applied the same hustle as always to growing relationships.

Fundamentals Always

John and Nancy had spent a lot of time and effort learning the BFRR investing system from Jaq. They were excited to apply their new knowledge and get moving in the direction of their dreams.

However, they had previously been trained in the fundamental approach to buy-and-hold real estate investing.

Every BFRR investor must do the same.

Just because we employ a unique strategy doesn't mean we forget fundamentals. The BFRR strategy is powerful, and it can change your life dramatically when applied – due to the ways it's different from the standard buy-and-hold approach.

However, the BFRR strategy is more similar to the buy-and-hold approach than it is different, and while the value-added through renovations is important, there is far more wealth creating potential on the back end – by holding and renting over the long term.

Thus, investing fundamentals must be applied to BFRR deals every bit as much as any real estate investment. This book isn't the place to discuss those fundamentals, as this is a big topic, and it has already been discussed in detail elsewhere. *Real Estate Investing in Canada 2.0* by Don R. Campbell is the Canadian industry standard on the topic. We recommend you read that book if you need a primer on the fundamental approach to investing.

Between John's ambitious approach and Nancy's methodical approach, it didn't take long for leads to come trickling into the couple's buying funnel.

As happens to many, John and Nancy made a few hurried trips to check out 'hot deals', only to find the deal was nothing special. Soon, John and Nancy developed the ability to separate real deals from fake deals.

After a few false starts, and after spending considerable effort researching target neighbourhoods and streets, they soon had a solid understanding of what a property would cost if it was in average condition and what they'd be willing to pay for it when they found it.

Within 6 weeks a promising lead came into their funnel, and they switched into negotiation mode. The prospective seller came into their system when John replied to an online advertisement of a property for sale in their target neighbourhood.

Rather than rushing, they took their time to properly negotiate a good deal. What follows is an email exchange between the seller and John:

John – Day 1

Can I get a street name? Also what are the property taxes and condo fees? Is it forced air heating?

Seller – Day 1

Good morning. It is on Cashflowsville Parkway. Condo fees are low $100 per month. Taxes are approx. $2000 per year. If you would like to arrange a time to view let me know.

John – Day 1

Is this a private sale?

Seller – Day 1

Yes, it is a private sale.

John – Day 1

Great. I have a couple more questions.

Was this a 3 bedroom converted to a 2 bedroom or always a 2 bedroom? Is there central air and heat? What is included in the condo fees? When are you looking to sell by?

Seller – Day 1

It does have both air conditioning and heating. It was always a 2-bed. The condo fees include maintenance of the gardens in the complex and all property insurance, so you don't need additional insurance. It is a well-maintained area with lots of good neighbours. I can be flexible with time scales in terms of closing. What is your time frame?

John – Day 1

I'm very flexible for closing, as we would plan to rent it out. Our concern would be the condition of the property and price.

What is the address of the complex?

Seller – Day 1

The condition is good. I would take an offer on the price. What were you thinking?

It's on Cashflowsville Parkway.

John – Day 1

I would have to take a look at it before we made an offer. I can come by today for 4:40pm. Would that be okay?

Also, why are you selling? And are you the owner of it?

Seller – Day 1

I am the owner. I am selling as I am moving into my fiancé's house. I can't make 4:40 today as I am in the west end of the city. Could you see it earlier around 1?

John – Day 1

I couldn't today but I could do 1:30pm on the weekend.

Seller – Day 1

That sounds fine it would actually be better for me too. Would you like to confirm 1.30pm on Saturday then? See you Saturday.

John – Day 1

Hi. Yes confirmed.

I looked in my database and noticed an ad from 2009 about renting the property for $1400. Is that what you are currently getting for rent?

Seller – Day 1

I was getting that amount. However it was a reduced rent. A property 2 doors down rents for I think $1200. It rents quickly.

I will see you Saturday at 1.30pm.

If you have any further questions let me know.

John – Day 1

It looks like the taxes are $2700 on the property not $2000.

Doing my numbers I couldn't purchase the property for more than $190,000. I don't want to waste your time and mine if you will not accept a price at that level.

Seller – Day 1

I would definitely entertain that level. If you were happy with the property I would accept $192,000.

This would be a fair price because I want a quick sale and that would be under market for the property. Shall we keep to the appointment at 1.30pm Saturday?

John – Day 1

I have spoken with my partner and we would like to meet you on Saturday. We would consider what you had proposed.

Let me know.

That would be fine. I can be there for 1:30pm on Saturday. See you at unit 33.

Seller – Day 1

Confirmed see you then.

5 days later...

Seller – Day 5

It's (the seller) from Cashflowsville Parkway.

I wondered if you had any news about your financing.

I can confirm that I would be able to proceed with a closing date of April 1st.

I look forward to speaking with you.

John – Day 5

I'm talking to my partner tonight.

Seller – Day 5

Ok. Thanks for letting me know. Speak to you tomorrow.

Seller – Day 5

Good morning, I understand you were speaking with your partner last night. Are you going to proceed with the purchase?

Please let me know and we can start the paperwork for April 1st closing date.

Note: At this point, you can start to see that the seller is starting to get antsy. He wants the deal to happen and is now pursuing John.

John – Day 5

My partner does not want to go forward with the project with the date and the price and I know that you were looking for 190k for April 1st.

I'm sorry. She wants 185k and I told her that you wouldn't go for it, as you were already meeting with an Agent.

Seller – Day 5

Hi. Thank you for letting me know. Obviously $185k is too low. I would go ahead at the price we discussed however not at $185k. If you change your mind let me know. I will be instructing an agent today.

4 days later...

Seller – Day 9

I have spoken with my partner and she and I have agreed we would meet you in the middle. We would be prepared to sell the property at $188k. We would hold off on instructing an agent if you could respond by 12pm today. Let me know.

John – Day 9

Can you give me 24 hours? I think this is reasonable and I am okay with it. I just need to talk to my partner. Is this okay with you?

Seller – Day 9

We feel it is reasonable.

I understand you need to speak to your partner. However we would like an answer sooner than 24 hours as if it's not a go we have another option to explore.

Please let me know. Regards

John – Day 9

I'm trying to contact him as we speak.

Seller – Day 9

Sounds good I will wait to hear from you.

Seller – Day 9

I have spoken to my lawyer this morning and we can get all the paperwork rolling as soon as tomorrow morning.

John – Day 9

I'm speaking to him (partner) at 8pm tonight and will give you an answer immediately.

Seller – Day 9

Speak to you then.

John – Day 9

We are going to have to pass on it at this time. Sorry.

Seller – Day 9

Ok, thanks for letting me know

5 days later

Seller – Day 14

Are you still interested in the Pickering house at $185,000?

John – Day 14

Do you have an agent already? This could be a problem.

Seller – Day 14

I can cancel within 24 hrs.

I am not concerned with the agent contract. He has a 24-hour cancelation policy. Are you able to close in April still?

John – Day 14

Have any repairs been done? Is it currently listed?

Seller – Day 14

What did you want done? Yes, it is listed. I just don't want to go through the whole arduous task of showing with agent etc. $185k is a very good price and if you can do that deal I will make it happen

John – Day 14

Ok. Let me talk to my partner.

Seller – Day 14

Sounds good

John – Day 14

Okay. We are interested at $185,000 but we need to close in middle of April because of a time conflict on another project.

And, we are asking that those permanent smoke/CO_2 alarms be put back in all floors of the property ASAP, as it is a fire concern.

Seller – Day 14

Ok, I will agree to the closing date of mid-April. I will meet the request of fixing the fire alarms.

Let's talk tomorrow and we can sort out all of the detail. Have a good evening.

John – Day 14

Excellent.

Note: this deal took 14 days to negotiate and that John eventually got the property for $5,000 less than he originally offered.

John met with the seller the next day and completed the offer. Both parties signed the offer to purchase, and John dropped off a deposit cheque at the seller's lawyer. The contract was given to the respective lawyers, and the deal was officially moving forward! John and Nancy tap-danced with excitement when John got home from getting the deal firmed up.

They were shocked that the deal played out just as Jaq described. It wasn't that they didn't trust Jaq, but they expected it to be different in practice than in theory.

By being neighbourhood experts they knew a deal when they saw it. This gave them the guts to wait for the deal to unfold. They refused to accept a poor deal. Let's take a look at the numbers:

Purchase Price: $185,000

Down Payment: $37,000

Closing/Holding/Renovations: $5,000

Cash Required for Purchase and Renovation $42,000

Renovations: New Carpets, Paint, New Toilet, Lots of Cleaning.

Property Type: 2-Bed, 1-Bath Townhome with Attached Garage

Based on their projections, this property would end up performing solidly. It wouldn't be a homerun, but it would be a typical BFRR deal. Some cash would be returned with the refinance, and the property would be a good long-term hold. They still had some work to do, but they were excited to get this far.

Celebrating

"What do you say we take the evening to celebrate?" John said.

"Well, it *sounds* like a great idea, in theory, but you and I both know the kids won't feed themselves and there's laundry to do, and there's Saturday morning soccer tomorrow," said Nancy.

"Yes, I know, but I also know my parents love having sleepovers with the kids. They know the whole routine, and could get the kids fed and to soccer on time in the morning. They managed to raise me after all, and what a stellar job they did! Laundry can wait until tomorrow and remember what Jaq said about celebrating success," said John.

"Well, I wouldn't chalk this one up as a success just yet. We still have to fix, refinance, and then rent this thing before I will consider it a success," said Nancy.

"You're right about, but even if this deal falls apart, it's a huge accomplishment to get this far. Think about what we've done. It wasn't long ago we were resigned to an uncertain and somewhat hopeless future – not knowing if we'd even be able to retire. Today, I'm a heck of a lot more confident about our life, all because we hired a coach and learned some solid investment and business principles. I feel like we're in control now, even though we have a long way to go. Let's go out and celebrate success instead of sitting at home lamenting how far we still have to go," said John.

"You make a good point. I'm proud of us for getting this far. I'm also quite confident about this deal. It fits the system and we did the due diligence. I'm sure the renovation expense will come in around what we predicted and the refinance will go as planned. You're right, let's go have some fun. You call your parents and I'll get the kids ready to go," said Nancy.

"Sounds like a fair deal," said John

The couple jumped into action and before long had their evening arranged. The kids were whisked away by the ever-helpful grandparents, and John and Nancy were left alone to get cleaned up and dressed for a night out.

That evening they basked in the glow of their early success. It was a great chance to relax and have some fun, but neither of them expected what would come next.

Old Demons Return

It was 6 in the morning the next morning, when John sat bolt upright in his bed. He looked like a possessed horror movie character, soaked in sweat, with wild eyes. There was a knot in the pit of his stomach, and he didn't know its source.

He wondered if it was something he ate the night before, although he had exercised admirable restraint and didn't overeat. He thought about the wine, but he only had one glass. That couldn't make him feel this way – could it?

He got up out of bed to get showered off, hoping that would help, but it didn't. He noticed along with his uneasy stomach and the cold sweats he was also paralyzed with fear.

He went to the kitchen, made coffee, and paced back and forth as he drank. He couldn't remember being this anxious before. Actually, there was one other time. When was that?

"Good morning, honey," Nancy said, waking John from the thoughts racing in his mind.

John was so startled he spilled coffee on his leg, "Ow! Darn! What the heck?" said John.

"Whoa, all just said good morning. I was going to give you a hug and tell you how happy I am, but now I'm not so sure I should. What's up with you? You don't look well," said Nancy.

"I'm not feeling too good. I don't know what it is. I'm anxious, jumpy, and have a queasy stomach. I woke up with the cold sweats, and I'm pretty sure it wasn't the food from last night. I only drank one glass of wine, so I don't know what's going on. Just as you came in the kitchen, I was thinking I've felt this way before, but I can't quite put my finger on what caused it," said John.

"I know exactly what it is," said Nancy.

"Really? What?" said John.

"This was how you looked when you got demoted at work. Honestly, you've haven't recovered since – until these last few months when we've been working on getting our first deal. It's almost eerie seeing you like this again. I had forgotten," said Nancy.

"Seriously? I didn't realize my anxiety was so obvious – then or now. It makes sense, though. We have a great property, and now we have to get it fixed. Yes, that's definitely it. The idea of managing the renovation is freaking me out. I've proven once that I can't manage," said John.

"Honey, everyone has setbacks. I still think it was your boss who fumbled, not you. I mean, who demotes someone after one little mess up? How about helping the person to grow better the next time? The only thing he achieved that day was to shatter your confidence. He didn't solve the problem. Didn't you tell me Thompson had a hard time on the next contract for the same reason?" said Nancy.

"Yeah, I don't know," said John. His thoughts ran wild as the demon he feared most made a return.

It only took a couple of moments for Nancy to recognize the glossy look in John's eyes. He was already showing signs of depression again as he drifted away from Nancy. The same question ran through his mind on repeat, "How on earth am I going to *manage* this renovation?"

They had only gotten a property under contract the day before, and now he only had a couple of weeks during the condition period to carry out the due diligence required before his personal moment of truth. John should have been excited, but instead he was paralyzed with fear and was in fact looking for the nearest exit.

From One Step to the Next

In this chapter, you saw how theory becomes practice by patiently following the system. You've also seen how anxiety and fear caused by old demons can negatively affect an investor.

As seasoned real estate investors know, you must learn how to experience and deal with fear, do your homework, and then follow through anyways.

In the BFRR investing world, the biggest source of anxiety and fear is around the fixing process and the costs associated with them. Unless you can be certain that the renovation process will be on time, on budget, and produce the required value lift, you will always feel stress about the renovations process. The next chapter deals in detail with the question of renovations and how best to execute them.

"If you're going to do something, do it right the first time."

Mike Holmes

CHAPTER 6

Fix

No Fix for Poor Execution

Have you ever heard of a renovation job going over budget? Of course you have. We all have. Renovation jobs go over budget all the time. This is the norm, not the exception.

It's true that money is made in real estate when you buy, but it's also true that an excellent deal can be turned into a bad deal by poorly executing the renovation.

The biggest problem renovators face is overspending, but there are many other small traps that investors can get caught in. All of them are some variation on bad management.

John has every right to fear bad management, but what he doesn't have the right to do is judge himself harshly for one perceived failure. Successfully managing a renovation on a BFRR project can be taught.

In the last chapter we discussed and demonstrated how to buy a great BFRR deal, but knowing how to buy isn't enough. You must also know how to properly execute the renovation phase. This chapter will show you the simple (but not easy) process of fixing a BFRR deal.

Leaning on Their Coach

After watching John mope around the house for a few days, Nancy was starting to get worried. They would soon close on their first BFRR deal, and Nancy needed John at his best to get through the renovation with success.

Their plan was for John to spend an hour or two each evening after work making sure the renovation was going smoothly. It might seem silly having John do that job since he was scared of it, but the truth was that neither of them were experts on renovating.

Early on when they were discussing the BFRR strategy, Nancy made it clear that she had no interest in managing the renovation project. John, on the other hand, admitted he wouldn't mind it *if he could overcome his fear*. Thus, they decided early on that John would manage the contractors.

There was no way they could do the renovation themselves, as quitting their jobs wasn't an option. They would have to hire contractors, but John wasn't feeling up to managing the workers once his depression set in. He'd heard horror stories about how renovation expenses quickly add up, and he thought for sure this would happen to him.

Nancy knew they had to get John out of his doldrums or the project would never pan out. She knew people create their own luck and if they believe something bad is going to happen it usually does.

Nancy knew John needed an intervention. She was starting to get anxious, too, so she decided to call Jaq and set up a meeting. Jaq was in no mood to talk to anyone, but he reluctantly agreed to meet Jaq.

"Why don't we hold the meeting at the property? We need to discuss the renovations process, anyways. I think putting the process in concrete terms will help alleviate John's anxiety. How does that sound? Could you get access to the property tomorrow?" said Jaq.

"I'm pretty sure we can. It's a private sale and we got to know the seller well. He's a great guy and he's not living in the property now, so I'm pretty sure he'd let us have access to develop our renovation plan[12]," said Nancy.

"Sounds great, shall we meet there at 7 o'clock?" said Jaq.

"Absolutely, see you there," said Nancy.

Nancy felt good as she hung up the phone. She knew if anyone could help John feel better it would be Jaq, and she knew the knowledge Jaq could impart would be empowering.

---

12   Go to www.theultimatewealthstrategy.com/tools to see sample renovation plans.

She felt John could manage a small renovation, but she knew it would be difficult while experiencing anxiety and depression. She was hoping meeting their coach would help.

It was precisely this scenario they hired the coach for. Nancy hadn't yet attached herself to John's fear, so she could see the forest for the trees. They were still very much in good shape, they just needed to get John through this process once.

A Pivotal Meeting –
60 Days after First Meeting

The next day came and went. That evening, when it was time to meet, only John showed up at the property.

"Where's Nancy?" Jaq asked.

"She couldn't make it. I don't know if we've been leaning on our babysitters too hard lately or what, but nobody took the job tonight. I'm sure all of this will slow down as we get through this first deal. What do you think?" said John.

"I know it will, but it doesn't really matter what I think. You look terrible John. You haven't been sleeping much, have you?" asked Jaq.

"How can you tell? I feel terrible. I'm not sure I'm up for this. Is it too late to back out?" said John.

"Yes, it is. Thank goodness for your quick decision making and jumping in with both feet. Because of that it's too late to back out now! Honestly, once you get this thing done you're going to wonder why you were ever so nervous about the renovations process. It's not that hard, and you'll find contractors to be some of the best people you'll ever deal with," said Jaq.

"I sure hope you're right, I just wonder if I won't invent some way to screw this up," said John.

"Listen, you should expect the unexpected. You know that from the flooding on your rental property. All we can do is prepare our best and move forward with the expectation that things will work for the best. The same applies with the renovation of this property. Being prepared is our job, but what concerns me is that right now you're giving into your fear. Take a good objective look at this. Your situation is great, and at this moment, all you have to do is get prepared and execute," said Jaq.

"Right. I guess I am buying into this story about my past failure a little too much," said John.

"A lot too much. The past is not always the best indicator of the future. Even if your so-called previous failure was terrible, which I doubt it was, then you *still* shouldn't think about it because it has no bearing whether or not you can execute this time. So, let's look at just the facts. Where are you on this deal?" said Jaq.

"Okay, so we already have our basic plan in place. As you can see, we purchased a townhouse. We paid $185,000, and our plan is to do cosmetic renovations, spending no more than about $8,000 on the renovation. We think the ARV will be between $220,000 to $230,000," said John.

"Okay, that sounds good so far. What else can you tell me?" said Jaq.

"Well, if we get the ARV we expect, it means our refinance will get us between $168,000 and $178,000 of mortgage funding (80% of $220,000-$230,000). Once we get the refinance we will return a big chunk of cash to our investor, and he will likely want to do another one after we rent this one," said John.

"That's a great plan. You'll find as you go along that this happens more often than you'd expect," said Jaq.

"Well, first we have to get through this one. If they're all as nerve wracking as this one I'm not sure I want to do a bunch more," said John.

"They won't be. You'll find there are very few problems that can't be solved. Right now, you don't even have a problem, except the one you've invented in your mind. From what I see here, this looks like a slam-dunk. As long as there are no expensive surprises, I can't see why this should be a difficult project. You're doing all the due diligence, right?" said Jaq.

"Yes, we've already had it inspected and got the condo documents professionally reviewed. There won't be any expensive surprised," said John.

"That's huge. Otherwise, it looks like a simple lipstick job, but you won't stop worrying about it until the job is finished, the refinance done, and the tenants moved in. If you've done the other stages of the due diligence, I can help you develop your renovation plan right now, and then you'll know your costs in advance. Is that the last major unknown?" said Jaq.

"It's the big one. I just hope having cost certainty allows me to execute like the buying system did," said John.

"It will. Of course there is a bit more to it, but we'll talk about that today," said Jaq.

"I'd like that. Based on some initial discussions with others and the fact that we know there won't be any big ticket items, we're expecting a lipstick renovation, but I don't know what that entails," said John.

"You will soon. Before we get started with the renovation plan, we should discuss the 4 types of renovations," said Jaq.

"4 types?" said John.

"Yep, although there are no hard and fast rules here – only general guidelines that help us think about how to tackle renovations. More accurately, these guidelines can let us know what kind of project we might be getting ourselves into," said Jaq.

"Guidelines are good. I'm fairly certain this is a light renovation because there aren't any big fixes necessary. It's all about surface appearance on this one," said John.

"Right, and from what I've seen and what you're describing, this one a *lipstick renovation*, which is the first of our 4 categories," said Jaq.

"How does it work?" said John.

"Well, for a successful lipstick renovation you must buy a good deal to begin with – it's the path of least resistance for creating value. On a true lipstick renovation, you just skim the surface of the property.

It's about paint, flooring, new lighting fixtures, perhaps some bi-fold doors, a countertop, perhaps an appliance or two, and maybe some smaller items like soap holders in the bathroom. Heck, on some lipstick renovations, the biggest impact you might make is by giving the property a thorough cleaning!" said Jaq.

"Cleaning was a big part of our early plan," said John.

"It makes a huge different. Something you need to know is that there are plenty of BFRR investors who turn over a lot of properties using *only this* renovation strategy. As long as you buy right, it's the easiest way to do a lot of deals because the renovation doesn't take much time or money," said Jaq.

"Cool, I guess our walkthrough will help determine if there's more than a lipstick renovation here, but I think we'll find this is a true lipstick deal. What's the next type of renovation?" said John.

"The next is what BFRR investors cheekily call the *lipstick and makeup* renovation. As the name would suggest it's still a light renovation, but it's a step up in the commitment required," said Jaq.

"That is cheeky. What's the difference?" said John.

"It's a lot like a lipstick renovation, but in addition to all the normal lipstick renovations, you also do things like replacing the kitchen cabinets, adding or replacing tiling, or replacing a bathtub. In theory it's not much harder than a basic lipstick but there are a few more risks involved," said Jaq.

"Wait a minute. Did you mention that a tub replacement would mean it's a lipstick and makeup renovation? If that's the case, then this deal is a lipstick and makeup. Our bathtub is 1970s green, so it definitely needs to be replaced," said John.

"Not so fast, we'll discuss that when we start developing your renovation plan – in a few minutes. I'll teach you a trick about bathtubs that should help you keep this a lipstick job," said Jaq.

"I'm skeptical, but you haven't disappointed yet, so I look forward to this tip," said John.

"You'll see. As I was saying, the lipstick and makeup renovation is still quite light, but instead of spending $5,000 to $10,000 you might end up spending $10,000 to $20,000. Of course, you should only take on a renovation like that if the value lift corresponds to the extra money spent," said Jaq.

"Gotcha. Anything else I should know about lipstick and makeup jobs?" said John.

"Yeah, a good rule of thumb is permits. Whenever a job requires a permit, there is additional complexity. On a small lipstick and makeup job, you might need a couple of permits – for example to replace a bathtub. The permit process swallows up a lot of new BFRR investors because of the added time of dealing with the city and inspectors. When replacing a bathtub you need only one small permit. It's not so bad, but it's still more complex than a basic lipstick job, which is why a lipstick and makeup style renovation is a perfect bridge to the next type of renovation," said Jaq.

"Do tell," said John.

"I call this third type a *partial gut* renovation. As the name suggests, this is deeper than the other two, which are pretty much surface level renovations. On this type of renovation you might add a legal basement suite or a third bedroom in a two-bedroom house. In addition, you'll do all the lipstick and makeup renovations we've already discussed," said Jaq.

"Sounds like a lot of permits," said John.

"Yes, it's a much more detailed process, and you'll be required to take out more permits than on a lipstick and makeup renovation. Still, it's not too complex. You should consider doing one in the future. The kicker with this level of renovation is that you'll be raising the value of the property *above* market value," said Jaq.

"How so?" said John.

"It has to do with the real estate principle of *highest and best use.* With the first two, you don't change the property to a *higher use* when you renovate. Instead, you just take the existing property and make it better. It's like giving an old car a tune-up. There is only so much you can raise the value of it by keeping it the same. On the other hand, if that old car is souped-up, restored, and is considered a classic, it might be worth more than the average. A partial gut does the same thing to a house," said Jaq.

"That makes sense. I'll be happy if I ever get confident enough to do a deal like that," said John.

"Confidence comes from taking positive forward action. You will get there in increments. It's important to remember, though, that the partial gut is slightly different than the first two," said Jaq.

"How so?" said John.

"Well, success in the first two types is entirely dependent on buying well. With a partial gut the buy is still important, but with the renovation you also change some fundamental characteristics of the property. Three bedroom homes are worth more than two bedroom homes. Basement suite bungalows are worth more than properties without basement suites, so the potential of a partial gut is enormous. You have the opportunity to add *significant* value with a partial gut, and if you add an additional suite you will add significant rental income for long term hold," said Jaq.

"Wow, partial gut renovations sound incredible, what's the catch?" said John.

"There's no catch. I'd just say don't do one until you're experienced enough to manage a larger renovation. Budgeting becomes more important as does having cash in reserve. Chances are, the renovation will take longer than a lipstick renovation. It will involve more holding time, which could be costly depending on the finance strategy used. Everything is bigger, more expensive, and more time consuming on a partial gut. In return for this additional risk, the payoff is higher," said Jaq.

"Great, you've told me about 3 types of renovations, but you initially said there are 4. What's the last one?" said John.

"The 4th is a *full gut* – the extreme makeover of the real estate world. Now, rather than just partially transforming the property, it's a full overhaul. On a renovation like this you might be literally replacing the roof – not just the shingles but the roof too. It's almost certain that you'll be replacing furnaces, doing wiring, plumbing, repairing a foundation, building an addition, turning a single family home into a triplex... well the list is too long to cover here. Everything is in play. When you buy a full gut property you need to get it for cheap and you have to expect several months of renovations. Even if you have the best team and suppliers in the world, you'll be spending in the neighbourhood of $100,000 for this type of renovation. It goes without saying that a total gut is a huge job that involves lots of permits, lots of cost, and lots of time," said Jaq.

"I can imagine. I think I'd be a nervous wreck doing a project like that," said John.

"Well, it's different than a simple lipstick renovation, but there are plenty of BFRR investors who succeed with full gut renovations. Remember, when you're done it's a totally different property, which means big rewards – like moving from 4 houses to a hotel in the game of *Monopoly*." said Jaq.

"Great analogy," said John.

"The thing to remember is the market for these types of deals is a lot smaller than the first three types. There are fewer properties in gutting condition than in lipstick condition. When you take on a full gut renovation, you're solving a major problem," said Jaq.

"Big problems need big solutions, which lead to big rewards," said John.

"You know the formula. On a full gut, you'll be dealing with grow-ops, hoarders, water or foundation damage, or properties being converted to multi-family. The risk is greater, but the value lift should be in the neighbourhood of $100,000. In fact, I've heard of people making much more than $100,000 on a full gut deal. I've also heard of people losing their shirts on gut renovations. It's exciting and risky territory," said Jaq.

"It sounds like it. I think I will steer clear of full gut renovations for now," said John.

"Since they take high skill and experience, I think that's a fantastic plan. Take your time before leaping into a full gut renovation, but when the day comes that you're ready, you'll find the profit potential is exciting," said Jaq.

"Cool, so let's talk about the property at hand. I was expecting to remove the bathtub, which in the schema you just shared would mean this would is a lipstick and makeup. I don't want to do any permits on the first deal, and you said there's a trick to avoid removing the bathtub. I'm eager to know this trick," said John

"We'll get there, but let's talk a bit about what we're trying to accomplish. Starting with the end in mind and thinking backwards is the best approach to renovation planning. Tell me, what's the first question we should be asking ourselves now that we're looking at this un-renovated property?" said Jaq.

"What needs to be done to this property?" said John.

"Well, if we were renovating our own home, or if we were renovators doing a quote for someone else, that's probably the exact question we'd ask. The problem with that question is that it's too open-ended. It could lead to over-renovating, which is a common problem," said Jaq.

"We don't want that," said John.

"Correct. You'll soon learn what all great BFRR investors know: there's always another renovation that *could* be done, but this doesn't mean you *should* do it," said Jaq.

"Right. We've already done our pre-purchase due diligence and we know this complex doesn't need a new roof, a new furnace, foundation work, windows, or anything else that could quickly get expensive. In fact, because this property is part of a condominium, many of those items are the domain of the condominium corporation, and we've gotten 3rd party verification that the condo corporation's reserve fund is well endowed to cover any future expenses," said John.

"That's a great start. Let's get back to our original question, though. Even though you've ruled out the big surprises, you still have to be vigilant against getting nickel-and-dimed to death on lipstick renovations. To avoid that you need to start with a solid plan and stick with it. Your goal is to bring this property up to normal market value by spending less money than the difference between what you paid and the ARV – significantly less," said Jaq.

"Right, so what's the question I need to ask then?" said John.

"The question is, 'What targeted renovations within my budget do I need to do in order to raise the value of this property to average market value?' The answer to that will be different on each property, which is why we're here today. We're going to see exactly what needs to be done," said Jaq.

"I guess that's a lot different than my question. I see how asking the right questions can make all the difference. Let's start upstairs with the two bedrooms and bathroom," said John.

As the two men walked up the stairs John could feel himself rising above his anxiety. Developing a clear renovations plan was the best thing he could do. Soon, they arrived at the master bedroom.

"The key to bedrooms is simplicity. A bedroom is a simple room, if you look at it, so don't complicate things. There are four walls, and in a simple two-bedroom rental property, such as this, there's a closet. That's it. Super simple. Your job is to make sure the doors, trim, and walls are freshly painted, the floors are new, the lighting fixtures are clean and new, and that the closet doors are clean and modern. This room is no different. The painting and flooring are part of the overall quotes you get for the entire house, so for this room you just need to price a new light fixture and bi-fold doors," said Jaq.

"Okay," said John, as he marked down the renovations in his notebook.

"Next, we have the smaller bedroom. It's exactly the same as the master bedroom, just smaller. The same rules apply here. Keep it simple. On top of the paint and floors, you again just need new light fixtures and new bi-fold doors," said Jaq.

"Should I add any new lights to enhance the lighting effect in either of the rooms?" said John.

"While that would be nice, you're doing a lipstick renovation, which means you don't want to do any wiring or open up any walls. Find the best light fixtures that maximize lighting in the room without paying too much for the fixtures. If you need to make it shine for the showings, just bring in a lamp that works in tandem with the lighting. Got it?" said Jaq.

"Right, I guess that's how people get off budget and off plan," said John.

"You got it. Remember one thing. This property will be a rental property, which means it has to be average, not extraordinary. Your plan is to bring it up to the average property value. There's a far bigger risk in over-renovating than under-renovating. With that said, you want it to be nice, clean, fresh, and have a new feeling, which is why we don't allow old beat up walls, flimsy bi-fold doors, or faded and dated light fixtures," said Jaq.

> **Renovating For the Market**
>
> The first goal of BFRR renovations is simple, modern, and fresh. However, this standard can vary slightly, depending on the market. Whatever the renovations, it has to appeal to the rental market in the area.
>
> Granite countertops would be typical in an upscale area, like the Beaches district of Toronto. Such renovations are necessary to attract good rent from the Generation Y tenants that live there, but granite wouldn't be a good idea in an area like blue collar downtown Oshawa.
>
> Knowing the rental market standard for the area and aiming for slightly above that standard is the BFRR investor's goal.

"Right, moving on to the bathroom," said John.

"The bathroom is an important room. Much like the kitchen, it's a space that can be easily over-renovated. You need to avoid that, but at the same time you have to get it right, to appeal to renters and impress appraisers. There are so many bells and whistles that *could* be added, and it's easy to get sucked into spending big bucks on bathrooms," said Jaq.

"We don't want that," said John.

"No, you don't. Adding all the bells and whistles to this bathroom could honestly cost $20,000, but when doing a lipstick job you'd never guess how much I typically spend. Here's a hint, it's not close to $20,000," said Jaq.

"We're trying to keep this entire renovation under $8,000, but I remember doing my bathroom at home and spending $5,000 just on the bathroom alone. This has been on my mind," said John.

"I typically spend between $500 and $1000 on bathrooms. That includes materials and labour," said Jaq.

"How is that possible?" said John

"Well, here we are in the bathroom. Let's look at how it's possible. What are the biggest items in this bathroom that you could see costing a lot of money?" said Jaq.

"Well, for starters there's the tub. That green color isn't fashionable anymore. I can't believe it ever was. In any case that will have to go. It must cost at least a thousand dollars or more for that. There goes your budget," said John.

"I agree that the tub is no good, but I disagree about removing and replacing it. When you start pulling out bathtubs, you're almost begging for bigger problems. You don't know what you're going to find behind an old tub. You must absolutely not take out the tub," said Jaq.

"Still waiting for the trick," said John.

"There are two solutions that cost peanuts and will make the bathtub spiffy. First, you can install a tub insert that goes overtop the tub, the old tile surround, and covers the walls around the bathtub. It looks great and provides protection against water seepage – it's a perfect solution for rental properties. The tub insert isn't always necessary, but it's a heck of a lot better than redoing all the tiling and replacing the tub," said Jaq.

"That sounds cheaper, for sure," said John.

"Hang on, there is another trick. You can also just paint the tub. Most people don't know this. You can turn this old green tub into a shiny white one for next to nothing. Using one of those simple tricks will save you thousands of dollars on every lipstick deal," said Jaq.

"You're right, I didn't know about either. That makes me feel better. The tiling around this tub is in good shape. It's just dated. Do you think I could leave it, and just paint it along with the tub?" said John.

"I highly recommend you do that. Don't turn this into a lipstick and makeup if you want to make money on it. Moving on, what else do you think would be expensive in this bathroom?" said Jaq.

"Well, the next two big items I see are the toilet and vanity. Those must be pretty expensive, no?" said John.

"There's an enormous range on those items. You can spend big money or small money. However, the better question to ask on a simple lipstick job is whether or not you even need to replace them. On my own projects, I probably change the toilet and vanity about half the time. Looking at this bathroom, I'd say you should replace the toilet. Change it to a low flow toilet to reduce water use, and keep an eye out for contractor packs at home improvement stores to save money on the purchase. If you do this, the toilet won't cost much over $100 including installation," said Jaq.

"Sounds good. What about the vanity?" said John.

"Leave it. With a coat of paint it will look great. Once you do that along with the other changes, this bathroom will be looking sharp," said Jaq.

John scribbled in his notepad, "Okay, here's the list so far: a) replace toilet, b) paint the tub and tiles, c) paint the vanity, d) replace the light fixtures, and e) paint the walls, trim, and door. What about some of the smaller things like soap holders and towel hangers?" said John.

"I assess these items on a job-by-job basis. If they look good leave them. Otherwise replace them. In this case I'd say you'd better replace the soap holders and towel hangers. It will add to the shiny newness of the room won't cost more than a few bucks. There you have it. That's how you spruce up a bathroom for under $1000," said Jaq.

"Okay, anything about the upstairs hallway I should renovate other than flooring and paint?" said John.

"Hallways usually have a linen closet. The same rule as bedrooms applies here. Make sure bi-fold doors are shiny and clean. If they're in good shape already, you don't need to replace them, but if they're hanging by a thread, you need to replace them. These doors look pretty rough, so I'd replace them along with the ones in the bedrooms. As we walk downstairs it's more of the same. You'll have to replace flooring and paint throughout. I'd also replace that ceiling fan above the stairwell. Ceiling fans are in the same category as light fixtures. You need them to be shiny and new but not fancy. Finally, take a look at those handrails. I wouldn't trust them to hold up a child, let alone a full grown adult. Put in fresh ones screwed to the studs. Let's head downstairs," said Jaq.

"Gotcha," said John as he scribbled in his notebook.

"It probably goes without saying that the main floor needs new flooring, paint, and light fixtures, but that pretty much does it for the living room," said Jaq.

"Which brings us to the original bank breaker – the kitchen," said John.

"That's what we think by default. The renovations TV shows seem to be trying to normalize $50,000 kitchens, which is ridiculous even for most homeowners. If you ask me it's an irresponsible use of a line of credit, but that's a whole different story," said Jaq.

"You can tell me about that later," said John.

"Now, you'll need to do this kitchen on a shoestring to bring it up to market value and stay on or under budget. There are a few tricks here, but to get started, let's go back to the original question, 'What targeted renovations, within my budget, do I need to do in order to raise the value of this property to average market value?' That question is even more important on the kitchen," said Jaq.

"Right. When I look at this kitchen the first thing I think is that the cabinets need to be replaced. But if the kitchen is anything like the bathroom, I'm guessing there are some tricks to save money. Am I right?" said John.

"You got it. There are some tricks to installing new cabinets, but the real trick is to not install cabinets at all," said Jaq.

"How so?" said John.

"Well, if you think about cabinets, they're just mini rooms to hold dishes. There's nothing inside, so you can make them look darn good just by surface work," said Jaq.

"Like painting a tub instead of replacing it," said John.

"Correct. Now, there are two steps to refurbishing kitchen cabinets on the cheap. First, paint them. I use a glossy porch and floor paint, which lasts for a long time and looks good. Second, install new hardware. Just as light fixtures are outdated, so are door handles and hinges on cabinets. Once you update these and paint, you'd be shocked how new a set of cabinets can look. Another option is to replace the doors along with paint and hardware," said Jaq.

"That probably saves a few thousand bucks, but what if I have to replace the cabinets?" said John.

"You can find cost effective solutions through online advertising websites or at habitat for humanity. You'd be shocked at what gets sold or donated. Remember those $50,000 kitchens we mentioned? Well, the old cabinets have to go somewhere. Often there's nothing wrong with these, and you can pick them up for cheap," said Jaq.

"Good point. Looking at these cabinets, I'd say I could get away with a paint and hardware replacement. What do you think?" said John.

"I'm counting on it. It will save you several thousand dollars and a lot of time. Next, let's look at the kitchen countertops. Now, this is something you should replace. Countertops are often horribly dated. Changing them is easy and quick, but don't use expensive countertops. Just use the simple multicolor ones that will absorb a few dents and hide scratches without being destroyed," said Jaq.

"I'm noticing a pattern here," said John.

"I hope so. The same goes for the kitchen sink and faucets. If they're horribly dated, go ahead and change them. It's another small expense, and looking at this property, I think it will be worth it," said Jaq.

"Are we getting close to being nickled and dimed here?" said John.

"When you tally all of these together after getting quotes and material cost estimates you will know for sure. If that happens, you can scale back renovations, but looking at this property, I'd say you're in good shape for spending under $8,000," said Jaq.

"Right, and I need to make sure it looks shiny and new for the appraiser and renter," said John.

"Correct, you need to give the impression that you're walking into a shiny new renovated property. This helps the appraiser agree with your proposal and makes tenants flock," said Jaq.

"Right. So, sinks, countertops, paint, and light fixtures are a must in this kitchen. Anything else?" said John.

"That fridge looks pretty good. Elbow grease will get it looking like new, but the stove has to go. See how it says 'Made in Canada'? That's a sure sign it's old, very old. Stoves aren't made in Canada anymore. The good news is that overseas manufactured stoves cost a lot less money than you'd think. Replace that stove, take care of the other renovations, and you'll have a sparkly new kitchen," said Jaq.

A Supply of Cheap Appliances

Using the BFRR strategy you'll soon find yourself buying a lot more appliances than you ever imagined you would, which means you'll have a good opportunity to build efficiency into your process. An excellent BFRR investor will always seek greater efficiency when doing a task or buying something repeatedly.

In this case, it means we need a consistent supply of quality used appliances. The best way to do this is to develop a great relationship with a top notch used appliance dealer.

Just as with cabinets, homeowners often upgrade appliances and get rid of quality working units. Take advantage of this fact.

You can buy multiple appliances each month and save a fortune by going direct to a quality used appliance dealer. Seek out the almost new stock, which looks outstanding but costs a fraction of the new price.

"That just leaves the front of the house and the basement," said John.

The two men walked outside.

"The cool thing about this townhouse is that the exterior is probably the condominium corporation's responsibility. Am I right about that?" said Jaq.

"Indeed, you are correct. We pay condo fees, and the condo owners collectively decide how the condo fees are spent. So, does that mean we don't have to worry about the curb appeal?" said John.

"Not exactly. There are small things you're allowed to do to the front such as paint the door and replace the mailbox. Take a closer look at the condo bylaws, but if I'm right you should do both of those, plus make sure you have a working light above the door. These dramatically spruce up the front of the property, which also helps attract tenants later," said Jaq.

"Gotcha. Should we head down to the basement now?" said John.

"Sure," said Jaq.

The two men went back into the property and down the stairs to the dingy basement.

"Okay, this was one of my biggest questions. I mean as you can see the basement is unfinished. It's just a concrete slab and a light. If I were asking my original question, I'd say I should finish that basement. I know that would break my budget, though," said John.

"You're right about that. There's a simple rule to finishing basements for BFRR deals. You only do it if it will add significant rental income. I'm not talking about a hundred bucks either. It has to add in the range of a thousand bucks of rental income, and the only way a basement renovation is going to add that much income is if you develop a suite, or if you're going to rent individual bedrooms in the basement to students," said Jaq.

"Sounds like a partial gut," said John.

"It is. If you add a legal suite, you're getting into the territory of development permits and zoning bylaws, projects that last months instead of weeks, and several tens of thousands of dollars, so the best strategy in this basement is to make sure it's spotlessly clean. There should be no cobwebs, piles of dust, or corners stuffed with unused materials. Keep it good and clean, don't spend any money on it, and move on," said Jaq.

"With that we've gone through the entire house. I'm feeling a lot better, but I still don't know what all this will cost," said John.

"I can tell you from experience that everything we just discussed won't be more than your budget of $8,000. Do you see how powerful buying right is? I mean you really don't have to do much work to this place. How much did you get this place for, anyways?" said Jaq.

"Well, we paid $185,000 and we expect it to appraise at $220,000 when we're done with the renovation. With $8,000 into the property in renovations, this means we'll be forcing about $27,000 of appreciation," said John.

"That sounds like a bread and butter BFRR deal," said Jaq.

"I sure hope so. We plan on doing another one like it soon if we can get this one refinanced and rented for the right price," said John

"That's a good plan, but let's finish what we're talking about right now," said Jaq.

Execution

"Didn't we just go through the whole house? What else is there?" said John.

"We went through the whole house and now you theoretically have a plan, but life has a way of throwing curveballs. Success is about execution," said Jaq.

"Now you sound like an NHL coach," said John.

"Exactly. Think about it. All hockey teams go on the ice with the same intention – to win. They have a plan, just like you to do right now, but it's the team with the best execution that wins. If you're a Leafs fan you know what I'm talking about," said Jaq.

"I sure do. They always look so good on paper, but they find a way to lose. Are you saying I might end up like the Leafs?" said John.

"Anything is possible, but the Leafs get paid even if they lose and you don't, so unlike them, I think you'll find a way to make it work. You just need to understand some basic execution principles to carry out your plan," said Jaq.

"That sounds good. As you know, executing on renovation management is my fear, but our conversation today is helping me get over that. The plan we just made was huge, but I wouldn't have even thought of execution," said John.

"Plan without execution is nothing. Now, the first principle of execution is *sticking to the plan*. We've just spent the last hour talking about the renovations needed to lift value," said Jaq.

"It makes me feel a lot more comfortable," said John.

"Right, well the plan is useless if you stray from it," said Jaq.

"I won't," said John.

"That's easy to say. It's another thing to do. A lot of investors get hammered by this. Remember, your goal is to create value, which seems like magic to some, but if there is any magic at all, it's simply that BFRR investors can say no to unnecessary renovations. Regular people can't, so they can't create value when doing renovations. I can't stress this enough. It's the secret to execution," said Jaq.

"I can do that. Once I have a plan in place I won't stray from it," said John.

"Good. The next execution point is the *budget*. We've just gone through the entire property, and you've seen what you need to do. Now you need to know exactly what it's going to cost in advance. You are still conditional in this deal. If you find your budget is too high to make this deal profitable, you can still walk away without penalty. You initially thought $8000 or less would be enough to renovate this place, but now's the time to find out exactly what you'll be spending. This is execution in action," said Jaq.

"Okay, so what's the process here?" said John.

"You know exactly what will be replaced, so it's time to do the grunt work. Get into the big box stores and the home renovation centres with your list and *price out materials*. Try to buy in bulk and remember to buy sturdy materials that don't cost much. You're installing baseline products here, and as much as you'd love a $500 toilet in your own home, a $100 one will do just fine in your rental property," said Jaq.

"Okay, so the first step is getting cost certainty on materials. What's next?" said John.

"Next is *material consistency* because you want to build repeatability into your system. By always using the same materials you can negotiate better deals, and by buying in bulk and you can use materials from one job to another. It also makes it easier for your renovation team when they know what color paint, what kind of flooring, lights, etc. It also saves you money in the future by ensuring you only need to do one coat of paint whenever the property is repainted," said Jaq.

"Right, I need to start thinking in terms of repeatability. This is advanced execution. What's next?" said John.

"The next step is to *get cost certainty on labour*," said Jaq.

"I've already got contractors coming in to give me quotes the day after tomorrow," said John.

"Great. You're one step ahead of the game, but there's something to do before any contractors show up. Now that we know what renovations need to be done, it's time to *develop a crystal clear scope of work*. If you aren't specific on this, you risk different contractors quote different jobs," said Jaq.

"What do you mean? It would be the same job wouldn't it?" said John.

"No. Every person brings a different understanding to each situation. This applies to contractors, too. Your goal is total clarity. Every aspect of the job must be laid out, so that each contractor is quoting exactly the same job," said Jaq.

"I would never have thought of that," said John.

"Your worry is executing on management. Well, guess what. Clear communication is true management execution. Not only will you not be getting apples-to-apples quotes, but you also risk having contractors tack on extra work or not finish tasks," said Jaq.

"How so?" said John.

"There are so many opportunities for miscommunication during renovations. If scope is not clear, then people assume. In place of clear expectations, they often fill in the blanks with their own beliefs," said Jaq.

"Can you give me an example," said John.

"There are plenty. Do the painters do one coat of paint or two? Do they caulk the windows and doors? Does the handyman replacing the toilet also dispose of the old toilet, or does he leave it on the jobsite? All of these considerations and a thousand more must go into your scope of work. Even if it seems small and silly, we put it in the scope of work and have the contractor sign off saying they'll do exactly as stipulated," said Jaq.

"So, the scope of work is like a contract?" said John.

"Absolutely," said Jaq.

"Right, so I don't have too much specialist work going on in this property. All of the contractors I called said they could do all the work that needs to be done," said John.

"That's good. This is possible on a true lipstick job, but as you start getting into the bigger renovation jobs you'll need specialists. You're in a perfect position here, where you can bring in one crew and they'll do the renovation without hassle," said Jaq.

"Any more execution tips?" said John.

"There's one thing that's important when developing a new relationship with contractors: *never make payment until work is complete.* In fact, if you're dealing with a contractor that demands money up front on a small job like this, you should treat it as a warning sign," said Jaq.

"Okay, I never thought of this," said John.

"It makes sense if you think about it. You're providing the materials on the job, so your contractors won't have much in the way if up front costs. There's no reason they shouldn't be able to wait a couple of weeks to get paid," said Jaq.

"It could be a sign of desperation," said John.

"Correct. Now, by all means pay a portion once certain targets have been hit, but don't pay up front. It's a sad fact that a lot of people have drug, alcohol, and gambling problems. There's just too much of a risk of that sort of thing to trust people you don't know," said Jaq.

"That makes sense. Anything else in the way of execution principles?" said John.

"*You must be available to take contractors' calls when the project is happening.* Yes, they should be semi-autonomous, but you're the project lead and you need to answer your phone when the contractor calls, or at least be able to call them back quickly. I'd love to sell you on the idea of a hands-off renovation process, but it's not realistic. You need to be there physically at times and available for calls other times. Are you planning on visiting the job site for an hour or two every day?" said Jaq.

"Yeah, I don't think I'd sleep well at night without knowing what was happening on the job site. I had planned on coming here every evening after work," said John.

"Good, but it's also a good idea to vary the time of day you go to the job site, especially if you have the same contractors working there on consecutive days. If you show up and they're not there, then call them immediately to find out what's happening. Replace contractors who cannot be there on time or do not follow through. They should at least tell you when they are not there," said Jaq.

"Right. I'll drop by at lunch sometimes, too," said John.

"Good. Your presence here it vital. Keep good notes about what you see as well as what the contractors tell you both face-to-face and when they call you on the phone. Keep great lists and *get materials to your workers as soon as possible*. If you plan everything well you can avoid too many trips to the store," said Jaq.

"There are some suppliers between my work and here. I was planning on stopping there whenever necessary," said John.

"Perfect. As the project lead you'll also have to do a bit of team leadership. Keeping the crew organized and on task is your job. The best and simplest way to do that is to *use the whiteboard system* on the job site," said Jaq.

"The whiteboard system?" said John.

"Yes, it's the simplest onsite management tool I know about. You start with the scope of work, and you just keep a list of jobs on the whiteboard. Every day when you go to the job site you ask the contractors about progress and check progress visually," said Jaq.

"Makes sense," said John.

"Never do a project without it. You also make notes under each job item stating what needs to be done and deficiencies noticed. Part of your scope of work will include a plan for repairing deficiencies, so you act as the lead inspector making sure the deficiencies are taken care of. The whiteboard is the system for deficiency fixing," said Jaq.

"I guess that's how I make sure I don't get stuck cleaning up sloppy work," said John.

"It's just human nature. People sometimes cut corners. I'm not asking you to micromanage anyone, but if contractors can see a reminder in words that you're aware of the tasks and deficiencies it keeps them moving in the right direction. It's also a reminder that you're not going to let anyone slip on quality. I always find this simple system helps get the job done faster, too," said Jaq.

"I can handle that. Actually, it's just the kind of simple tool that will help alleviate my anxiety," said John.

"That's great, but there are two more items before we say goodbye. First, give *yourself a cushion – on both budget and timeline*. I always add an extra 10% to the budget," said John.

"Why? I thought we calculate with precision," said Jaq.

"We do, but overages happen – it's what we call "getting nickel and dimed to death". We calculate everything down to the penny, know our costs inside out, and try our best to stick within those prices, then we budget 10% extra so we're not surprised by overages," said Jaq.

"Kind of like we did by creating a reserve fund when we bought the property, right?" said John.

"It's a lot like that, but the reserve fund is used less often and is replenished by cash flow. It seems like the 10% cushion is commonly used despite our best efforts. The best BFRR investors I know are obsessive about costs. They seek ways to save a hundred dollars here or a thousand dollars there, because they know that over time the accumulation of those small saving adds up to tens and even hundreds of thousands of dollars, which over time raises ROI," said Jaq

"Okay, we will definitely budget for overages," said John.

"And *timeline overages,* too! Always ask yourself how going over on the timeline will affect renting the property and carrying costs. A timeline overage can become a cost overage because it can raise your carrying costs and/or delay your income. Great BFRR investors do everything to avoid timeline overages but are prepared if it happens. Don't let a whole deal hinge on a week or two. You have to be comfortable knowing if you do go over that everything will work out," said Jaq.

Jaq paused for a moment. Took a look at John's eager face and continued.

"Listen, you've learned a lot here tonight. It's time to go home, get some sleep and let this all sink in, but I want to know how you're feeling first. You had anxiety about the renovation process, but how do you feel after this discussion?" said Jaq

"A heck of a lot better. Right now I think I can handle this renovation. I don't think my anxiety will completely disappear until it's done, but I'm not as worried now as I was before. I feel like I'm following a clear map now. I'm going to head home and start organizing. I know the kids will be in bed soon and Nancy is eager to help me prepare so everything will be ready for this renovation," said John.

Jaq smiled to himself. He remembered how thrilling the first renovation project on a BFRR deal is and all of the doubts he had. He recalled how the thrill of the first deal turns into pride and confidence over time and how the strategy helps people gain financial security and momentum.

"That's a great idea. Excellent preparation leads to excellent execution, which leads to excellent results," said Jaq

The two men walked out of the property, locked the front door, and said their goodbyes. John smiled to himself for the first time in a few days.

"This is really happening," he thought.

Principles of a Successful Fix

Use this checklist for renovation planning and execution:

- **Planning**
  - Create Renovation Plan – What exactly will be fixed?

- **Execution**
  - Stick to the Plan
  - Develop a Clear Scope of Work – What will be done and how?
  - Develop a Budget – Source and price materials and labour
  - Don't pay contractors until work is complete
  - Be available to take calls from contractor
  - Visit job site every day
  - Supply materials quickly when needed
  - Use the whiteboard system
  - Give yourself a budget cushion

The Crossroads between Buying, Due Diligence, and Fixing

You've just learned how to properly set up and execute a BFRR renovation project. This chapter included tips on how to plan, prepare for, keep on budget, manage, and execute a successful project.

Each of these components is necessary to move from buying, through due diligence, and into the fixing phase. As always, having knowledge is important, but without action knowledge is nothing.

Now that we've discussed how to fix a property, it's time to demonstrate what the fixing phase looks like in practical terms. Read on to see how John and Nancy turned their understanding into action and how John overcomes his fears by taking steps towards his goals.

"It was character that got us out of bed, commitment that moved us into action, and discipline that enabled us to follow through."

Zig Ziglar

CHAPTER 7

Getting the Job Done

Action Creates Success

Have you ever expected something to be difficult or even impossible only to find out later that it wasn't nearly as hard as you expected?

This is exactly what happened to our friend John when he finally took on his first renovation project. He found that with the right team and the right preparation that it wasn't that difficult in the end.

John was overwhelmed with fear because he'd never previously broken the process down into a series of small parts before. Working with Jaq enabled him to see the process for what it was.

This chapter shows how John used the simple method of small forward steps to overcome his demons and execute a great renovation project.

The Fixing Process

John left his meeting with renewed confidence. He was starting to see how his supposed past failures were more due to failed process than anything else. He took previous failures as a personal failing, but in fact they were caused by a lack of education and support.

This time he was slowly introduced to a successful process, and John started to see different results. This time he had a coach and a network of like-minded investors to turn to for help.

The success started to manifest with a great buy, but John wasn't out of the weeds yet. He needed to execute on the renovation, and after talking to Jaq about it, he knew the best way to make sure of that was to prepare to the best of his ability and follow the principles of execution.

He and Nancy got to work over the next couple of days and did all of the tasks he and Jaq had discussed. They found the work wasn't as hard as they'd imagined, but it took persistence.

Getting a price on every material was slow and painstaking, but this arduous task was minimized by the knowledge that the materials list would only have to be made once. After preparing it the first time, then they could add materials piecemeal as they needed a new one, or if they found a better deal. They saw how developing this materials list over time was a system that would make every deal easier in the future.

After completing due diligence and preparation it was soon time to close on the deal. When the day finally came John went to the project site on his lunch break to let the contractors into the property.

It was a running start. Due to excellent preparation, the renovation process *started on closing day.* John installed his whiteboard in the living room, spent a few minutes reviewing the job plan with the contractors he'd sourced, and before getting out the front door, he could hear the workers pulling out the old flooring.

John smiled to himself, "So this is what management execution feels like."

Execution

Within a few days John and his renovation team were into full gear with the project. As planned, John dedicated some time to the renovation every day, and he was seeing results from the process.

"So that's 4 rolls of 2-inch green painter's tape, three transition strips to match the laminate flooring, and 2 electrical outlet cover plates?" said John. He was talking on the phone to his contractor Randy.

"Yep, no big rush, but we'll need those tomorrow," said Randy.

"I'll stop by the store and pick them up on the way there tonight. You'll have them in plenty of time," said John.

"Thanks. What time will you be here tonight?" said Randy.

"I get off work at 5 and it will take me probably 45 minutes to pick up the material and get to the property, so let's say between 5:45 and 6:00. Why do you ask?" said John

"We'll probably be here. We usually shut down between 6:00 and 6:30. This whiteboard system is great. I was hoping we'd see you today and we can update the board for tomorrow," said Randy.

"Um, ah, yeah, that's a good idea. I'll be there with the supplies and we can spend a few minutes updating the whiteboard. See you later," said John.

"Yep, see you this evening," said Randy.

John was stunned. He wasn't barking orders at the contractors. He wasn't pushing them to finish. The whole thing was different than he expected, including the way the contractors treated him, too. It felt like a team effort, which was a feeling he was familiar with as a member of teams, but never as lead. The best part was that the job was on schedule (and everything looked great).

The contractors seemed to want to get the project done as much as he did. Everyone did their job with no questions asked and there was no drama. It was almost… boring.

Randy came highly recommended by Jaq and several other members of the Real Estate Investing Club. He didn't fit John's preconceived ideas of what a contractor was like. Randy's professionalism was refreshing, and John secretly promised himself he would stop believing in stereotypes.

Randy was a regular guy that conducted business well. He showed up on time, he worked the whole day, and he knew what he was doing. There were no issues once the price and terms were set. Randy just went to work.

John wasn't so naïve to think every contractor was the same or that every job would go so smooth, but he was happy Randy was professional and that this first job went smoothly. He was again grateful for having hired Jaq. The recommendation to use Randy alone was priceless.

Preparing for the Next Phase

Meanwhile, John and Nancy were busy preparing for the next step.

"I spoke to the mortgage broker today. She said the appraisal is scheduled for next Wednesday. I told her the renovations would be finished on the Tuesday after that, is that right?" said Nancy.

Their daughters were in bed, and John and Nancy were doing some evening work in preparation for their first BFRR deal.

"Yes, they might even be done on Monday the way it's going. I'm going to head over to the property this weekend and make sure everything is on track. I should know more precisely by this Monday, so if we need to reschedule the appraisal for a day or two later we can let them know earlier," said John.

"Perfect. Where are we with tenants?" said Nancy.

"The ads have been up since Monday and I've gotten 6 calls already. It looks[13] like we're going to be able to rent it for $1,275, which will give us solid cash flow. I'm

---

13   Go to www.theultimatewealthstrategy.com/tools for access to our free tenant questionnaire. This valuable tool will help you select only the best tenants for your property.

showing the place to 3 prospective tenants on Friday night," said Nancy.

Showing Before Completing Renovations

There are both positives and negatives to showing a property before the renovations are complete. Some BFRR investors show properties to tenants before renovations are complete, but others advertise and show the property only when it's finished or very close, rather than in mid-renovation.

The reason for waiting is the possibility that the renovation goes long. Nothing is worse than signing a lease with a new tenant only to find out they can't move in due to ongoing renovations.

The best strategy is to plan for a renovation to be completed mid month, and if renovation deadlines aren't met then there will be enough time to complete the renovation before the month ends. This ensures the property doesn't sit vacant for a month after fully renovated.

Plan your closing dates accordingly and work hard to meet timelines.

"Have they all filled out the rental applications we got from the local Real Estate Investing Club?" said Nancy.

"Yep. Based on what I'm seeing, two of them look like solid leads," said John.

"Great, so it looks like we'll have tenants in the property for April 1st, that's better than great – a one-month turnaround for $40,000 of equity and solid cash flow. This is looking like how Jaq described it would," said Nancy.

"Yeah, but we have a long way to go. Things have been going along so well that it's got me a bit suspicious about something going wrong. I keep waiting for big surprise," said John.

"Well, all we can do is prepare to the best of our ability, so let's go over these numbers again," said Nancy.

The couple crunched numbers, prepared documents, and made phone calls until it was time for sleep. They were moving one step closer at a time through excellent preparation and execution.

Action to Results

You've just seen how John overcomes his fear and executes an excellent BFRR renovation project. John applied the knowledge he learned from Jaq into practical action, and the result was boring old success.

The renovation is a major component of the BFRR process, but the next stage – refinancing – is equally as important. Just as excellent buying leads to an excellent fix, so does an excellent fix lead to a successful refinance.

As you'll learn in the next chapter, there is a science to pulling off a successful refinance. You might be surprised to find out this process is more active than passive. Read on see how to apply the science of successfully refinancing.

"Money won't create success, the freedom to make it will."

Nelson Mandela

CHAPTER 8

Refinance

Getting the Bank on Board

Have you ever been baffled or intimidated when dealing with a bank? If so, you're not alone.

Unfortunately, the banks don't always do what we want them to. If they did, we'd have unlimited mortgage financing with 0% interest, and there would be no qualifying process.

Since this dream will never come true, and since we need to take action rather than wait for miracles, we must work within the banks' guidelines. The biggest mortgage financing challenge in BFRR investing is getting the bank's appraiser to give us the value we want.

We predict ARV on a property, but how do we make sure the appraisers agree?

This is an important topic. You've already learned how to buy and renovate. If those phases have been carried out well, then you're already on the way to success. However, to complete the project and give yourself the best chance of success, you must execute on the refinance as well.

This topic is vital to finishing out a BFRR deal strong.

Nearing the Big Day

"I've got some good news and some bad news, which one do you want first?" said Diane, the mortgage broker they'd been working with. Instantly, John's heart started pounding. He immediately thought this was the big kick in the teeth he was expecting.

"Let's start with the bad news," John said with a gulp.

"The appraisal came in low. I know you were expecting $230,000, but the appraisal came in for only $210,000," said Diane.

John took a minute to digest the news. It was horrible. It was earth shattering. It was awful… actually, it wasn't that bad. All it meant was that stupendous return they were expecting from the refinance would now only be… incredible. They would still be able to give Bill a chunk of his money back, but it just wasn't as much as he was hoping for. John quickly breathed a sigh of relief to himself.

"What's the good news?" said John.

"The good news is you got the financing! Not only that, you got an incredible interest rate – only 3.5% over 5 years," said Diane.

John did some quick calculations in his head. Indeed, the cash flow was going to be nice. He went from horror at the anticipation of bad news a few moments earlier, to now feeling like he was in the driver's seat.

It was still a week before April 1st, which was their projected refinance date. John felt better knowing that the refinance would at least come through, so Diane's good news was welcome, but John was still cautious, as he wanted to make the right financing choice.

"Oh wow, that is great, but I need to speak with Nancy before we go ahead with that mortgage. Can I have a day before I commit to that?" said John.

"Absolutely, give me a call tomorrow or the next day to let me know what you want to do," said Diane.

"Will do. Thanks for everything. Talk soon," said John.

John called Nancy as soon as he'd hung up the phone with Diane. After explaining the situation the couple decided to set a meeting with Jaq to see if he had any ideas about what to do.

Tilting the Playing Field

The next day at their meeting, the topic was the lower than expected appraisal with Jaq, "I just don't know what happened. We had good reason to believe the townhouse would be worth between $220,000 and $230,000. Why would the appraisal come in low?" said John.

"Appraisers don't always act rationally, and as much as they would like to pretend otherwise, there's plenty of bias in the appraisal process," said Jaq.

"So, how do we overcome this problem? Are we now stuck with this valuation?" said John.

"Well, you should have called me. Didn't we agree that we'd speak before every step of this process? I could have given you some great tips before you got that first appraisal. Anyways, what's done is done, and you don't have to accept the first appraisal. There's a lot you can still do, although it's best to intervene before the first appraisal," said Jaq.

"The first appraisal?" said Nancy.

"Yeah. Never accept the first appraisal if it doesn't suit you, especially if you have good reason to believe the value is higher than what the appraiser gave you and *especially* in this case, considering you didn't intervene," said Jaq.

"Intervene?" said John.

"Yes, don't be passive at any phase of the BFRR process, including the refinancing and appraisal," said Jaq.

"Wouldn't another appraisal be the same as the first one?" said Nancy.

"Of course there's always that risk, but you won't know the outcome until you try. I've seen second appraisals come is as much as $30,000 higher than the first one. It's definitely worth the effort to get the appraisal you want," said Jaq.

"That's great news. We have to give it a try. So what do we do?" said John.

"Well, I will run through some of the most tried and true ways to help ensure you get the appraisal you're seeking," said Jaq.

"My note taking pen is ready," said Nancy.

"First and foremost is *knowing your ARV.* Remember how much I stressed knowing your property values for the buying component of the BFRR strategy? Not knowing pre-renovation and post-renovation value can sabotage refinancing simply because you don't actually know," said Jaq.

"We can rule that out as a problem. We studied the values closely and we have very good reason to believe this townhouse should value in the range of $230,000 after our renovation," said Nancy.

"This is important because appraisers can't identify a value when there are no comparable properties sold in the previous 90 days. I seen exampled where one property was appraised 3 times in one month by 3 different appraisers. No repairs or improvements were done to the property and the appraisals came in at $196,000, $210,000, and $206,000. Have there been any recent sold properties in the same complex with similar value to your ARV projection?" said Jaq.

"Yes, and there was also a few that sold lower. However those ones were in rougher shape. They weren't in top-notch post-renovation shape like our unit. The lower sold properties also didn't have a garage as ours does. The other unit that sold for $230,000 also had a garage," said John.

"Okay, so chances are the appraiser used those lower ones to base his appraisal on, although it looks like he didn't consider the differences between yours and the lower ones," said Jaq.

"I don't think he did," said Nancy.

"It's our job to make sure the appraiser has all the information. If your ARV calculation is reasonable based on comps, then the appraiser must also see it that way. Unfortunately, many rookies believe they will get higher than market value because of their renovations," said Jaq.

"We're good on value. What else can we do for the next appraisal?" said Nancy.

"Were you onsite when the appraiser went through last time?" said Jaq.

"Umm, no. Should we have been?" said John.

"Yes. The comps may be available, but who is to say the appraiser will use the right comps or understand the story well enough to give you the appraisal you're looking for?" said Jaq.

"You really think their appraisal would change based on what we tell them?" said Nancy.

"It happens all the time. In fact, appraisers love it because it can make their job easier. You see, appraisers want deals to close just like anyone else in the process. The more deals that die as a result of low appraisals, the more friction they cause. Officially, as a group, they're supposed to be unbiased, but on a personal level, appraisers want deals to close. They just need good reason to appraise at the value you want," said Jaq.

"So, clear communication is important again," said John.

"Yes, but remember that on a refinance they don't have such a guideline. If you can be there with them and *subtly let them know what the property should appraise at,* it makes their job easier," said Jaq.

"You mean we just tell them the appraisal we want?" said John.

"If you're subtle and respectful, there's nothing wrong with giving appraisers some guidance," said Jaq.

"So how do we subtly let them know what the property should appraise at?" said Nancy.

"First of all you tell them the value you're looking for. To back up your claim you provide them with the comps you based your ARV on. Yes, they will likely have access to all the same comps as you, but there's a good chance they used others or didn't see the same reasoning as you when looking at comps. It really helps when you show them the exact proof and why they should use that proof," said Jaq.

"It's that easy?" said John.

"If they're going to give you the appraisal you want, they need proof. If they were ever questioned on their process, they need to be able to provide that proof. So give them the proof and tell them the story of why," said Jaq.

"I guess it really never hurts to ask for what you want," said Nancy.

"Never. Influencing the appraiser is about creating a compelling case for your desired valuation, which means talking about the exact renovations you did and why they're added value to the property. This is especially important if you did HVAC renovations, which they'd never see on their own. I would also show them before and after pictures to give them a visual representation of how much the property has improved. Finally, give them a ballpark figure about how much money you spent on the renovations," said Jaq.

"Should we just show them the receipts?" said Nancy.

"I wouldn't do that. As BFRR experts we can renovate for less money than others. Appraisers are used to the normal expenses for renovating, so just tell them approximately how much it would have cost if you took a normal approach to the renovations. This will fit the story already inside the appraisers head, and they will be impressed that you spent the money on the renovation," said Jaq.

"Are you telling us to lie?" said John.

"No, be forthright with them. Tell them that you're an expert and that as a result you spent a lot less money than the average person would. Tell them what the average person would spend and provide examples," said Jaq.

"What else can we do?" said Nancy.

"*Develop a personal relationship with the appraiser.* Now, I'm not talking about being their best friend or taking them out for dinner. I'm just suggesting you be informal and polite. It doesn't hurt to ask them about their family. This is especially important over time as you will end up dealing with the same appraisers over and over," said Jaq.

"What do you mean?" said John.

"As long as you're reasonable and as long as your values are reflective of the market, you'll find that appraisers get easier to deal with over time. They will trust you and your valuations," said Jaq.

"Anything else?" said Nancy.

"Sure. It's also vital *to show the property as well as possible.* It's incredible how many investors spend big money on renovations, and then at the last and most important minute they cut corners that affect appraisal value," said Jaq.

John shuffled uncomfortably in his seat as Nancy glanced over at him.

"What?" said Jaq.

"Well, I kind of, sort of left a bit of a mess in the basement. There were some construction materials down in the basement and some of the dust from the basement tracked up the stairs. It was all there when the appraiser went through. But, I thought they were supposed to be impartial and look at the permanent aspects of the property. I thought they were supposed to ignore a little dust," said John.

"They are *supposed to*, but humans just aren't the rationale animals we pretend. We're influenced by our emotions, and often the emotions that make a difference operate below conscious thoughts. Dirt and dust are

powerful to the subconscious mind of the appraiser," said
Jaq.

"Okay, well we didn't coach the appraiser and we left
a mess. I guess we know why we didn't get the appraisal
we were seeking," said Nancy.

"That might well have done it, but why leave it to
chance. Do more than is necessary," said Jaq.

"Such as?" said John.

"*Show the appraiser the rental income.* Once the
appraiser sees that the higher mortgage amount is
justified by an excellent rental income, they soon become
more pliable. It shows them that you're aware of what
you'll be earning on a property and that you can therefore
justify the higher mortgage you're looking for, I bet your
appraiser didn't know you're going to get $1275 for this
place, did he?" said Jaq.

"Nope, and we know this is high for the market, so it
would have helped. Anything else?" said Nancy.

"As you get more appraisals, you'll find the low ones
are often done by the same appraiser. You'll get to know
the appraisers in your area find that there are some that
habitually appraise lower. You can *instruct your mortgage
broker not to seek financing with certain institutions* if
they hire lowball appraisers," said Jaq.

"We can do that?" said John.

"Of course. You're the one who will be affected.
Always take control of your situation, and if you don't
want to avoid a certain lender you can always just wait
to see which appraiser calls. If it's the one you know is

a lowballer, you can simply *cancel the appraisal*. Try to reschedule with a new appraiser," said Jaq.

"That sounds like interference," said Nancy.

"It is interference, and there's nothing wrong with it, but I'd like to mention just one more. You can *renovate for curb appeal,*" said Jaq.

"We were kind of restricted on this property given that it was a townhouse," said John.

"Right, but when you purchase a single-family property renovating for curb appeal is one of the best strategies for bumping up appraisals. When your appraiser steps out of the car to see a gleaming new renovated beauty in front of him, it's hard not to believe the property should be worth more. It's human nature to be attracted to shiny objects," said Jaq.

"Right, but won't we blow our budget on such renovations?" said Nancy.

"There are ways to do it for cheap that still looks outstanding. It doesn't' apply in this case, but always remember this method," said Jaq.

"Okay, so is that it?" said John.

"Well, what we just discussed are all ways to directly improve prospects for a better appraisal, but let's not forget that the refinance is part of the larger strategy that also includes the initial purchase and potential partnerships, " said Jaq.

"Do you mean that we might not even want to bother with a refinance in some cases?" said John.

Standard Equity Removal Methods

Above, we've discussed the most common way to remove equity – the standard refinance. This conversation is the most important since it will be the most oft-used method in your BFRR refinancing repertoire.

1. **Refinance** – The gold standard. This is simply going back to the bank and getting a complete refinance of the property after renovations have been complete.

2. **HELOC behind 1st Mortgage** – This can be a great way to top up financing and remove equity.

   When getting the initial mortgage using this product you simply ask the bank to register a higher charge than. The bank will only advance funds based on what you pay up front, but it will advance more funds later, after you've done renovations and raised the value.

   Another benefit is that this product is often interest only, so it is can be a lower monthly payment than a mortgage.

3. **Blend and Extend** – Use the Blend and Extend Option for the difference between the first mortgage and the reappraised value.

   Once the value is lifted post renovation, this unique mortgage product 'extends' the length of the term and 'blends' the different interest rates together.

Integrated Strategies

"Not exactly. The end goal of a BFRR is usually to refinance with a bank for the long term. Within that goal you can be creative about the overall strategy, and at times this might mean holding a property for a little while before getting the refinance you want," said Jaq.

"I thought we always wanted to refinance immediately," said Nancy.

"You do, but there may be times when waiting for a bit is a better strategy. If you do everything in your power to get the appraisal high enough to refinance, but it still doesn't come through, then you might be better off just putting this property on a 1-year mortgage, then refinancing again in 1 year and taking our more equity at that time," said Jaq.

"Or maybe we just leave it on the open mortgage we currently have it on?" said John.

"If the cost of the higher interest rate doesn't kill you, then this might be an option. The advantage of keeping it on the open mortgage is that you can try for the refinance before one year is over. The disadvantage is that you won't return any of the costs to your investor," said Jaq.

"Right, well a 1-year mortgage or keeping it on the open mortgage might be best, although we want to give our investor back some of his money. Still, I think we should try again and this time influence the appraiser," said John.

"Good to hear, but always remember that *refinance strategies are part of larger strategies* even though the

basis of BFRR always stays the same. There are different
ways to skin the proverbial cat," said Jaq.

"What does this mean?" said Nancy.

**Integrated Strategies for Entrance and
Refinance**

- Open mortgage and refinance
  - Cash to buy and refinance (can use cash, RRSP,
    RESP, TFSA mortgage, or line of credit)
  - Borrow from LOC then refinance and cash out
- Private lender and refinance
- Eco grants
- Leave 1st mortgage on property, take temporary 2nd
  mortgage
- Joint venture partner lives in property
- Raise Value over time and refinance
- Vendor Take Back and refinance
- Assume original mortgage and refinance

"I hope you have a bit of time. This is a big topic
because there are few limits to creatively putting deals
together. As long as execution is legal and ethical you're
free to go for it – find the most creative way possible to
put together a deal. If you do, you'll be the toast of the
local Real Estate Investing Club, but just remember one
thing before you chase the most creative deal possible,"
said Jaq.

"What's that?" said John.

"Sometimes the most creative methods are rarely used for a reason. Don't use a creative strategy just because it's different. Use a strategy because it's the best one for you, your partners, and because it meets your goals. Just buy good deals and the right strategy will appear," said Jaq

"Gotcha, so what are they? We already know about the strategies of buying on the front end with bank financing and bank financing the refinance, putting a HELOC behind a 1st mortgage, and the Blend and Extend strategy. What are the more creative integrated strategies?" said Nancy.

"The next one becomes more available to investors once they get momentum and have plenty of investor money available. Many investors at first think money will be hard to come by, but it comes flooding in when a track record is established. We end up finding money is available and it's good deals that are in short supply," said Jaq.

"We're looking forward to this day, but what's the strategy?" said Nancy.

"Well, when cash is aplenty, you may be able to use *cash to buy and then refinance.* A joint venture partner usually supplies it but you may have cash enough to do it yourself at some point," said Jaq.

"Right. So how does it work?" said Nancy.

"The partner puts up the cash to do the initial purchase and renovations. The funds might come from cash in a partner's bank account, their line of credit, or from a self-directed RRSP, RESP, or TFSA (Registered Retirement Savings Plan, Registered Education Savings

Plan, or Tax Free Savings Account) account. The partner will then qualify on the refinance mortgage. They'll get all or most of their initial investment back at the time of the refinance. Alternatively, the cash might come from your own bank account or line of credit before refinancing with a partner or yourself on mortgage," said Jaq.

"So, the main point of this strategy is to use cash on the front end and refinancing to get the cash back," said Nancy.

"Correct, but it's not to be confused with the next strategy, which is to *borrow from someone's line of credit* to buy, and then refinance with a bank mortgage. This line of credit might come from a family member, a friend, an acquaintance, or an investor. Whatever the case, the point of using this strategy is to secure a preferential interest rate. This is a good option, and many family members and/or friends love the opportunity to lend their line of credit so they can make a bit of money without doing any work. An added perk is that many of the people who start out lending money from a line of credit end up becoming long-term joint venture partners," said Jaq.

"That sounds like a good option, and I'm pretty sure I could think of a few people who might be good candidates to borrow LOC funds from," said John.

"Great. Next is to *borrow money from a private lender and then refinance.* This one is a bit more advanced, but it's definitely achievable and in some cases is the best option. Keep in mind that private moneylenders are professionals. This means they charge a premium. Whereas you could probably borrow someone's line of credit for 8-10% or even less, you'd probably be facing a 12-15% interest rate from a private moneylender. On the positive side, these professionals can usually get you the money fast – almost immediately. They have their own system of due diligence based mostly on the value of the property, so as long as the deal is strong enough they'll usually lend on the property quickly. Private moneylenders' process is to register a mortgage, which means you're legally in the same position as you would if you borrowed from a bank. If you can refinance fast, this works, otherwise, the cost of borrowing adds up quickly," said Jaq.

"I don't think I'm quite ready for private money, but I could see it down the road," said Nancy.

"Absolutely. Don't rule it out. Once you get to be an expert on your neighbourhood, you'll know what a great deal looks like and how long renovation turnarounds take. You will feel comfortable using private money as confidence goes up," said Jaq.

"Right. What other strategies are there?" said John.

"The next strategy is *to leave the current mortgage in place and take a temporary second mortgage.* This is a way to pull some equity out of a property. However, if you do this, you need to be certain that you can refinance quickly, since placing the second mortgage on the property will likely make your total loan value very high. To employ the 2nd mortgage strategy make sure you've significantly lifted the property's value and that you'll be able to fully pay out the 2nd mortgage with room to spare once you've executed the refinance. It will probably work better on a partial gut than a little lipstick deal," said Jaq.

"Wow, there are a lot of integrated strategies within the BFRR strategy," said Nancy.

"It's true, and there are more possibilities. Any combination that's legal, ethical, and works is available. Another is to *bring in a joint venture partner who pays more than the amount of the current property value.* This is designed to get the active investor some cash-in-pocket immediately and is most-used by investors who've chosen to forego a traditional career and invest full time," said Jaq.

"Is this ethical?" said Nancy.

"Great question. Of course we never do anything that isn't ethical. The investor has to know you're doing it and why you're doing it. It's not about skimming money without the investor finding out," said Jaq.

"Right. I see what you mean. So, how does it work?" said Nancy.

"The joint venture partner brings some combination of money plus bank financing for the original purchase. On top of that they supply the money for the renovation, and in addition they pay the active investor a little extra. Once the refinance is executed, all the money is returned to the investor as always. Your goal is to get as much of the money back to the investor as possible after the refinance, " said Jaq.

"Any tricks to doing this properly?" said John.

"Well, with the added money used to pay you, the property must still cash flow. It would irresponsible to sacrifice cash flow for an immediate payday. Also, this strategy is best when doing more than a lipstick renovation. The expected value lift on these bigger renovation projects is significant, and the time commitment of the active investor is higher, therefore getting some cash for the active investor up front is justified," said Jaq.

"That sounds like one for the future. Anything else?" said Nancy.

"Yes, there are more. You can *joint venture with someone who will live in the property and benefit from a low down payment.* Because the property will be the partner's primary residence, it becomes a candidate for 5% down payment. You then do your renovation and lift the value. Because the down payment is so low, there's a great chance you'll return the joint venture partner's entire down payment," said Jaq.

"Sweet deal," said John.

"For everyone involved! A 100% return of cash invested in a short time is remarkable, and if you're strategic enough you can even buy a property with a suite, so in addition to the joint venture partner living there, a tenant can also add to the cash flow. If you do it this way, you can by a single family home or a duplex with 5% down, but a 3-plex or 4-plex will require 10% down," said Jaq.

"It sounds like an awesome strategy," said Nancy.

"It is, but there are two drawbacks. First, you have to account for CMHC fees. CMHC has to insure every property with less than 20% down payment, and they charge thousands of dollars for it. This is an extra expense to consider. Second, since the owner is required to live in the property, you're limited in how many of these deals you can do. In other words, you can't rely solely on this strategy. Just do these deals as they come available," said Jaq.

Mortgage Fraud and You

We've just discussed a great strategy (partner lives in the property) that, when used correctly, can accelerate your investment career, along with your partner's financial situation.

Unfortunately, this strategy is also one of the most abused strategies.

Many 'investors' pretend the partner will live in the property, but never have any intention of staying for long. They reason that as long as the partner lives in the property for a little while, that they were 'in essence' telling the truth/

Don't be fooled by this self-deluding 'logic'. It's called mortgage fraud. Banks and law enforcement officials don't take this matter lightly, and it's a serious crime. When investigating these matters, it's easy for the officials to tell whether or not the partner in question had real intention to live in the property for the long term.

Participating in dodgy dealings could sink you as an investor. We urge you never to mess with your future or that of your partner – it's simply not worth it.

Use this strategy only if intentions are pure and if the partner plans to live there for the long term.

"I like the sounds of that idea, and I know a few people who have enough money for a 5% down payment mortgage and don't yet own their own home. Perhaps some of my acquaintances might consider this option," said Nancy.

"It's a great way to get started as both an investor and a homeowner. You'll find other candidates from your circle come forward if you help one family first," said Jaq.

"Right! I'm getting this impression the BFRR strategy can be a great way to help people too," said John.

"You've got that right. A lot of people win when you execute the strategy – motivated sellers, investors, realtors, contractors, and of course yourself. There's one more strategy I'd like to talk about, and it's a longer-term value creation strategy where you *buy a property and raise the value over time before refinancing*," said Jaq.

"That sounds different. I thought the whole point of the BFRR strategy was to create equity up front and pull out some cash right away," said John.

"Typically, it is, but what if you could buy a great deal that produces cash flow immediately, and you could finance the renovations over a period of time – say 5 years – using only cash flow produced by the property?" said Jaq.

"Sounds okay," said John.

"It works, and if there's one thing BFRR investors should be it's pragmatic. This strategy is often used on small multi-family properties with say 4 units or on a block of 4 townhomes. If the asset produces enough cash, then it will carry the overall mortgage for a few weeks or months while one of the units is being renovated," said Jaq.

"As long as the cash flow is good, I don't see anything wrong with this," said John.

"You're starting to sound like me! When doing this strategy, you only renovate when you have a vacancy. Just let tenancies take their natural course, and with each vacancy you renovate another unit. You will increase the value of the property every time you renovate a unit. The goal is to raise rents after each renovation, and therefore raise the property value. It's similar to a normal BFRR deal, but it takes longer to execute," said Jaq.

"I guess we don't always have to be in a rush," said Nancy.

"Sometimes, quickly isn't better. For example, imagine you typically purchased properties with a partner because you needed cash for purchase and renovations," said Jaq.

"Sounds like us," said John.

"Sounds like most investors. Then, imagine you gathered enough cash to do a deal like this by yourself but you didn't have the cash to renovate immediately. In such a case, you'd have to pay for the renovations with cash flow," said Jaq.

"What's the advantage of doing this instead of just partnering?" said Nancy.

"Well, after a few years you would be the proud *solo* owner of a great small multi-family building. The longer you own such a property, the more profit you earn. So, being a solo owner, and owning longer rather than shorter make this a great deal. You'd make more money on such a deal over the long term," said Jaq.

"So, be flexible for whatever works best," said John.

"Exactly. Strategies are important but secondary to fundamentals. If you buy a fantastic deal and execute the renovation, any strategy will work because you've applied the magic of value creation – even if that value creation is over a longer time horizon. It's like a license to print money," said Jaq.

"Any more?" said John.

"There is a couple more. You can purchase the property with a *Vendor Take Back (VTB) and then refinance later*. VTBs are more often used in commercial real estate, but they're used often enough in residential real estate that you should be try to use them whenever possible. In fact, I make it a habit to ask every seller if they'll do a VTB," said Jaq.

"Why is that?" said Nancy?

"Well, if I can buy a property with as little of my own or my partner's money as possible, why wouldn't I? If I can get in with a VTB it makes one less trip to the bank. Of course, when doing a VTB you need to refinance with bank financing after raising the value of the property, so you'll deal with a bank anyways, but using a VTB can make your buying process smoother, and often you can secure a great deal," said Jaq.

"Cool, what's the last one?" said Nancy.

"Finally, we can *assume the existing mortgage and refinance later*. When using this strategy and the VTB entrance strategy, you'll have to bring some cash also, as the value of the mortgage assumed won't be the same as the purchase amount," said Jaq.

"So the cash need is no different than a normal mortgage then?" said John.

"It depends. As long as the mortgage being assumed has terms you can accept, then mortgage assumption can be a great strategy. Just remember that you or your partner must qualify on the assumed mortgage. After the value of the property is raised, or at the end of the mortgage term, you'll refinance just as with any other BFRR deal," said Jaq.

"Interesting. We came here to discuss refinancing. We got that and a lot more," said John.

"Right. There were two separate but related discussions. First was how to make sure your refinance goes well. Second was to craft a whole strategy that includes the entrance, partnership, and renovation," said Jaq.

"You were right about one thing – that was a big discussion. I think we need to get going. Is there anything else?" said Nancy.

"No, that's about it. Let me know how your refinance plays out and we'll talk soon," said Jaq.

The three of them gathered up their things, said their goodbyes and headed for the door.

"I have a feeling that next time we chat we'll be having a much different conversation," said Jaq as he got into his car.

John and Nancy looked at each other. "What do you think that meant?" said Nancy.

"He has quite a flair for the dramatic, so I have no idea, but I'm sure we're in for quite a ride now that we're almost through the first one," said John as he and Nancy headed home.

Talking to the Mortgage Broker

After their meeting, John called the mortgage broker, Diane, and requested she seek financing with a different lender. They explained to her that they needed a better appraisal, and to their surprise she totally understood.

"That appraiser has a bit of a reputation for lowballing. It shouldn't be a problem to secure financing from a different lender," said Diane.

John smiled at the memory of Jaq telling him the power of using a BFRR expert mortgage broker. He knew a 'normal' mortgage broker would not have understood his request to pursue a different avenue.

"I'm fairly confident we'll get it this time," said John.

He smiling again into the phone, knowing he now had the knowledge to tip the odds in his favour.

Tipping the Scales

A few days later John was onsite with the appraiser doing subtly persuading the mortgage broker in all the ways Jaq taught Nancy and him.

"Anything I need to know about this property?" said the new appraiser, Garrett.

"I'm glad you asked. I wanted to make sure you got all the information to make your appraisal with. There are a few things. First off, we strongly think the property should appraise for $230,000," said John.

"Do you have good comps?" said Garrett.

"Absolutely. There are some that show lower sales, too, but I wanted to point out the differences. First, none of the lower comps were renovated, but as you can see this one has been thoroughly renovated. Second, the higher comp was an identical property that sold for $230,000. Just like this one, it was also renovated, but more importantly, it had a garage, just like this one," said John.

"I think I missed that one in my initial research. Thanks for sharing. That will make a big difference," said Garrett.

John smiled, and the two men continued their conversation. John clearly communicated with Garrett and subtly persuaded him using a logical and intelligent explanation for everything.

John felt confident when he left, and he wasn't surprise a few days later when he got a call from Diane telling him they'd gotten the appraisal.

The Numbers

Total Cost (Purchase, Holding, Renovation): $190,000

After Repair Appraisal: $230,000.

Mortgage (80% of $230,000): $184,000

Created Value: $40,000

Money Left In Deal: $6,000

On paper, this deal perfect for John, Nancy, and their partner Bill. When they finally got the appraisal and financing in order, they learned that they had created $40,000 and only left $6,000 in the deal.

However, they still had to get an excellent tenant into the property, and to do this they had some more work to do.

From High Activity to Low Activity

You just learned how to tip the scales in your favour for getting an excellent appraisal value on a BFRR deal. Getting the value lift is what makes the BFRR deal so powerful and effective, so this chapter covered some vital territory.

Value lift is big, but mortgage pay down and appreciation is where the true wealth-creation takes place. This is why the rental period is the make or break time on any BFRR deal.

Unfortunately, too many investors who believe the work ends when the purchase, renovation, and refinance are over.

This could not be further from the truth. In reality, the work just begins when you move into the property management phase. Many think property management doesn't make much of a difference, but the truth is that it's a high return on investment activity.

All of your efforts up to this point can be sabotaged without excellent property management over holding period. The high activity purchase, renovation, and refinance may be over, but the lower activity property management phase is just beginning, and this chapter is dedicated to maximizing your property management efforts, which will help you achieve a top end return on investment.

"Service to others is the rent you pay for your room here on earth."

Muhammed Ali

CHAPTER 9

Rent

Property Management Magic

Have you ever heard of a landlord with tenant problems? Perhaps a better question is: have you ever heard of a landlord without tenant problems?

If you've been in the game for a bit, you'll know that landlording comes with its own set of challenges. A lot of landlords hate it, and this dislike is driving people to leave the real estate business too early.

Tenant trouble is the biggest factor that makes investors quit and keeps potential investors from purchasing real estate, and this makes sense. Why? People work hard at their jobs, so the idea of spending evenings and weekends sorting through the goop of human drama isn't an exciting proposition for most.

But it doesn't have to be this way.

Up until now, this book has focused on the steps to acquire and finance a great BFRR deal. These are important phases of the BFRR process, but this enormous effort could all be undone without excellent property management.

Put positively, all the effort comes together when the property is finally rented. The eventual success of the project will be decided by the rental period.

So, this chapter is critical to your BFRR success. Landlording is an art and a science. The more you practice it, the better you will get at it, but by using the wisdom in this chapter you will be miles ahead.

Read on to find out *why* it's important and learn *how* to execute on this oft-forgotten but critical phase of the process.

The Property Management Problem

"Whew!" said Nancy.

It was the first Friday night since the first BFRR deal, and she was ready to flop down on the couch and forget about real estate for the rest of the night. Getting the property purchased, renovated, refinanced, and rented felt like a big effort.

"It will get easier. I'm sure of it. It's like going to the gym, having a kid, or any other new challenge in life. The beginning is the hardest part. A rocket uses 95% of the fuel used to escape the atmosphere, right? We just have to get out of the atmosphere," said John.

Nancy giggled.

"I never knew you were such an astronaut. If I weren't along with you for the ride, I'd probably think you were talking nonsense right now, but I know exactly what you mean. In our case, the 'atmosphere' means working with minimal job security until retirement and barely scraping by into old age. Out of the atmosphere for us means financial freedom, and it's a ride I want to take," said Nancy.

"I'm glad you liked my metaphor. I'm sure we'll get there. One of the hardest parts is over. Most of the activity happens during the transaction, renovation, and refinance period. Once the property is in the portfolio, the job becomes one of property management, which when it's done properly shouldn't be nearly as much effort as the transaction period, but I have to admit I'm a little bit nervous about the property management, too," said John.

"Why is that?" said Nancy.

"Well, I know we can do it, but if I had to choose a full time job, it probably wouldn't be property management. With a BFRR deal the post-renovation property needs fewer renovations than a normal buy-and-hold property, especially during the first 5 years when the renovations are fresh. This is important because the benefit of market appreciation and mortgage pay down often takes time," said John.

"Right, and fewer renovations means easier property management, right?" said Nancy.

"It should, but let's not forget all the petty problems we have with our tenants. With only two properties we get calls every single week," said John.

"True," said Nancy.

"Some of those calls are for small renovations – the type we probably won't have to deal with on a BFRR deal – but many of the calls are unrelated to renovations. We've just added a 3rd property, and if we're going to do this thing properly we'll be adding several more. I'm confident we can get the properties rented out, but I'm not so certain I want to be taking tenant calls for the next 5-10 years," said John.

"Neither do I. Tonight for example, I just want to relax. The thought of a tenant calling and needing us to run out is terrifying. Does real estate success mean never having a free moment to do anything other than tend to the needs of tenants?" said Nancy.

"I sure hope not – I want to get this rocket ship out of the atmosphere. I can handle the idea of the busy periods where we'll be adding a property, renovating it, and refinancing it, but I'm having a hard time coming to grips with the idea of managing many properties. Dreading the sound of the phone isn't a good feeling. It makes me shy away from wanting more property, which will sabotage our plan for financial freedom," said John.

"Well, this is something we should figure out soon because if we don't, we might burn off all of our fuel before we get out of the atmosphere," said Nancy.

"If there's one thing I've learned through all this is how much Jaq's help can help us get unstuck. I'll call him now. Do you have time to meet with him next Friday at 5:30 at the Equity Café?" said John.

"I sure do," said Nancy.

John called Jaq to set a meeting for one week later, and then John and Nancy settled into a relaxing evening at home – luckily there were no distressing calls from their tenants that night.

A Property Management Primer

John and Nancy got out of their car ready to walk into the Equity Café to meet Jaq when they heard the all too familiar sound of John's cell phone ringing.

"Ugh," they both said.

John looked at his phone. They both knew it was likely a tenant.

"Hello," said John.

Nancy stared at John as he listened.

"Really? Why? Can't you just send it by email transfer?" said John.

He paused for 30 seconds – rolling his eyes several times while listening.

"Okay, I'll be there in about 2 hours. See you soon," said John.

As John was on the phone, Jaq joined them at their table, "What was that about?" he said.

John sighed deeply.

"It was one of our tenants. He pays his rent, but there's always some drama about it. It's getting tiresome.

One month he was late because of some circumstance or other. I can't remember why. The next month his cheque bounced and we had to chase up the money. There were a couple of other events. This time he told me he can only pay by cash and that his car is in the garage, so he can't drop off the rent. I have to go to his house to pick it up. It's a pain, but I'm going to head over there after we leave here," said John.

"That sounds distressing. Imagine if you had 30 tenants doing the same thing. You'd never have time for anything but tenant problems," said Jaq.

"Yeah, that's what we're thinking. It's why we wanted to meet today. We love the idea of creating financial freedom with the BFRR strategy, and we don't even mind the business of buying, renovating, and refinancing, but we're not sure we can handle the daily grind of multiple tenants. The few we have are a big enough commitment. How do you do it Jaq?" said Nancy.

"I don't do it," said Jaq.

"Oh, you hire a professional property management company, then? Or do you just neglect your tenants?" said John.

"Neither. Well, these days I have an in-house management team, but I self-managed a large portfolio for several years before handing things over to a property management company. I never did what you're about to do tonight," said Jaq.

"Okay, that can't be chalked up to luck. We find we're running around after our tenants all the time. They're like the kids we never wanted," said Nancy.

"It's not luck. I should qualify what I just said – I did run around after tenants for the first year or so until I learned the ropes from some of the masters of the trade. Once I learned how, I found there were very few times it was necessary to do this kind of legwork you're getting involved in. Tenants should be doing most of it themselves, and when you teach them how it's not that hard to do," said Jaq.

"Teach them how? Do we have to run a course on being a decent person – someone who takes care of life responsibilities?" said John.

"It's not quite like that, and I urge you to change your perception of tenants first. Consider this: your tenants *are decent people*, but they've been taught by repetition that they can get away with certain behaviours. There are many sloppy landlords out there. Some tenants have gotten into the habit of pushing the boundaries and knowing they can get away with it. They might know how to be *decent people*, but they don't know how to be *decent tenants*. There is a difference," said Jaq.

"I'm not picking up your point," said John.

"Well, tenant problems are one component of landlording. Eliminating most of those is one of the most important jobs a landlord has. If you don't, you'll end up with a bunch of problem tenants, which is unacceptable. Improper property management causes more investor burnout than any other problem. On a side note – burned out landlords are a great source of future BFRR deals," said Jaq.

"Thanks for the tip, but let's get back to fixing tenant problems. I brought my notebook. I'll be thrilled if we can minimize tenant problems with better knowledge," said Nancy.

"Prepare to be thrilled then because you most definitely can minimize tenant problems. I'll lay it out for you today in broad strokes. Of course, your property management education will be ongoing, but perhaps I can help you understand some of the most important principles today," said Jaq.

"Please do. We've never thought about it systematically. Ever since we bought our first property we just threw a tenant in it and hoped for the best. Generally we've scraped by, but there have been enough problems that we haven't enjoyed the experience. Heck, I can't even imagine it being enjoyable. It's like enjoying a trip to the dentist," said John.

"Many investors have one or two bad experiences that colour their perspective towards all future tenants. Listen, *property management might never be as much fun as the acquisition, renovation, or refinancing aspect of BFRR investing*, but it can be deeply satisfying because it's your best chance to develop long-term relationships. A landlord-to-tenant relationship is an important one, and I even think you can have a positive impact on your tenants' lives if you do it right," said Jaq.

"Really? We find that becoming friends with our tenants is usually a bad idea. The only times we've done that we were burned," said John.

"That's true. You'll notice I didn't mention anything about being their friend. I said you could develop real relationships with tenants. There are different types of impactful relationships than just friendships. Most of us had at least one teacher who left a big impact on us, but we wouldn't say the teacher was our friend. We can positively influence people without being their friend, and that's what I'm talking about here," said Jaq.

"How does a landlord positively impact a tenant?" said Nancy.

"By being an excellent landlord. It might sound simplistic, but it's true. Now listen, the best reason for being an excellent landlord is to get excellent results, but the added benefit is having excellent relationships. In fact, the first principle of landlording is that excellent relationships lead to excellent results," said Jaq.

"That sounds wonderful, but the relationship breaks down quickly when the tenant starts doing silly things like not paying rent on time," said John.

"Why do you put up with that?" asked Jaq.

"I don't put up with it, I always tell them that they have to pay on time," said John.

"Right, but human beings respond to real consequences not nagging reminders. Tell me, what would happen to you if you started showing up late to work every day?" said Jaq.

"I'd be given a warning within a week and would be fired within a month," said John.

"In other words, there would be real world consequences that you couldn't accept," said Jaq.

"There would," said John.

"So, you make a point of getting to work on time, don't you?" said Jaq.

"Every day. So, are you saying I need to evict my tenants for paying rent late? I thought you said it was all about relationships," said John.

"It *is* about relationships, but as long as you have tenants taking advantage of that relationship, it's not a good relationship. When a tenant signs a lease, they're making a commitment to pay the rent on time. Every time they don't, they're breaking their commitment and denigrating the relationship, but it's not their fault," said Jaq.

"Of course it is!" said John.

"No, it isn't. It's hard to hear, but it's *your* fault. They've done it in the past to other landlords and gotten away with it. You help nothing by letting it continue," said Jaq.

"But, I don't let it continue. I always tell them..." said John.

Jaq interrupted, "Telling them is nothing. Showing them is everything. The *real world* has proven their behaviour okay in the past, since they've never experienced real world consequences for paying late. In this way a bad tenant continues along. They believe they're upholding their end of the relationship. Your job is to train them out of that," said Jaq.

"Training tenants sounds like a lot of work," said John.

"It's not as much work as you might think, because once you implement your system, each tenant will quickly get the picture. Plus your screening will get better. You become an excellent landlord when you get great at systems and building proper landlord-tenant relationships," said Jaq.

"Okay, so you're saying once we implement a landlording system then we'll have better relationships? This is new to me, as I've never thought of being systematic in relationships before," said John.

"The two are intrinsically connected. How would you feel if your company suddenly didn't pay you on payday?" said Jaq.

"I'd be livid," said John.

"Of course. You provide your company with a service and in return they have a very systematic relationship with you. Part of that system is that they pay you on time. No exceptions. In return you show up to work on time and you do your job. No questions. There are many other parts to the system. You likely receive some sort of benefits, have specific holidays, and have pre-defined working hours, am I correct?" said Jaq.

"Indeed you are," said John.

"Right, inside your company there is a set of rules. The same works in a landlord-tenant relationship," said Jaq.

"You said that right, there are so many rules in the landlord tenancy act," said John.

"Right, but the rules don't just apply to you! The tenant has to uphold their end, too. A tenant's most important responsibility is to pay rent on time, yet it's the most common problem between landlords and tenants," said Jaq.

"Good to know we're not alone," said Nancy.

"It happens to everyone, but what separates the pro landlords from the amateurs is how you deal with this common problem. You need to act like your company would if you failed to show up for work. Treat it like a business. Install a system of consequences to immediately correct the behaviour. If the behaviour isn't corrected, then take steps to end the relationship – just as your company would if you didn't show up to work," said Jaq.

"So, it's all about relationships, but we have to fulfill a role within that relationship – a much different role than normal," said John.

"That's correct. Relationships are the most important aspect, but to develop proper relationships we *must implement a set of effective systems*. The two work hand in hand. Without systems it's impossible to have excellent relationships, and without commitment to the relationships, the systems are difficult to develop. You need a solid reason to be systematic, and I can think of no better reason than having excellent relationships, which will make your real estate business a huge success and you a power investor," said Jaq.

"Okay, so the first and most important component is the relationships, but systems sound like a close second. I'm not accustomed to thinking of systems as being helpful in relationships. It almost seems mechanical and cold. How do we make it human?" said Nancy.

"There are simple principles of conduct that you should adhere to – it's a matter of human decency. You could call this your 'system of conduct'. It's a rule bound set of principles that will help guide your behavior when interacting with tenants," said Jaq.

"I failed ethics class in university, so don't get too deep on me here," said John.

"My system of conduct is simple: at all times I strive to be *solution oriented, civil, and staunch.* Being *solution oriented* means when there's a problem you move immediately onto the solution, which is usually the application of a policy from your system. Don't waste a moment playing the blame game. *Being civil* just means you never stoop to an unprofessional level. Keep it professional at all times. *Staunchness* means you don't bend your predetermined set of rules. This is the kind of character required to build a successful relationship with your tenants," said Jaq.

"I've been guilty of breaking all three of those in the past, but tell us more about systems. I've never thought of property management like this before," said John.

"Systems and relationships work together. The systems are the platform the relationship is built on. For example, if the tenant wants a repair, there must be a system in place for them to request it. They don't just call you whenever. In addition, there must be a system in place for you to respond appropriately. It can't be haphazard," said Jaq.

"What would this look like?" said John.

"The normal unsystematic way would look like this. First, the tenant would call the landlord's cell phone directly. Next, the landlord would react, trying to figure out how to deal with it immediately. Then, the landlord might even drop whatever she is doing and go to the property. After that it's just a scramble to get the fix done," said Jaq.

"It's like you've been watching me on hidden camera," said John.

"It's not just you. This is the standard. In this schema, the onus is on the landlord to fix something, but that's just the way the landlord has set up the relationship. They have to react. Being reactive never works in landlording. Being systematic does," said Jaq.

"So, what would a more systematic approach look like?" said Nancy.

"A more systematic approach would require a procedure for the initial communication from tenant to landlord. I have maintenance request forms in all of my properties, and when a tenant wants work completed, they fill out the maintenance request form," said Jaq.

"That does sound systematic. How does it work?" said Nancy.

"First, the tenant must detail the work they're requesting on the form, but the form also explains that the work may or may not be completed. If the request isn't deemed urgent, there is no requirement to do any kind of work. A shower that doesn't work would have to be fixed immediately, but a wall blemish wouldn't," said Jaq.

"So, you don't necessarily do what they ask?" said Nancy.

"No, I look at the maintenance request form and make a judgment whether or not it's urgent. If the renovation needs to be done so the tenant can live a normal life, then I handle it right away. Since the request form is detailed, it helps me decide if the work is urgent or if it can wait until a more convenient date," said Jaq.

"That would be handy. I can't tell you how many times I've rushed over to a property to fix trivial things," said John.

"It happens all the time. Listen, sometimes the tenant request is legitimate, yet it's not an emergency. There are really three types of requests. First, there are emergencies where you drop everything and move. Next, there are urgent maintenance requests, where you take care of it right away. Finally, there are non-urgent requests, where you batch the work in it with a routine maintenance visit," said Jaq.

"I've never thought of them as separate categories before," said John.

"You need to start. Without this systematic approach, you'll never know the difference and will end up treating every maintenance request the same. Distinguishing them and making thoughtful decisions will ensure that you take fewer trips to a property. You can even avoid a trip yourself by sending a handyman," said Jaq.

"That *sounds* great, but I doubt our tenants would follow the system. They'd just call us directly like they do for everything else," said John.

"Of course. This is how they've been trained. Why do they have your direct phone number? Tenants need a specific number for maintenance. When they reach that number, they will hear an answering machine, and they have to leave a message detailing their maintenance request. If you set it up that way, they'll find there's no way around the maintenance request form. Building a process even eliminates frivolous maintenance requests," said Jaq.

"Wait a minute, are you saying that tenants shouldn't even have my number? Now you have my attention," said John.

"I'll tell you what I do. I subscribe to a virtual phone system called *Grasshopper* – others I know use *eVoice or Canada One Voice*. These systems allow unlimited phone numbers. I manage the whole system behind the scenes and can set the phone number to go directly to an answering machine or directly to my phone. Most of my lines go directly to an answering machine, especially the lines that are set up for things like maintenance," said Jaq.

"That sounds awesome, but what do you do when you have a genuine emergency, like my flood? Surely the tenants need your direct phone number for something like that?" said John.

"No. What they need is a good set of rules about what to do in certain kinds of emergencies *along with* an emergency contact number. When my tenants call my emergency contact number, I receive an immediate notification on my phone. No matter where I am I can immediately deal with a real emergency. I take emergency calls seriously and respond quickly, and since I don't get a lot of emergency calls, I know the ones I do get are serious. What you find is that there are few real emergencies, and when a tenant has been trained they don't call the emergency number frivolously," said Jaq.

"So, what do you do with the other calls that go to answering machines?" said John

"I respond to them at a predetermined time. I don't answer requests when they come in. Instead, I set aside a time to listen to all messages, usually once per day on a regular weekday, during working hours. I always get back to tenants in a reasonable amount of time, but I don't cancel life events for non-emergency situations. Heck, I don't even look at messages outside business hours for non-emergencies," said Jaq.

"I like the sounds of that. Are there any other kinds of systems we should know about?" said John.

Jaq chuckled.

"What?" said John.

"You need a system for *every aspect of landlording*. I'm not trying to give you a comprehensive list here; I'm just speaking in broad strokes. We don't have time to discuss every system to manage a portfolio of rental properties," said Jaq.

"Where could I find them all?" said John.

"There are manuals and courses you can take, or you can do like so many others and develop your own systems over time. If you do it yourself, the rule is to treat every circumstance as though it could happen over and over again. If it did happen again how would you like to handle it simply and efficiently? Ask yourself that question and develop a system to solve the problem if it happened again. Remember also that for every system you also need to develop a way to communicate it to the tenant or whoever else is involved – this is all part of your system," said Jaq.

"Sounds like a lot of work," said John.

"Two things. First, it's not remotely as much work as *not* developing systems. Second, it's a lot less work if you adopt others' systems. Learn from others' mistakes," said Jaq.

"Good point. We need systems," said John.

"It's a must. Relationships are number 1, but without a solid platform of systems you can't develop great relationships. The trick is to get started building systems as soon as possible. Treat it with the energy you do acquisitions, and you might even enjoy it," said Jaq.

"Really, how is that possible?" said Nancy.

"Well, most people don't think of property management as a money making activity, but consider this – the value lift from the renovation and refinance phase brings a one time payment. On the other hand appreciation, mortgage pay down, and cash flow continue as long as you own the property. It means what you do after you own the property will bring greater monetary reward than the front end. Property management pays," said Jaq.

"Of course. If the property isn't tenanted, there's no income. No income means no profit. That's easy to see," said John.

"That's the obvious one, but there are more ways that excellent property management makes you money," said Jaq.

"Such as?" said John.

"We've talked about systems. Well, one of the most important systems is the system for improving cash flow. As an excellent landlord you need to be relentless in your pursuit of better cash flow. $50 per month might not seem like much, but imagine if you improve cash flow by $50 per month across a portfolio of 30 properties," said Jaq.

"That's good dough," said Nancy.

"Now imagine you do that every year. $50 across 30 properties is an improvement of $1500 per month. Then you do it again a year later. It's the equivalent of adding another salary to your income every other year. Do you think you'd like that?" said Jaq.

"Of course we would, but you're talking about a lot of properties here," said Nancy.

"True, so let's take a much smaller example. You own 3 properties now. Imagine you never bought another, and then imagine that with excellent property management you could add just $200 of monthly income from the 3 existing properties you own? It amounts to $2400 per year. Then you do this year after year. After 5 years it's an additional $12,000 annual income. Would you like $12,000 extra income yearly?" said Jaq.

"Those months we barely cover off our expenses wouldn't be so stressful, and we'd hire a handyman more often than doing the work ourselves," said Nancy.

"Yes, which would lead to less burnout and more acquisitions. You see, most people think of adding to their real estate income all at once, but a methodical, systematic, and relentless landlord understands that big financial rewards are the result of seeking small improvements year after year," said Jaq.

"Are those kind of results really possible?" said John.

"Of course they are. You're already ahead of the game when you start the holding period with a great property. However, the results are compounded when you apply the system of improving cash flow," said Jaq.

"I see the benefit, but how does it look in practice?" said Nancy.

"Start by thinking of what cash flow is made up of. To have cash flow, total income has to be more than total expenses. There are two basic components of cash flow. To improve it, you can raise the properties' income or reduce its expenses. The system is to do quarterly and yearly analyses to determine whether or not you can improve on either side," said Jaq.

"In a strong market it's common to raise rents regularly, perhaps even every year. How else do you consistently improve income?" said John.

"Raising rents is the most common way to *increase income*. As long as you stay within the rent control laws there's nothing wrong with raising them as much as the market will accept. Another is through targeted renovations, which you'll take care of during the fix phase. Other common methods are to rent your property as a furnished suite, add a coin operated laundry, rent parking spaces or garage storage, rent basement storage, or add a basement apartment," said Jaq.

"There are a lot of good ideas in there. As I get more comfortable I'd especially have no problem doing a basement apartment addition," said John.

"In the right circumstance it's a great way to add income on a new BFRR deal, but don't write it off as a strategy for existing properties. Doing it when you purchase is great, but many proactive landlords are doing it to existing properties as well. You can sometimes refinance this kind of deal. If you have equity, it might not cost you much cash. Also, if you own a property by yourself you can bring on a joint venture partner who would pay for the addition of the suite and in return they get a percentage of the ownership in the property. You two had two existing properties before you started doing BFRR deal, right?" said Jaq.

"Yes," said Nancy.

"Well, you might want to do an analysis on each of those properties to see if a secondary suite makes sense," said Jaq.

"One of our properties might, especially since we've owned it for 4 years now, and it's appreciated in value. Maybe we could refinance it and add a suite without spending much of our own cash," said Nancy.

"That's the way to think. Proactive landlords strategically think of every way to raise income, but they also *decrease expenses*. Some of the most common ways are to refinance when interest rates are better, re-amortize the mortgage, and analyze and eliminate. I personally analyze my expenses every 3 months. I discover inefficiencies almost every time. Each time I find one I give it the axe. It feels like cutting off a monster's head – even if it's just $25 per month. Money saved is as good as money earned. I know the power of compounding income and the negative power of compounding expenses," said Jaq.

"I'm pretty good with numbers, and I've already started putting together the templates for running regular reports in *Quickbooks*, so I'm pretty sure I could handle the regular analyses on our expenses," said Nancy.

"Perfect. *Quickbooks* is great, so is *123 Landlord,* or you could always hire a bookkeeper. It usually costs about $20 per property each month for a bookkeeper. However you do it, you'll be spending your effort where it yields results. Keeping up to date reports for cost analysis is a high yield activity that is often left undone," said Jaq.

"Looks like the work is just beginning," said Nancy.

"In many ways it is, but this is a lot less intense as the buy, fix, and refinance. Here it's about consistency," said Jaq.

"Jaq, it's been illuminating as always. We still have a lot to learn about landlording, but for the first time I feel ready to improve my landlording game, and I actually think it's possible," said John.

"Great. That's what I'm here for. Based on what I saw with your acquisition process, you two are good at executing. Improving management is no more difficult than finding, renovating, and refinancing properties. All it takes is the will and you have plenty of that," said Jaq.

"We do, but we were hung up on the hopelessness of landlording. It used to feel like a treadmill. Now we have a different perspective about landlording, I know we can do it. Thanks for everything," said Nancy.

They said their goodbyes and John and Nancy went home to discuss how they were going to improve property management skills.

Meanwhile Jaq sat back in his chair, took a deep breath and felt enormous pride. He was proud of his protégés John and Nancy, but he was proud of himself, too.

This kind of success was why he'd entered the coaching business. Nothing gave him greater satisfaction than sharing the right knowledge at the right time to overhaul investors' perspective.

Landlording Process

In this chapter you learned about some of the mistakes that many landlords make. In addition, you also learned how proactive landlords seek to implement and improve systems and relationships.

We can't stress the importance of landlording enough. It's the difference between being a flash in the pan and being a long-term success, which is what BFRR investors all want. Doing one deal is great, but how do you move from one to many? How do you repeat over and over again?

In the coming chapter you'll see how successful BFRR investors are able to build momentum by adding multiple properties in a short period of time.

"An investment in knowledge pays the best interest."

Benjamin Franklin

CHAPTER 10

Becoming Investors

Invest, Earn, Repeat

Have you ever gotten used to doing the same thing over and over again? In life we often look for new adventures, activities, and friends. Often, this behaviour is harmless, but in real estate it can be a success killer.

Why?

Every time you change business models or directions you are forced to learn a new set of skills, and there are just a bunch of new considerations every single time an investor changes.

As a BFRR investor, the true method of creating momentum is to do the same kind of deal over and over again. If, at some point, you decide to change directions, please make it a small change in order to capitalize on already-earned knowledge, connections, and skills.

In this chapter, you will see how John and Nancy use the power of repetition to build up their real estate investing momentum.

Building Momentum

John called his old friend Bill not long after the property management conversation. The recent success had sunk in and he and Nancy were as adjusting to the new responsibilities of a new management style. They were experiencing growing pains but starting to see the power of systems in their property management process.

John thought it was a perfect time to get together with Bill for one of their monthly 'boy's night out' events, which consisted of telling bad jokes, drinking a couple of beers, chatting about life, eating something unhealthy, and watching violent sports on TV. On this day however, they had a more interesting topic to discuss.

"Okay, let me get this straight. I gave you $45,000 for a down payment and renovation expense on a rental property," said Bill

"That's correct," said John.

"I know that property will bring us cash flow, mortgage pay down, and market appreciation over the next 5 to 30 years depending on how long we keep it," said Bill.

"Indeed," said John.

"I know we'll probably double our money before selling, so I'm happy about that. The money I worked hard to save for years is now working for me, rather than me working for money," said Bill.

"Sounds like real estate to me," said John.

"Right, but now you're telling me you're giving me a $42,000 cheque already, which is a 100% return of my initial investment... after just a month, and we still own the property?" said Bill.

"That's what I'm telling you, and moreover, the refinance kicked back an extra $4,000 on top of that, so our contingency fund is covered. You don't have to bring cash for that," said John.

"How is this possible?" said Bill.

"That's the power of the BFRR strategy that I told you about," said John.

"Wow. So, when can we do it again?"

"What do you mean? I thought you were out of cash," said John.

"Not any more! I got all my cash back! Oh, and we have some more socked away. Don't get me wrong, we're not high rollers or anything, but we received an inheritance a couple years of ago. We paid off our mortgage and put the rest in the bank. We didn't know what to do with it since we didn't want to put it in mutual funds – until the opportunity to invest with you came up. Anyways, we won't need any more. You'll just keep recycling our money, right?" said Bill.

John laughed at Bill's enthusiasm. He also smiled inside.

"Well, that won't happen every time. Still, Nancy and I would love to do another great deal like that one. First, we need to rest for a bit, but we'll be looking for another one soon," said John.

John couldn't believe this was happening already. All along, Jaq said doing a solid deal would attract money to future deals. He believed Jaq, but didn't think it would happen so fast.

"By the way, you said you paid off your mortgage. Did you know you can probably get a significant line of credit with that equity," said John.

"Yeah, I know all about the home equity line of credit, it's impossible to ignore since the bank starts sending you junk mail about it the day you pay off your mortgage. We ignored it because we don't want to buy a boat or a cottage. What did you have in mind?" said Bill.

"Well, you're smart for not wanting to spend the money on liabilities, but have you ever considered how good an investment tool a line of credit could be? Interest rates on a line of credit are low," said John.

"I've never thought of using a line of credit to buy a property. Is that really a good idea?" said Bill.

"I wouldn't own a property long-term on a line of credit, but we could use it to buy a property and renovate before putting traditional bank financing on the property. It would be just like one we just did, but rather than use bank financing on the front end we'd use the line of credit," said John.

"If you get me an immediate return like you did on the first one, you can do whatever you want with my line of credit!" said Bill.

"Great, I haven't been to Vegas in a while," said John.

"For an investment!" Bill clarified.

"Of course. The benefit of using the line of credit is speed. You don't need to arrange bank financing since the line of credit is already available and this can help in many ways. For example, it might be the difference between getting and not getting an outstanding deal," said John.

"So, you use the line of credit as short term financing to buy and renovate a property before using bank financing over the long term?" said Bill.

"That's correct. Anyways, Nancy and I would be thrilled if you wanted to do another deal whether with cash you or a line of credit, or some combination of both. We appreciate the trust," said John.

"Well, I trusted you as a friend on the first one, now I trust your track record. I've never heard of a result like what we just had. I have a few buddies at work who would like to chat with you, but let's get my second one done before we tell them, okay?" said Bill with a chuckle.

"You have the next deal reserved, I promise you that! Oh, and the fun is just beginning. This property promises to throw us money as long as we keep it, especially with excellent property management," said John.

The two quickly devolved into their teenage selves as they ate, laughed, and watched hockey. John was starting to settle into this BFRR real estate investor thing.

Maybe he was management material after all, or maybe he was a frustrated entrepreneur waiting for the right opportunity all along.

"Luck is when preparation meets opportunity."

Seneca

Getting Back to Work

John and Nancy were watching TV one night when John had the strangest feeling.

"It's like our lives have gone back to normal. Our new property has been rented for a month and the excitement of the first deal has died down. I wanted to take a break after that first deal, but now I'm getting bored. I never thought I'd miss it so much," said John.

"I've noticed you pacing. We said we'd relax for a bit and then evaluate if we wanted to do another one. I know I do. The hardest part is to learn from the first one. I'm confident we can do another one," said Nancy.

"I didn't realize I was pacing. I agree. I'd like to do another one, and Bill is on board. In fact, I spoke to him the other day and he told me he's secured a line of credit. He's prepared to use it for a short-term entrance strategy on a new BFRR deal," said John.

"Grab your computer, honey. I know you're dying to start looking for properties. There's no time like the present," said Nancy.

Bill smiled, grabbed his computer and started searching. The hunt was on for the second property.

Repeating the Process

John and Nancy found they worked well together, as they both excelled in different roles. John loved hunting down properties. Initially, he employed a lot of hustle, but he soon saw that relationship building was a more effective way to find great deals.

In addition to finding deals, John also managed the renovation. Nancy was great with the books, back-end systems, and due diligence. With property management, Nancy ran ads and filtered candidates, but John did all the showings and face-to-face meetings.

Within a couple of months they found another suitable property, closed on it, and only a month after closing had it refinanced – much like the first one. Bill continued to be thrilled and word about their investing prowess started to spread.

People were taking note and people started to see John and Nancy as experts. This was embarrassing for John and Nancy as they felt they were just following a proven strategy. They didn't invent the system, and they didn't think they were brilliant. Still, people assumed they had special investment powers.

John and Nancy were modest whenever people approached them to invest their money. It wasn't a tactic – they were genuinely honored by others' belief in them.

John and Nancy *always* treated investors with utmost respect. They knew their role was important and that investing other people's money is a big responsibility. They knew their actions would affect others' ability to retire, pay for a child's education, or travel the world.

They never took it for granted that the money would continue to flow towards them without extreme care. This humbleness served them well as they spent the next couple of years becoming experienced BFRR investors.

Mostly they focused on lipstick and makeup renovations, employing different combinations of entrance, joint venture, and exit. Just as Jaq had originally told them, they started to see opportunities to do bigger jobs including some partial gut renovations. Their confidence and capabilities grew with each deal.

Over the next two years John and Nancy did 8 deals in total. The first few were much like the first one – their cookie cutter template for BFRR deals. However, as Jaq had suggested would happen, they found opportunities to try more creative strategies.

Whatever the circumstance and strategy, each deal followed the system and the fundamental principles – to create value for the short term while holding the property for the long term. By being creative and flexible, they found there were more great opportunities to get into fantastic properties.

Let's take a look one of the deals they did late in the first year of their BFRR investment career:

Single Family Home Case Study #1: The Smoker's Townhouse

The Numbers

Type: Townhouse

Purchase Price: $145,000

Down Payment (20%): $29,000

Closing/Holding/Renovations: $8,500

Cash Required for Purchase and Renovation: $37,500

Refinanced Value: $170,000

Net Value Created: $16,500

Cash Returned: $20,000 (Difference between original mortgage $116,000 and new mortgage of $136,000)

Money Left in Property after Refinance: $17,500

Equity Return on Cash Remaining (EROCR): 94% (Net Value Created/Money Left in Property with Refinance)

Yearly Cash Flow: $3,000

Yearly Mortgage Reduction: $2,622

Yearly Profit Before Appreciation: $5,622

First Year Appreciation (at 3%): $5,100

Total Annual Equity Growth and Profit: $10,722

Annual ROI Assuming 3% Appreciation: 61%

Strategy Type: Purchased with Investor's Line of Credit Then Refinanced and Rented

John and Nancy became keenly aware of the power of real estate repetition over time. With this in mind, they kept their eyes and ears focused on doing deals similar to others they'd already done in the past. As their very first deal was a successful townhouse BFRR deal, they looked for similar townhouses in the same neighbourhood.

They found the smoker's townhouse on the MLS and moved quickly. The listing agent was a realist and had listed the property for $153,000 even though other properties in the same complex had sold for $170,000. John and Nancy found out that the seller was motivated, but they knew at that price it wouldn't last long.

Still, the property was outdated and stunk of smoke. In fact, the smell was so overpowering (and the tar stained walls and ceilings so dreary) that it was driving away buyers even at the low price.

Not wanting to waste any time, John and Nancy did as much pre-purchase due diligence as they could and wrote an offer with no financing condition. The only condition on their offer was an inspection condition.

The property went into a multiple offer situation, but John and Nancy got the deal! They found out later from the real estate agent that their offer of $145,000 was lower than the competing offer, but because they didn't have a finance condition the seller chose their deal.

From this, they learned the value of purchasing with an investor's line of credit. They won this deal because of their ability to close quickly.

The Renovation

John was getting more comfortable with hiring contractors and he'd gotten beyond his fear of managing a small renovation job. He learned it was simple process like everything else.

The renovations were simple on the smoker's townhouse. The biggest part was smoke smell and stain remediation. It involved a good wall cleaning, stain blocking primer, two coats of paint on the walls, and two coats of stain blocking ceiling paint.

Next, John had the crew rip out the old carpets and install new ones. He also had his crew install new lighting, new trim, and a tub insert. The total cost of materials and labour was a hair over $6,000. The total cost for renovations, holding, and closing was only $8,500.

Refinance

By using all of the skill at each phase of the process, John and Nancy were able to get the townhouse refinanced at a value of $170,000. This was an excellent revaluation. It put them up near the top of the comparable values of other recently sold properties in the townhouse complex.

With the excellent refinance value, John and Nancy were able to return all but $17,500 of their investor's line of credit. It was agreed that the investor would pay out the rest of the line of credit with cash.

The plan was to hold the property for the long-term and eventually refinance it again 5 years later when the mortgage expired.

The market fundamentals were strong and mortgage pay down was a given so long as they could keep it rented. This meant that at the end of 5 years they have every expectation that they'd be able to return the rest of the investor's $17,500 and split a significant chunk of cash on top of that.

The 2nd Refinance – Looking 5 Years into the Future

Five years later, the original mortgage term ended and they were able to refinance the property again, taking more equity. Refinancing again at an 80% loan-to-value on the newly appraised value of $220,000 they received a mortgage of $176,000.

Since the initial mortgage had been paid down to $130,000 over the 5 years of holding, it meant the partners took $46,000 of equity out of the property. After paying the money partner out for the remaining $17,500 they'd left in the property, each partner received an additional cheque for $14,250.

In addition to this nice little kick back, the investors each retained $22,000 ($44,000/2) of equity in the property. They allowed the cash flow to pile up in the reserve fund and every now and again dipped into it for small renovations.

The smoker's townhouse was a very average deal in the realm of BFRR, but it's worth pointing out that the property returned over 40% annually on cash invested.

The smoker's townhouse wasn't a homerun – rather it was a solid single. As every baseball player, coach, and fan knows, hitting singles is the way to win games. Homeruns are flashy and fun, but piling up singles is the surest path to success.

Case Study 2: The Squirrel House

Contractor Partnership on Private Money Purchase

John was out looking for deals one day in the middle of the second year of their BFRR journey when he came across a property with an industrial sized garbage bin on the front lawn. It was the size of an international shipping container, and John knew it indicated that something significant was happening with the property.

Likely, it meant the property was getting a big renovation, which increased the odds it was owned by a motivated seller, so he placed a sticky note on the door asking the owner to call him.

He soon received a phone call from a realtor who was listing the property on behalf of the bank. They'd taken repossession of the property, and would list it for sale with the realtor when the property was renovated.

John's proactive approach paid off. Over the following week, he spoke to the realtor several times and learned much about the property. By speaking to the realtor before it was even listed, he and Nancy were able to get their homework done before anyone else even knew the property was for sale.

Thus, they were well prepared, and they got the property under contract the same day it was listed with the realtor.

Although John was fully on board with relationship building for finding deals, he still kept his hustler instincts. This was a good thing because it was his relentless pursuit of a good deal that led him to put a note on the door of the property.

The Numbers

Type: Semi-Detached

Purchase Price: $175,000

Closing/Holding/Renovations: $25,000

Cash Required for Purchase and Renovation: $60,000

Refinanced Value: $250,000

Net Value Created: $50,000

Cash Returned: $60,000 (Difference between original mortgage $140,000 and new mortgage of $200,000)

Money Left in Property after Refinance: $0

Equity Return on Cash Remaining (EROCR): INFINITE (Net Value Created/Money Left in Property with Refinance)

Yearly Cash Flow: $4,200

Yearly Mortgage Reduction: $3,856

Yearly Profit before Appreciation: $8,056

First Year Equity Growth at 3% Appreciation: $7,500

Total Annual Equity Growth and Profit: $15,556

Annual ROI Assuming 3% Appreciation: INFINITE

Entrance Strategy

The property required a quick purchase in order to satisfy the bank, as they wanted the property off their books. In order to close quickly, the property was purchase with $200,000 borrowed from a private lender's line of credit at 8% per year, which John and Nancy would make monthly payments on while carrying. The $200,000 of borrowed funds was enough to cover the purchase, closing and renovation costs.

It was a great opportunity, however this deal was John and Nancy's first departure from the basic lipstick and makeup jobs, and John didn't yet have the expertise to manage this renovation himself.

John had already been in discussion with an excellent contractor named Anthony about one day partnering on a deal. This was the perfect deal for John and Nancy to partner with Anthony, as the job required an expert contractor's touch. They agreed to split all the profits 50/50 after expenses were paid out.

The Renovation

John and Anthony liked the property from the first time they viewed it, as they saw the immediate potential to add value. As strange as it might seem, they got excited it might be a great deal when they found there were squirrels living in the attic.

Good BFRR investors know that squirrels aren't too hard to get rid of, but that most other buyers will be very shy of them. The critters' presence scares people away.

The squirrel mafia had taken over and left little 'presents' all over the place, and not acorns, either. The inside of the property was dilapidated but it had a solid structure. John and Anthony figured that the renovation would require a *partial gut*, which involves all of the surface level renovations of a *lipstick and makeup* renovation along with some bigger items like a furnace, a new bathtub, and a few others.

Leveraging Anthony's experience, John learned a lot about executing partial gut renovations, including how to navigate the permit process.

The Refinance

After the purchase and 3 months of renovations, John and Anthony had accumulated $25,000 of expenses for closing costs, holding, and renovation. When the renovations were complete they refinanced the property and rented it out, as planned.

The bank appraised the property at $250,000, which meant John and Anthony received a mortgage of $200,000 (80% of $250,000) and were thus able to repay the private lender back the $200,000.

They were left with $50,000 of created equity in the property (20% of $250,000) and were certain they'd benefit over the long term from appreciation, mortgage pay down, and cash flow.

It's important to note that since they used private money to pay for everything on the front end (including purchase price, renovation costs, and closing costs) and because that entire amount was paid back upon refinancing, the rate of return on this property was infinite. When you invest $0 every dollar earned is created money.

Additional Benefit

The partnership allowed John to get the deal done and give him the experience of overseeing a partial gut renovation while still having a motivated general contractor on board.

This would serve John well as he took on bigger projects along his BFRR journey – including one where he added a second suite to a detached bungalow.

John and Nancy were always looking for new and creative ways to put together deals and become better BFRR investors, and their partnership with Anthony was a great education.

A Summary of Success

At the end of the first two years of their BFRR journey, John and Nancy owned 8 fantastic properties with their partners. In every case they used very little or none of their own money, which enabled them to leverage what they could have achieved on their own.

Attracting money to their deals was no longer an issue. In fact, they had a waiting list of investors ready to invest with them. The results they achieved couldn't be replicated anywhere else, therefore investor money came flowing towards them. In those first two years they learned the old truth that money follows money.

With every investor they met, John and Nancy realized that everyone else was as disillusioned with the standard methods of investing as they were. With every conversation, they learned there's nothing as attractive as a BFRR deal.

Their only competition (if you can call it that) came from their tiny tight-knit community of BFRR investors. Let's take a look at the sum of what John and Nancy created over two years and 8 deals:

Total Purchase Price + Expenses: $1,660,000

Total Value After Renovations: $1,870,000

Value Created From Renovations: $210,000

Total Appreciation Growth: $280,000

Portfolio Value 5 Years Later: $2,150,000

Yearly Average Portfolio Appreciation: $56,000

Yearly Cash Flow: $37,800

Yearly Mortgage Pay Down: $41,000

On cash flow alone, which is a small portion of the wealth created, John and Nancy had added the equivalent of an average worker's salary ($37,800) income (split with partners). The mortgage pay down, which was the second smallest component of the real estate pie, added up to the equivalent of yet another salary ($41,000 per year).

With appreciation they were earning on average more than $50,000 per year. In other words, each property was a gift that kept on giving.

These investments would have been great without the value lift at the front end, but results were superlative when you consider the initial value creation. In a matter of two years, John and Nancy had transformed their financial picture.

If they had decided to stop after those two years, John and Nancy would have had more than enough money to retire comfortably. The fear of not being able to provide for the family in retirement was now gone, but more importantly the grinding frustration, boredom, and lack of fulfillment from John's job was a thing of the past.

With his real estate success and the financial momentum they'd built up, John became more confident at work. He was no longer scared to take risks and started enjoying it more. His colleagues were drawn to his new energy.

What once troubled John was no longer relevant, and in many ways he was a different person. He'd entered the positive cycle of action where success feeds action, and action feeds success. Because of this cycle, money flowed towards him and Nancy.

They felt stable in the system they'd developed, but were now starting to think bigger.

It was around that two-year mark when John suddenly remembered Jaq's cryptic words the day they walked away from the conversation at Equity Café when they brainstormed the options for getting a better refinance. At that time he mentioned something about things getting interesting.

John finally knew what he meant.

Investors Ever Growing

In this chapter we saw how BFRR investors can build momentum over a two-year period. Most successful BFRR investors have similar stories. Money starts streaming in their direction after the first couple of good deals, and like John and Nancy, most real-life investors also seek out bigger deals and bigger challenges after an initial period of success.

This is natural human progress. For most investors it means taking on a small multi-family project. The following chapter will focus on making the move from single-family BFRR deals into small multi-family projects.

*"If you're not growing,
you're dying."*

Unknown

CHAPTER 11

Small Multi-Family

Incremental Change

Have you ever noticed that challenges get easier over time? This phenomenon is true across the board – this includes real estate challenges.

There is nothing wrong with sticking to the same thing forever, but investors often find their skill level has grown beyond their original strategy, and playing a bigger game makes sense.

It's great to do a BFRR deal that will put out one unit of rental stock at a time. Such a deal would make a nice return for both active and money partner, but it's dead simple.

Many investors correctly reason that it's much harder to do a deal 3 or 4 times larger that would put 3 or 4 units of rental stock into the market, so why not do it? Everyone would make more money, and the challenge forces the investor to grow.

This was exactly what John and Nancy did when they decided to move into small multi-family BFRR deals. They key to their transition lay in the fact that it was an *incremental change*. 95% or more of the skills they developed by doing single-family BFRR deals could be carried forward into their new venture.

This chapter details the small changes that BFRR investors must make when transitioning from single-family to small multi-family.

Preparation Conversation

In the two years since becoming battle proven investors, John and Nancy had come to view their role as important. They were responsible for making money grow, improving the quality of neighbourhoods, and for providing safe and affordable housing for tenants.

However, it became apparent they were ready to manage a bigger challenge.

As members of the local Real Estate Investing Club, they had met other investors that were investing in small multi-family buildings using the BFRR method. After two years of doing single-family deals, their thoughts turned to small multi-family.

From what they'd heard, it wasn't much harder to do a small multi-family deal than a single-family home.

However, it was still a change, so they wanted to consult their real estate coach, just as they did with every previous step.

After the first couple of single-family deals they didn't lean on Jaq as heavily as they did in the beginning, but John and Nancy knew how a conversation with their real estate coach[14] could help get them moving in the right direction.

As John reflected on the journey, he couldn't believe it had only been two short years since his despair-filled conversation with Bill at the Equity Café..

He knew Jaq would never take credit for everything he and Nancy accomplished, but the truth was they would never have been able to do what they did without their coach, which was why John called Jaq right away, as his mind turned to small multi-family BFRR investing.

"John, great to hear from you. It's been a while. How is the journey of life and real estate treating you these days?" said Jaq.

"Life is pretty much the same as the first day I met you Jaq. Worried about the future, hate my job, and ready for change," said John.

"Seriously?" said Jaq.

Usually it was Jaq gently ribbing John, but this time John shocked Jaq into a reaction. For the first time, Jaq was speechless.

---

14 A good coach will take you further faster. Visit www. theultimatewealthstrategy.com to find a real estate based wealth coach that fits for you.

When John broke out laughing, Jaq knew the joke was on him, "I take it things are better than that? Good one John. Great to see you're not taking life too seriously," said Jaq.

"Well, there is one kernel of truth in what I said. I don't hate my job and I'm not worried much about the future, but I am ready for a small change," said John.

"Ah yes, you're ready for the next level," said Jaq.

"You were expecting this?" said John.

"Of course. It happens to everyone. What seemed insurmountable in the past becomes routine. Tell me, how many BFRR deals have you done now?" said Jaq.

"We've done 8 and it's been about 2 years since we first started," said John.

"Correct me if I'm wrong, but putting together and executing BFRR deals almost feels routine by now doesn't it?" said John.

"I guess you could say that. I've never thought of it in that way before, but yes it is, and we're thrilled with the results, but we're thinking we can get even better results by doing small multi-family deals, which is why I called you," said John.

"It's a logical next step," said Jaq.

"We think so, and we wanted your take on making the move into small multi-family investing. Do you think it's a good idea, and are there any big unknowns that we might not be aware of that make it riskier or more difficult?" said John.

"Your path is a lot like mine. I moved from single-family success into small multi-family. It's like this: cash flow is better with small multi-family and you benefit from economies of scale, but there's not much dramatically different other than that," said Jaq.

"It can't be that simple," said John.

"You have to be fixated on expenses and timelines, as the purchase price and renovation expense numbers are bigger. Think about it. If you buy a duplex, it means you have 2 units to renovate rather than 1. If you throw the same amount of labour at it, you'll to take longer to finish the job. This can surprise some people when they first get started," said Jaq.

"I can imagine that," said John.

"Or imagine if you do a private money deal and it ends up being vacant for a while during the renovation. The cost of borrowing adds up quickly. You have to plan for bigger jobs and ensure that you have enough cash to pay for the renovation and for staying power. With those things in place, you'll be ready to tackle the job," said Jaq.

"So it's just a bigger scale. I'm pretty sure we could adjust for that," said John.

"You definitely can. It's still a matter of buying the deal right, executing the renovation, refinancing, and getting great tenants in the property for the long haul," said Jaq.

"We've gotten good at that little system by now," said John.

"Exactly, and it's repeatable, but with small multi-family buildings there are some cool little bonuses you don't get from single-family properties," said Jaq.

"Such as?" said John.

"Such as coin-operated laundry. It doesn't make economic sense to install one on a single-family property, but it does on a small multi-family. This creates additional income," said Jaq.

"Right. Any other benefits?" said John.

"Yes. The single-family market is driven by emotion, whereas the multi-family market is income focused. This means your yield per dollar spent will almost always be better on a multi-family property. The price you pay for a multi-family property compared to the rent you collect is better. These numbers make it a more investor friendly play than the single-family market, which is driven by emotion," said Jaq.

"Right, and since value is dependent upon the total income of the building, there's opportunity in buying undermanaged properties. A good BFRR investor can turn these properties around by improving the tenants and the rent roll. That's what I've heard anyways," said John.

"This isn't the same John I first met. You sound like a pro now. I guess you are a pro now... Yes, you've heard right, and it's an even more powerful strategy when dealing with bigger buildings, but let's not talk about larger multi-family buildings for now," said Jaq.

"I agree. My mind isn't there yet. I think jumping into 2-4 units is appropriate. You're still talking to the guy who once thought he couldn't manage a small townhouse renovation, remember?" said John.

"Oh yeah, I'd almost forgotten about that guy! Well, now you know that with some planning, budgeting, and focus, a small renovation is a breeze. A slightly bigger one is similar with a bit more complexity in terms of numbers and timelines, so it's probably the appropriate step," said Jaq.

John felt that he and Nancy could handle the task of investing in small multi-family BFRR deals, but it was great to get the same feedback from his mentor. He left the meeting determined to start planning and looking for deals right away.

The Action Phase

John and Nancy dove into the new process with the reserved excitement of veteran investors. Rather than starting with a big set of unknowns, as they did when they first started as BFRR investors, they now confidently moved towards their goals with each step planned out in advance.

Drawing on their experiences with single-family BFRR investing, they applied the same lessons to small multi-family buildings. Their learning curve with small multi-family properties was less severe than their initial BFRR learning curve.

John and Nancy both agreed that keeping things simple by focusing on undermanaged properties needing lipstick renovations was the best strategy, as they knew they'd be able to raise values by raising rents.

Furthermore, they knew the long-term play on a small multi-family building was about the excellent cash flow and mortgage pay down potential, so they searched for solid deals where they could raise the value through targeted renovations.

John and Nancy had been speaking to an investor named Jane who was ready to commit money to their first small multi-family project.

Jane had $80,000 available to invest, and she wanted to use the money as efficiently as possible. John and Nancy went to work on a plan to help her get the most out of her money by investing in multiple properties. To that end, they put together a plan they called the 'recycled money' strategy, which would allow Jane to get 2 properties for the price of 1.

The Deal –
A Big Duplex with Plenty of Options

John and Nancy quickly learned that much about finding small multi-family deals was similar with single-family deals. First, they did a thorough study of their target neighbourhoods in order to become familiar with property values.

Next, John did a locally targeted ad campaign and pored over online and newspaper ads. He drove every street in the target neighbourhoods and looked for properties that appeared neglected, empty, or under repair. Finally, he asked his real estate agent to send him regular listings in his target neighbourhood.

John filtered leads for a while before finding a power of sale property that interested him. The size of the property caught John's attention, as the bottom floor apartment was 2600 square feet with 4 bedrooms, two bathrooms, a study, and an attached two-car garage.

It was an apartment in name only. In fact, the bottom floor alone was much bigger than most houses. The top floor apartment was also large at 1400 square feet with 3 bedrooms and 1 bathroom.

Overall, there was 4000 square feet of living space in the duplex. The size alone was great, but it was also located on a tree-lined street with all single-family homes. This made it more attractive because it would ensure a high-end renter.

Each of these single-family homes was worth $400,000 or more, but the list price on the duplex was only $225,000. John and Nancy knew it had potential based on that discrepancy alone. They knew that if nothing else they could convert the property back into a single-family home and it would likely be valued around $400,000.

This was but one possibility for the property. They also knew the cash flow would be strong and that the property would be easy to fill with great tenants once it was renovated. John and Nancy were confident about this because of the size of the property. Each suite was huge, which would help them attract tenants once renovated.

The property was also zoned for commercial use, which gave them more options. They thought that (depending on land use bylaws) they might be able to change the use of the property.

The upper apartment had been used as a commercial unit when it was last occupied, however when John first saw the property on the MLS the upper unit was vacant due to renovations. Still, the potential for commercial use was another option to put aside for later thought.

Another long-term option – one that John and Nancy preferred above others – was to convert the duplex into a legal 3-plex or perhaps even a 4-plex some time in the future. They knew the building was big enough for this possibility and that if they ever decided to add an extra suite (or two) that the cash flow on the property would be stupendous.

With all this potential, you might be surprised to find out that they almost didn't pull the trigger on the deal.

You see, they were also committed to keeping their first small multi-family deal simple. When they first looked at the MLS photos it appeared the property had baseboard heating rather than a modern forced air system. John thought that a big HVAC job would be too complex on their first small multi-family deal, so they almost passed on it.

After letting it slide for a couple of weeks, the property showed up in their email inbox again – this time it was listed at $200,000, which made John sit up and take notice. The price alone made him think twice about the property, even if he would have to install a new heating system.

John's jaw dropped when he looked at the property details again and realized the property *did* have a modern forced air furnace, but only in the lower apartment.

It was only the upper apartment that had baseboard heating. This slight difference was a big deal for John. It was far less risky to have only one of the two units on baseboard heating. It would be easier to rent just the upper unit with baseboard heating than it would the other units. John knew he wouldn't have to upgrade the HVAC system right away, so he went to see the property right away.

On first seeing the property, John got an idea why it wasn't selling in spite of the fact it was an outstanding deal. The property appeared to need a lot of work, but he realized most of the issues were in the upper unit. Still, he didn't think it was that bad and kept an open mind.

The lower unit was in great shape, but more importantly had a committed tenant already renting it. Of course the tenant loved it. It had 4 bedrooms, 2 bathrooms, a study, a double garage, and rented for only $1000 per month! To top things off, the tenant ran her pet grooming business out of the front window. This was legal, as it was zoned for commercial use.

He had mixed feelings about keeping the existing tenant because, on one hand, the unit could fetch a higher rent if he were to renovate and re-rent it. On the other hand, he could save the renovation cost and keep a flow of income while renovating the top unit, if the tenant stayed. In the end, he decided to keep the tenant in spite of the low rent she paid and just focus the renovation efforts upstairs where they were most needed.

The upper unit needed the normal lipstick upgrades John was accustomed to along with a few others (roofing and windows). After his analysis, John knew it was the baseboard heating, roofing, and windows that were scaring other buyers away.

He smelled opportunity, and even though the renovation was a bit more complex than he wanted on his first multi-family it was no more difficult than some of the renovations he'd started doing on single-family deals. John knew enough tricks by now, that he was confident he could fix this property on a tight budget and turn it into a great cash-flowing property.

Of the 8 windows on the upper unit, 7 of them required replacement. By this time, John had developed a relationship with a great contractor that did windows. With labour and material each normal-sized window cost around $200, which meant John would spend about $1400 on windows. It was a significant expense to add to his normal rock-bottom renovation costs, but it was acceptable considering the potential for value lift and cash flow.

The property also needed re-shingling, which John again preferred not to do unless the deal was strong, as it was in this case. He even started using a veteran trick known as a 'nail-over'[15] to save money on roofing. As the name indicates, you can do shingles by just 'nailing

---

15   Go to www.theultimatewealthstrategy.com for more practical and useful renovation tips.

over' the existing shingles rather than removing them. This process costs significantly less than a traditional shingling job where old shingles are removed.

The down side of a nail-over is that the shingles don't usually last quite as long as a normal re-shingling, however the cost savings are worth it when the goal is to get a property renovated and re-rented quickly. In this case it was the difference between a $5000 shingling job and a $3500 shingling job.

Rather than lasting 25 years the shingles may only last 20 years on a nail-over. John decided to do the nail-over, knowing that the shingles wouldn't last as long. Instead he chose to keep a tight budget, and rightly reasoned that if he still owned the property in 20 years that the cost of re-shingling at that time would be well worth it.

Taking the shingling expense together with the windows, John added just under $5000 to the cost of his normal lipstick renovation. The cost was more, but the upside was so high that it was well worth it.

Even at list price, the deal was superlative. Still, John wanted a discount off the $200,000 list price. He offered $190,000 and got the deal after the bank completed their normal power of sale process.

The Numbers

Type: Duplex

Purchase Price: $190,000

Down Payment: $38,000

Closing/Holding/Renovations: $12,500

Cash Required for Purchase and Renovation: $53,000

Refinanced Value: $230,000

Net Value Created: $27,500

Cash Returned: $32,000 (Difference between original mortgage $152,000 and new mortgage of $184,000)

Money Left in Property with Refinance: $18,500

Equity Return on Cash Remaining (EROCR): 147% (Net Value Created/Money Left in Property with Refinance)

Yearly Cash Flow: $7,560

Yearly Mortgage Reduction: $3,840

Yearly Profit Before Appreciation: $11,400

First Year Equity Growth at 3% Appreciation: $6,900

Total Annual Equity Growth and Profit: $18,300

Annual ROI Assuming 3% Appreciation: 99%

The 'Recycled Money' Strategy

John and Nancy had gotten into the habit of returning as much money to their partners as possible after refinance. They did this because they both kept full time jobs and therefore didn't need immediate income, but what's more, they did it because returning money to investors creates immense goodwill.

Investors are unaccustomed to getting a huge return on their investment within a few short weeks, so they're blown away when they partner with a BFRR investor and get a cheque within a couple of weeks or months. Returning money fast is an excellent strategy for impressing investors and ensuring a non-stop flow of capital to your BFRR deals.

More importantly, when joint venture partners receive a large chunk of their initial investment back they're able to re-invest quickly. The average investor with $60,000 to $100,000 tucked away for investment can only do one deal using a traditional buy-and-hold approach, but by using the power of the BFRR strategy, investors can purchase multiple properties with the same amount of money.

John and Nancy referred to this as their 'recycled money' strategy. Just as the name suggests, it allowed John and Nancy to 'recycle' the same dollars more than once for multiple property purchases.

Rather than sinking $50,000 to $60,000 into one property and waiting several years to get that money back (as would be the case with a buy-and-hold investment), John and Nancy's strategy was to give most of a joint venture partner's money back after the refinance, which the partner would then reinvest in a second deal.

They employed this recycled money strategy with Jane, and it allowed her to maximize the $80,000 she had available for investing.

Flow Of Jane's Investment Cash

Initial Cash Available: $80,000

Cash Invested in Deal #1 (see above): $50,500

Cash Returned from Deal #1: $32,000

Cash Left In Deal #1: $18,500

Jane's Investible Cash Remaining After Deal #1: $61,500

Jane's Portion of Yearly Return on $18,500 Invested: $9,150

Doing Another Deal – The Mouldy Duplex

It didn't take Jane very long to get excited about the idea of getting more of her money working as hard as the original $18,500 was working. She, like so many other disillusioned Canadians, was aware that there were few options for an investor to earn a good return on a safe investment. She knew that finding active BFRR partners like John and Nancy was rare, so she was thrilled to put her money back to work on another deal.

Just as John and Nancy had planned, they went to work on another deal to get Jane's money working again. They'd had such success on the first duplex project that they decided to try it again with another duplex.

John started searching for properties similar to the first one. This time it took a few months to find a suitable duplex, but eventually such a property showed up on

John's radar, and before long he was once again looking at it.

The property had been sitting on the market for about 3 months by the time John saw it, and when knew why the moment he walked in the door. It only took about 5 seconds to sense the unmistakable smell of mold, a problem that drove away buyers. Heck, it was a problem that would have driven him away a couple years earlier.

However, as he got more experienced, John stopped being scared of problems. In fact, he'd developed the ability to see problems as opportunities to add value – a useful skill in the BFRR world.

He knew the best way to get the deal he wanted on this property would be to first get it under contract and then do a thorough inspection. His goal with the inspection would be to gather the evidence, so that he could renegotiate to get the price he (really) wanted.

From his initial viewing of the property, John knew both units would require basic lipstick renovations, but to find out how to remedy the mold issue, John needed to do a thorough inspection.

When John was at the property doing his initial viewing, he found out that one of the units was empty and in fact uninhabitable due to the mold in the basement (and the mouse poison that was spread around).

John learned that the upper unit was being rented for only $700 to the owner's friend. This tenant was supposed to be renovating the property while he lived there, which explained the low rent. It was a kind of trade off, but the friend wasn't making much progress on the renovation, and the property remained in a sorry state of repair.

By the time John made his offer, the property had been on the market for over 3 months. That, along with the fact the friend was living in the property to fix the problems, were good signs the owner didn't have much money available and likely wanted to sell quickly. Armed with this knowledge, John managed to negotiate the price down to $180,000 from an original list price of $209,000.

Even with the property under contract, the deal wasn't a guarantee, as John still had to complete the inspection and find out how severe the mold problem was.

John's inspector, Mike, found out that the mold problem was in fact a foundation problem, which became a mold problem. The house was resting on an old block foundation that allowed moisture to pass through. This moisture was seeping into the walls. It was so bad that one entire basement wall was black with mold.

Mike recommended John call a foundation specialist to take a look at the property, but he wasn't sounding the alarms. He believed there was a good deal to be had here, as he suspected the foundation could be repaired without much expense.

The foundation specialist gave John a quote for $3,500. This price shocked even John, as he was half-expecting the fix would cost $10,000. If it was that high, John knew he wouldn't do the deal. Keeping an open mind ended up making John and Nancy (and Jane) a lot of money.

It turned out there was a special process for repairing block foundations without any digging. The process involved drilling into the foundation every 8 inches and pumping grout (which is waterproof) into the block. The grout then fills the cavities of the block, which therefore stops any moisture from penetrating the foundation. It's a relatively inexpensive fix compared to digging up and resealing the exterior of the foundation (the traditional way).

When he found out the cost of the foundation repair, John knew he'd buy the property, but he still didn't want to pay out of pocket for the fix, so he asked for a further $2,500 discount off the deal.

The seller held firm at $180,000, but the real estate agents eventually agreed to take the $2,500 ($1,250 each) out of their commission, which meant John got the discount to pay for most of the foundation repair.

In his experience, John found realtors were often more than willing to discount their commission to get a deal done. On this particular deal, the discount for the foundation repair was vital. Without it, John would have had to pay out of pocket – something he was allergic to, the way others are allergic to mold.

The Numbers

Purchase Price: $177,500

Down Payment (20%): $35,500

Closing/Holding/Renovations: $17,500

Cash Required for Purchase and Renovation: $53,000

Refinance Value: $230,000

Net Value Created: $35,000

Cash Returned: $42,000 (Difference between original mortgage $142,000 and new mortgage of $184,000)

Money Left in Property with Refinance: $11,000

Equity Return on Cash Remaining (EROCR): 318% (Net Value Created/Money Left in Property with Refinance)

Yearly Cash Flow after Refinance: $10,440

Yearly Mortgage Reduction: $3,790

Yearly Profit before Appreciation: $14,230

First Year Equity Growth at 3% Appreciation: $6,900

Total Annual Equity Growth and Profit: $21,130

Annual ROI Assuming 3% Appreciation: 192%

In terms of numbers, this deal was similar to Jane's first deal, but as you can see the ROI was significantly better because John got this property at a better price, and because of the stronger cash flow.

John expected to spend more on renovations on this second small multi-family deal than he did on the first, but even the additional renovation expense didn't harm the numbers on this deal. In truth, the cost of renovations was still inexpensive, and the extra cost was well worth the mind-blowing return.

Jane was thrilled. She couldn't believe she owned the $230,000 worth of cash flowing real estate assets and was out of pocket less than $30,000. Using the strategy meant she *still* had cash available to keep investing, and her total return on cash invested was stupendous – just under $20,000 (on $30,000 invested)!

Flow of Jane's Investment Cash

Cash Invested Deal #2 (see above): $53,000

Cash Returned from Deal #2: $42,000

Cash Left In Deal #2: $11,000

Jane's Investible Cash Remaining After Deal #2: $50,500

Yearly Return on $11,000 Invested (50% ownership): $10,565

The Next Couple of Years

John and Nancy added several more properties to their portfolio over the next couple of years – usually using their 'recycled money' strategy as they'd done with Jane.

Their pace of acquisitions was similar as the first two years when they were purchasing single-family homes, but the difference now was that each time they added a property, it amounted to at least 2 units and sometimes more. This made a significant difference to their portfolio and cash flow numbers.

John and Nancy's (Sort of) a Bummer Story

Most everything went smoothly for John and Nancy in their first few years, but it would be unrealistic to say there were no problems. When buying multiple properties, the law of averages states that once in a while an investor will run into unforeseen circumstances.

Most unforeseen problems are mitigated using the BFRR strategy because there is additional value created. When unforeseen and unpleasant events happen, it's nice to have additional equity as a shield between oneself and potential disaster.

When we think of disaster in real estate, the first thing that comes to mind is a property that ends up costing the investor money instead of making money. Losing money is the opposite of what we seek.

When done correctly, losing money in real estate isn't nearly as common as it is in mutual funds or other institutional investments, where it's the rule rather than the exception, but it still happens more often than it should. Usually, it's a result of buying wrong, not having enough equity in the property to begin with, and then being hit with an unexpected expense.

The unexpected expense is never fun, but unexpected problems can be mitigated if the principles of BFRR investing (buy under market, create value) are followed. This was exactly what happened to John and Nancy on their 5th small multi-family deal.

The property started out looking like it was going to be the best deal they'd yet done, and they were expecting to earn over $800 of cash flow every month.

Luckily, everything was done well on the front end, so the coming series of unlucky events didn't cause a calamity, rather a nuisance.

John found the property one evening, as he was driving to the job site of a different deal. Out of the corner of his eye, he saw a "For Sale" sign in the window and called the number right away.

After negotiating a good deal, John and Nancy purchased the property for $210,000. They budgeted $8,000 for renovations and stayed relatively close to that price. They refinanced for $235,000, which meant they received a decent cash return right away, and they expected the property to be a cash cow for several years to come.

One more point to note: John and Nancy put $5000 of investor money in the reserve fund, as they always did. This is what many investors call a 'sleep at night fund' because of the peace of mind it provides in case of dramatic setbacks.

The trouble started about a week after they put the first tenants (two university students) in the property, when John received a call on his emergency line. After implementing property management systems over the years, John knew calls to his emergency line meant real emergencies.

He followed up on the call immediately and found there was raw sewage gurgling up the drainpipe in the basement. He got the mess cleaned up and remediated, and it wasn't too expensive, as the tenants caught the problem before it reached the walls or carpets. However, the drain line had to be cleaned out, which cost a few hundred dollars.

John thought that was the end of it, until he received a call one week later for the exact same problem. Again, he got the problem cleaned up, but this time he realized there was a bigger problem. Why else would it happen again? He brought in a sewage drain line expert to find out what was wrong.

The plumber used a camera scope to investigate and found a tree root had grown through the sewage line. This meant the line would need to be replaced.

John and Nancy had no choice but to replace the drain line. Luckily the $5,000 in the 'sleep at night fund' was more than enough to cover the repair, as the total bill for both times the sewage backed up and the cost of replacing the line was around $2500.

This all took place within a couple of weeks of buying and renting the property, which meant the renovations budget was thrown out the window and the reserve fund decimated. John was now sleeping a little less well at night, but the property still looked like a winner.

After the drain line problem, things went smoothly, and the reserve fund was built up over the next several months. Thank goodness for cash flow. However, almost a year after the original 'crappy situation' another problem arose.

It was fall then, and John received a complaint from the tenant about the furnace not working. Again, the tenants perceived this as an emergency problem as the weather forecast was calling for sub-zero temperatures. After hearing about the problem, John agreed it was an emergency. It's never good to let a property get too cold. Tenants can get sick and pipes can burst, so John went to investigate immediately.

After looking around himself he called in the experts who could come as early as the next day. In the mean time, John taught his tenants the art of staying warm overnight in a property without a furnace.

The HVAC experts showed up the next day and started doing their investigation. Their findings shocked John and Nancy. It was their closest call (ever) to a true landlording catastrophe.

The HVAC specialist found that the chimney had collapsed on the inside, which meant the carbon monoxide gas that was supposed to be vented out was actually pouring back into the property. As you can imagine this would be a disaster, probably worse than a fire. Carbon monoxide poisoning is more likely to kill than a fire, as it can go undetected. Tenants can be poisoned to death without warning. Of course, there is supposed to be a warning system – the carbon monoxide detector.

When John got news from the HVAC specialists about the collapsed chimney and the dangerously high levels of carbon monoxide in the property, he immediately checked the carbon monoxide detector and found that a single AA battery in the device had been installed backwards, which rendered the device useless.

He couldn't believe the series of events that had unfolded. If the furnace worked properly, there's a good chance the collapsed chimney wouldn't have been discovered.

Furthermore, if the weather had been colder for a few days longer (with a working furnace) a lot more carbon monoxide would have poured into the property. With no working carbon monoxide detector in place, a serious catastrophe was highly probably.

As it turned out, the furnace breakdown ended up saving the tenants' lives.

John and Nancy thanked their lucky stars and added a few new procedures to their growing landlording procedures manual. Number one on the list was to personally change the batteries in smoke detectors and carbon monoxide detectors themselves. In this case, they had let tenants do it, which resulted in the battery being incorrectly installed.

The HVAC specialists quoted them for a new furnace, but they found the cost of buying a new furnace was too great, so they decided to rent a furnace system instead. This allowed them to save a lot of money. In the end, this situation wasn't so expensive, just stressful.

After having the chimney fixed and new rental furnace installed, things went back to normal and they hoped they'd seen the end of their problems with this property.

However, when the next summer rolled around they faced another big expense. This time it was an air conditioning unit that conked out, and when it happened they simply paid for a replacement from the overused reserve fund. Luckily, it had been replenished again by cash flow in the interim.

This story is more of a precautionary tale than a horror story. The expenses incurred from the unexpected problems could have been much worse if the cash flow wasn't outstanding and if the BFRR principles weren't followed (creating value and buying under market). Having the reserve fund in place saved John, Nancy, and their investor from great pain.

4 years after the property was purchased it had appreciated by $40,000. This made the difficulties experienced much more palatable.

More than anything this situation taught them some lessons. The biggest of which was to review their insurance policies and safety procedure to protect against major catastrophes and liability if one should every happen. They had been close to disaster and never wanted to go there again.

The Next Step

In this chapter we saw how BFRR investors can move from single-family investing into smaller multi-family properties. Both the single-family and small multi-family niches are excellent niches, and if you so choose to invest solely in either or both of these niches, you can have an excellent investment career.

However, many investors eventually choose to move into larger multi-family investments as they become more professional and confident. The following chapter breaks down the biggest concerns when investing in larger multi-family properties.

If you choose to execute the BFRR strategy on larger multi-family properties you'll need to further your education on the topic of multi-family investing, however the following chapter provides an excellent primer on the topic.

"Your dreams should be so big that they both scare and excite you at the same time."

Bob Proctor

CHAPTER 12

Larger Multi-Family Buildings

Stepping Into the Big Time

Have you ever shocked yourself by how far you've come by taking a series of small steps?

Small steps forward day after day is the way to tackle any large major undertaking, but unfortunately many people, including investors, fail to take this consistent approach to growth.

John and Nancy never set out to go beyond single-family BFRR investing, but they did delve into the process, day-by-day, month-by-month, and year-by-year. The total result was that they grew as investors (and people) beyond what they originally set their sights on.

Taking small steps every day led them somewhere they didn't expect to be, but when they got there, they were pleasantly surprised.

They realized that they were ready to step into what many would call the "big time" of real estate investing, proper multi-family properties, after 2 years of single-family and 2 years of small multi-family focus.

In the last chapter, we saw how they made the incremental transition from single-family to small multi-family BFRR investing. In this chapter, we'll see how they made the somewhat bigger leap into larger multi-family deals.

The Next Step

During years 3 and 4 of John and Nancy's BFRR career they gained enormous momentum as investors. They'd moved strategically into small multi-family building investments and were now power investors in that realm.

With the 12 deals they'd done in small multi-family, and the 8 single family deals they did in the years before, they now co-owned 38 units with their joint venture partners. Theirs wasn't a small real estate portfolio anymore.

While they were very happy continuing to do small multi-family deals, there was one significant factor that made them want to move into larger multi-family properties – they now had access to a larger pool of investment capital. They'd earned it through networking and marketing, but most of all the access to money was a reward for outstanding results.

They knew with the money available that they would have no problem funding a larger deal. This fact, along with the experience and expertise they'd developed over the years, tipped the scales in their minds, and made them decide to try larger multi-family investing.

They knew that with one or two deals, they could double the amount of units in their portfolio. This fact played a big part in their decision to step up.

They liked the idea of significantly growing their portfolio, but they also liked the idea being able to add many units, while doing a similar amount of work as they did with small multi-family buildings.

Sure, the numbers were greater, and yes there was more due diligence involved, but when they considered that they'd be able to add 10 times (or more) as many units with each purchase, they soon realized the work involved for one larger multi-family building would be a far more efficient use of time.

John had moved from fear of real estate deals to empowerment. He now had the confidence to do a larger multi-family deal, and he was ready to get going.

Four years earlier, the though a deal like this would have been absurd to John. At that time he was fearful of a simple renovation job on a small townhouse, but John had changed. The positive circle of action and results lifted his confidence, and now the whole world looked different to him.

Consultation With Jaq

As had become habit whenever a big task was ahead, John and Nancy called Jaq for some advice about moving into larger multi-family deals. They knew how important it was to not reinvent the wheel, and they knew Jaq had been there before them.

Within a couple of days of calling, they were back at the Equity Café, sitting across from Jaq, a man who'd become their friend and trusted mentor over the years.

"How does it feel to be here?" said Jaq.

"It's surreal to remember the person I was a few short years ago, as I sat there lamenting everything with Bill and being a victim in my life," said John.

"You've come a long way," said Jaq.

"Well, we're ready to go further still. We're ready for bigger multi-family buildings," said John.

"Great. They're a bigger challenge, but there's such reward waiting at the end that it's well worth it. Are you ready to get straight into it?" said Jaq.

"Let's do it," said Nancy.

"Moving into larger multi-family properties is a significant change. It's a different game that requires you to play by different rules on several fronts. Yet, the fundamentals of real estate and the BFRR strategy remain the same. In fact, most successful apartment building investors do some version of the BFRR strategy," said Jaq.

"What do you mean by that?" said John.

"This is the realm of professional investors. These are people who understand that if you *can* add value to an asset, it means you *must* add value to it. You've already been doing the same thing on a smaller scale, which makes you uniquely prepared to move into bigger apartments," said Jaq.

"That's what we thought, but we were wondering if it's a lot harder to find a good deal," said Nancy.

"When a good deal comes up the competition can be stiff. You might do fewer deals, but because you're adding multiple units each time you purchase a property, you don't need to do as many deals. It's worth being patient and taking your time with multi-family buildings," said Jaq.

"I can see that, but you mentioned a lot of competition. With smaller properties I always liked to have an inside line and be the only one negotiating with a seller. Are you saying this won't be possible with larger multi-family properties?" said John.

"It's often more competitive, but this just means you negotiate differently. The first principle is to get a property under contract as soon as possible. If you don't, another pro will, and chances are you won't get another chance on that property. Make your offer quickly, and remember that you can re-negotiate as you find out more about the property," said Jaq.

"I've been doing that for years already on smaller other deals. That's what the inspection is for," said John.

"Absolutely, but the due diligence period with larger multi-family properties is even more important than it is with smaller properties. This is because there is more at stake and greater risk. I recommend getting 30 to 60 days due diligence as a condition on any multi-family offer," said Jaq.

"That seems like a long time. I'm used to a week or two," said John

"I know, but it's impossible to complete the due diligence on a multi-family property in a week. Not only that, but you often need time to secure funds to put the deal together," said Jaq.

"That should not be a problem for us. We have money waiting," said Nancy.

"It's one thing having investors ready, but having all the money secure is another matter," said Jaq.

"We have many investors that would love to invest with us, but not many of them would have enough available to do a bigger deal like this on their own," said Nancy.

"That's what I'm talking about. You might have to put 3 or 4 investors together to do a deal. It's one reason why you need a longer due diligence period," said Jaq.

"Right. What are the other reasons due diligence would take so much longer than with a small multi-family property," said John.

"First, when you're shopping for a multi-family property the seller will provide you with *the financials*, and you use that as part of your basis for moving forward with the purchase of the property. However, it's not wise to take the financial numbers provided by the seller as the gospel truth. Of all the multi-family buildings I've purchased or analyzed, I've never once seen a perfectly accurate set of financials," said Jaq.

"How do you make sure you're getting the right numbers then?" said John.

"*You have to investigate every single income and expense claim.* Some of them are easy to verify, but some take work to find answers to. You can't skip this process or even do a lazy job of it. The stakes are too high. If you're off on a utilities bill estimate on a small building, it might mean the difference of $50 or so, but on a big building it might be thousands of dollars per month difference, which alters the bottom line," said Jaq.

"Right, so doing the numbers in detail is vital. No wonder due diligence takes so long. What else is there?" said John.

"Another aspect is the *building due diligence.* When doing a home inspection on a small property you always want to bring in your home inspector to find problems with a property, and that's an option with a larger multi-family property, too. However, I find it's much better to not hire a building inspector for a couple of reason. First, the building inspection is quite expensive on larger multi-family buildings," said Jaq.

"Wait, are you telling me you don't inspect a multi-family building?" said John.

"No, we actually do a more thorough inspection than a building inspector can do. You see, a building inspector is a generalist, and they will look at all the major components of a building. If they have doubt about a building component, they write on their inspection report to see a specialist," said Jaq.

"Sounds reasonable," said Nancy.

"It's reasonable but not effective. You end up with an expensive report telling you to get a bunch of specialists to come through and check all the areas of the property. This report doesn't give you specific costs to repair or even specific recommendations," said Jaq.

"Right, but we need specifics in order to move forward with a purchase," said Nancy.

"That's right, and there are two choices. You can hire an inspector then bring in specialists, or you can go direct to the specialists. A lot of professional BFRR investors skip the building inspector and go straight to the specialists, said Jaq.

"Okay," said John.

"There are other benefits, too. When you bring in specialists immediately, you can also get quotes from them on fixing each problem. Oh, and I don't just bring in one specialist for each component of the property. I bring in 2 or 3 roofing specialists, 2 or 3 HVAC specialists, and so on. The property is a beehive of activity during the due diligence period," said Jaq.

"That makes sense. I guess you want serious proof when you come back to the bargaining table," said John.

"Bingo. How is an investor supposed to get a good sense of the purchase price for a building if they don't have a good sense of the renovations that will be required after purchase? Just as your property inspection helps you get a better deal on a smaller property, you will use the quotes from all of your specialists to do the same on a larger multi-family building," said Jaq.

"Right, so what else is involved in due diligence?" said John.

"Another big difference between larger multi-family and single-family or small multi-family is *financing*. Buyers have to qualify for a mortgage on properties with fewer than 4 units, but when the property is 4 or more units, it's the building that qualifies rather than the buyer," said Jaq.

"So, does that eliminate the problem of bank's lending limitations?" said Nancy.

"Well, it means you're now playing by different rules. On one hand, it's fantastic because you no longer have to go through the process of qualifying an individual's income, but on the other hand it means the bank is quite stringent about the building," said Jaq.

"What do you mean?" said John.

"Banks don't want to own real estate. They qualify individuals on residential properties because they need proof the person could pay if something went wrong. With a commercial building they want assurance that nothing will cause the building to stop earning an income. In essence, they qualify the building instead of the buyer," said Jaq.

"Right, that's reasonable. So, are you saying the requirements to qualify a commercial building might be harder than qualifying a person on a residential purchase?" said Nancy.

"In some cases, yes. One of the requirements is to get a phase 1 environmental report. Banks won't advance funds until this is done. This is a minimum requirement and usually costs the buyer about $3,000. Multi-family buyers have to spend that money knowing full well it might result in not buying the building," said Jaq.

"That seems like a reasonable risk for the potentially huge reward," said John.

"It is, but it sometimes gets more expensive. If there is anything in the phase 1 environmental report that the bank doesn't like, they may request a phase 2 report. These typically cost $10,000 or more," said Jaq.

"Yikes. I'd hate to spend that and then not buy the property," said John.

"Exactly, that's why a lot of successful BFRR investors go back to the seller and negotiate for them to pay for all or part of the phase 2. Sometimes you get it, sometimes you don't. Either way the stakes are higher, and you don't get the 10 grand back," said Jaq.

"Bigger reward, bigger stakes," said Nancy.

"Here's the kicker: if the phase 2 report makes any recommendations to remediate environmental issues you have to either pull out of the deal, pay to fix what the report suggests, or negotiate with the seller to comply with the environmental requests," said Jaq.

"Right, and negotiating that could take time. I think I'm starting to see why 60 days is a good condition period," said John.

"You need it. Multi-family is costlier and riskier, so you need to do your due diligence, as will the bank. They won't lend until their own due diligence requirements are met," said Jaq.

"Are there any other expenses we wouldn't see on small multi-family deals?" said John.

"Sure. *Mortgage application fees* are one. The investor pays to apply for a mortgage on a commercial property. With small properties, the bank pays mortgage brokers, but on commercial mortgages it's the investors have to pay," said Jaq.

"I've heard that, but doesn't the investor only pay when they actually get the mortgage?" said Nancy.

"No. It might seem crazy, but due to the amount of work required on each commercial deal, the mortgage broker needs to know you're serious and needs to know they will be reimbursed even if the deal falls through, hence the application fee," said Jaq.

"I understand that. The stakes are higher and they need to protect themselves. Any other big expenses?" said John.

"Yes. Whereas you might be able to get by managing your own properties on single family or small multi-family, it's highly recommended to *use professional property management* on larger multi-family buildings," said Jaq.

"I understand that from an efficiency point of view, but I suspect this isn't the reason you have in mind," said Nancy.

"That's correct. When you step into the commercial realm there is a new world of regulations involved. Only an expert property manager can navigate these regulations," said Jaq.

"Aren't their fees exorbitant?" said John.

"If it's a building around 20-units or so, you can expect to pay between 3% and 10% of the gross rent collected on management. If there isn't enough income on the property to pay for professional property management, you should not buy the building. It's as simple as that. From this day forward as you move into larger multi-family buildings, you must always include professional management in your expense calculations," said Jaq.

"I guess I'll get used to spending that kind of money eventually," said Nancy.

"Try not to think of it as spending money. A good property management company should actually save you money because they can get discounts on labor and material. In addition, their fees may be tax deductible. Ask yourself what is your time worth? Good management is money well spent. If you were to do it yourself, you'd likely never buy another building again. You would become the bottleneck in your own business," said Jaq.

"Anything else?" said John.

"Just remember that you need deeper pockets and that everything takes longer. Otherwise, it's still real estate and it's still the BFRR strategy. You have to know your ARV, and you have to plan for a longer renovation period. There won't be any 2-week turnarounds on a multi-family project. More often than not, you should plan a year or more to get the renovations all complete," said Jaq.

"Great, thanks for this. I think I can handle it, and we're ready to make the move. The next time we all speak, Nancy and I may be the owners of a larger multi-family building," said John.

"I don't doubt it. You're both excellent at meeting new challenges. Best of luck," said Jaq.

They parted company once again and John and Nancy started searching for a larger multi-family building.

Putting the Deal Together

John and Nancy dove in with both feet as usual. They knew it was a different task than finding a single-family or even a small multi-family building, but they were undaunted.

John found it frustrating to know other experienced multi-family building buyers were always ready to pounce on a good deal. This removed some of the advantage John had built up during their single and small multi-family career.

He was expert at seeking out deals that hadn't yet been listed with a real estate agent, and even properties listed weren't often coveted by other professionals. So, competing with true professionals on every deal was frustrating. Still, he remained patient and stuck with the process.

Before long a good-looking deal on a 17-unit apartment building came across John's desk. Knowing the potential, he moved quickly, and within 5 minutes he was on the phone with the realtor.

John asked the realtor if he could come see the property the same day. The agent was hesitant, as he was being inundated with calls about the property. John pushed for it, though, and the realtor relented. John canceled a couple of other commitments and found himself in the property within 3 hours of seeing the listing email.

Getting in quickly was a major coup for John, as it gave him the negotiations jump on other hungry investors. He knew from doing his advanced research that this property had potential.

The Numbers – Part 1

List price: $799,900

Comparables: $1,500,000 to $1,700,000

Potential Value Lift: $700,000 to $900,000

As you can imagine, this deal attracted much attention from other multi-family investors. This kind of equity upside brings a pro real estate investor out of their seat the way a homerun does for a baseball fan. John and Nancy had hit plenty of singles, but this looked like it could be their first legitimate homerun.

Over the previous few months, John had been thwarted several times while looking for multi-family buildings. Often the properties he was interested in were under contract before he could even see them. Not this time.

His suspicion about the level of competition for this property was confirmed when viewing the property, as the real estate agent's phone rang a dozen times during the hour long showing. John heard the realtor book viewing appointments for that evening and the entire next day. He knew if he wanted the property he'd have to act quickly, decisively, and come in with a strong offer.

During his viewing, he noticed the property needed a lot of work, but that the cost to do the renovations wouldn't come near the amount of equity that would be created by doing the renovations, since rents could be dramatically raised with renovations.

He liked this standard of value lift rather than the emotional standard often found in the single-family realm. There is no 'emotional lift' built into the value of multi-family buildings.

Hardscrabble multi-family investors aren't prone to getting excited about the color of the kitchen cabinets or Feng Shui. They don't often pay more than market value based on a property's income and market acceptable CAP rates, therefore the only way to force up the value of a multi-family building is to improve the property's income.

Cap Rate

Capitalization rate – more commonly referred to as "Cap Rate" – is a key formula to understand when evaluating real estate from the perspective of an investor looking for income properties. The Cap Rate helps you determine how long it will take for your investment to pay for itself. CAP Rate is often used by realtors when marketing investment properties.

The formula is as follows: Annual net operating income divided by purchase price/cost.[16]

---

16   Source: http://www.fredhelps.com/secrets/investment-cap-rates-explained

Sometimes improving the management of the building is enough to lift overall rental income. Perhaps the building isn't in bad shape, and filling vacancies is just a matter of more aggressive marketing or cleaning up the curb appeal of the building.

In other circumstances, the building charges rock bottom rent because the property is run down. As the renovation for each unit is completed, it can be rented for more money. Over time, a building's rent roll is raised dramatically by renovations. John knew this would be his strategy on the 17-unit building.

By comparing the values of well-maintained properties in his target region, John knew the 17-unit building was a great opportunity. With a list price of $700,000 to $900,000 below the going market rate for a well-maintained property, it was clear this property required *both* renovations and better management (let's face it, the two go hand-in-hand).

As John kept digging the true picture became clearer. The realtor explained that only 5 of the 17 units were rented. This explained the rock bottom list price, as the rent roll was a fraction of its potential.

The property was run-down and ugly. This was the main reason for the lack of renters, but the poor rental situation was also partially explained by tired management.

The owners had self-managed the property and were fatigued. They didn't love real estate, nor did they have working property management systems. As a result, they were now selling the property at a much lower price than they could have fetched if the property was well cared for and managed.

On his initial viewing of the property, John saw several ways he could add value and attract new tenants.

The Renovation Plan

1. Change the suite mix from five 1-bedroom and twelve 2-bedroom units to three 1-bedroom, four 2-bedroom, & ten 3-bedroom units.

2. Complete all the plumbing that was started by the original owner

3. Bring building up to fire code

4. Add new windows where necessary

5. New tile in entry

6. Expand laundry facilities and increase laundry cost

7. Paint

8. Improve curb appeal

9. Add new kitchens in each unit – including new fridge and stove

10 Install security cameras

11. Paid parking stalls

12. Raise tenant profile with professional management

On his initial inspection, John didn't see any major deal-breaking expenses. He saw that most of the renovations would be equity building cosmetic renovations like shiny new kitchens, paint, and tiling.

In addition, he saw an opportunity to do psychologically important improvements like adding security cameras and charging for and enforcing parking.

The parking problem was a unique improvement opportunity John planned based on something the realtor mentioned. He said building residents often complained about other people using the parking lot. The tired landlords didn't or couldn't spend any effort solving or minimizing this problem.

John knew that by cleaning up the parking lot, charging for parking spots, and monitoring and towing rule-breakers he could improve the feel of the building for tenants. This kind of simple and creative 'upgrade' got John excited to do the deal.

He moved quickly.

The Numbers Part 2

Accepted Offer: $825,000

John knew the property would attract several offers. Therefore, to have a shot at it, he and Nancy crafted an above list price offer. The list price was $799,900, and although John was accustomed to getting discounts off list, he also knew what a smoking hot deal this 17-unit building was.

However, John knew there would be more opportunity to negotiate later, and he knew the current owners had run out of money and would be excited by extra cash. He knew it would give him a better chance at getting the deal ahead of the other hungry investors.

Yet, he hadn't given up on price. He still had the inspection process, which was often an excellent chance to drive down the purchase price. He planned to use the inspection to dig up problems and use them as leverage to negotiate a better deal.

John and Nancy always used the inspection this way, but this time the process was different. As Jaq suggested, they brought in a team of specialists instead of relying on a generalist inspector. To get it all done, they had to move quickly during the 30-day inspection period.

It was a busy scene on inspection day. John and Nancy brought in a multi-family roofing specialist, an HVAC specialist, a foundation specialist, and a whole army of other contractors. Each of the contractors had agreed to provide a quote within a week so John and Nancy would be armed with sufficient evidence to re-open negotiations.

The specialists did what specialists do best – find ways they could possibly charge for work. When your life's work is to replace boiler systems, every boiler looks like a boiler that should be replaced or at least serviced. This was exactly what John and Nancy wanted, and they planned to use their specialists as evidence to renegotiate.

Each specialist provided a quote for work that would need to be done soon, but based on direct conversations with his team of specialists, John knew much of it could wait. There was a difference between what *could* be done and what *needed* to be done.

However, John and Nancy knew most of the bigger, non-cosmetic renovations could wait for 5 years. This would be enough time to improve the building, raise cash flow, and therefore raise the value. In 5 years they'd have the option to wrap the big renovations into a refinance or pay for them with cash flow.

In the meantime, their plan was to do only the cosmetic work, bring in tenants, and raise the rent roll. This was their plan, but the sellers didn't need to know that.

They just needed to know that John and Nancy were going to be stuck making big repairs to major building components. Using the quotes as leverage, John and Nancy went back to the seller and asked for a significant discount. They got the discount, but it was only one part of the puzzle.

The Numbers Part 3

Final Closing Price (after renegotiating): $740,000

Discount Off Purchase Price: $85,000

Assumed 1st Mortgage (from existing remaining mortgage from the seller): $450,000

Vendor Take Back: $150,000

Down payment: $140,000

Renovations: $160,000

Multi-family buildings often come with opportunities for creative financing. This one was no different, and John and Nancy used all the creativity they had to reach the financing solution on this property.

The first piece of that puzzle was the existing 1st mortgage on the property for $450,000, which amounted to more than 60% of the eventual sale price.

Securing this (through a mortgage assumption) was a coup. It meant they only had to come up with an additional $290,000 to purchase the property.

John and Nancy wanted to get as much of the remaining $290,000 covered without having to dig into existing cash, so they proposed the sellers carry a Vendor Take Back mortgage. Sadly, the sellers didn't accept their first proposal, but they did agree to carry a $150,000 VTB using the same terms as the assumed mortgage.

All told, $600,000 of the $740,000 purchase price would be financed at 4.5%. The icing on top was that John and Nancy wouldn't have to make any payments on the Vendor Take Back until the mortgage term ended 13 months later, when it would all be due as a balloon payment.

John and Nancy still required a total of $140,000 for the down payment and another $160,000 for renovations. The renovations would cost more than $160,000, but this number was what they needed to get the renovations started. As the units filled up, they'd be able to fund the late round of renovations with the money from the cash flow.

They expected it would take the entire 13 months (until the mortgage term ended) to get the property renovated, new tenants in, the rent roll raised, and the value bumped up. At that point, they planned on refinancing the property to pay out existing debts on the property.

They had a significant pool of investor's money to draw upon for this deal and they wanted to make some money for their investors, but the deal was so fantastic they also wanted to keep it for themselves.

This grand slam would set them up for life.

They needed $300,000 of cash to cover the down payment and renovation expense ($140,000 for down payment and $160,000 for renovations), so using investor money was required.

So, how were they going to manage to keep sole ownership?

The solution was to borrow $300,000 in private funds to cover the down payment and renovations. This way, they could help their investors earn a strong return, yet they'd maintain total ownership.

John and Nancy borrowed the entire $300,000 secured against equity they had in other properties. They borrowed at 10%, which would result in $30,000 or more of holding costs over 13 months.

This additional cost added to the risk on the property, but the upside of solely owning this building was worth it. The property was a game changer and would put them in the upper echelon of investors.

Carrying Through

Putting together the deal was a huge task and required immense skill from John and Nancy. The confidence they'd built up over the years of single-family and small multi-family investing helped them to put the deal together, but it took pure fortitude to carry out the plan over the next 13 months.

It's one thing to do a quick turnaround deal with smaller numbers with a refinance after a month. It takes a higher level of gumption to do a deal with much big numbers over a much longer time horizon.

Still, it was worth it and they were ready for the challenge. Spending $740,000 to purchase the property, then adding $160,000 to renovate and another $30,000 of holding costs would still leave them with around $500,000 of available equity depending on the eventual appraisal and financing.

Much of that would have to stay in the property after refinancing, but if they were able to secure a mortgage for 70% (of the predicted ARV of $1,500,000) they'd be able to pay off all the financing and still take more than $100,000 of cash for themselves.

Cash flow was negative when John and Nancy acquired the building, but they threw labour and resources at the property from the moment they took possession and were able to get the 12 vacant units renovated within three months. This effort ate up the entire $160,000 of financed money they'd earmarked for renovations.

The leases on the remaining 5 units were all due to expire over the course of the next 8 months, and the plan was to replace them all when their leases were up.

The tenants in these units were bottom-feeders, and none of them were interested in staying around with raised rents. When John and Nancy made it clear to them the building was changing and their rents would be going up, none of them renewed their leases.

The tensest part of the process was trying to get the building leased up during the holding period before refinance. It only took 3 months to renovate the original 12 vacant units, but it took much longer to get those units all re-rented.

The building needed 10 units to be occupied before it would generate positive cash flow. Naturally, John and Nancy were eager to get the building leased up, but it was a precarious situation, as renting to the wrong tenants could be a major setback. They had to be choosy about the tenants they selected, and they were battling against the building's poor reputation from the previous owners.

It was an uphill battle and a huge relief when the 10th unit was leased 6 months after purchasing the building. One month later (7th month of ownership) 12 units were leased and the monthly cash flow for renovating started piling up. By the 11th month all of the units were renovated, and finally on the 12th month of ownership (one month before the planned refinance) the last unit was rented.

John and Nancy were cool through it all, but it would be a lie to suggest they weren't feeling pressure as the months went by. Their goal was to have every unit full and the rent roll up raised in time for refinance at the end of month 13. They were thrilled when it happened and the refinance appraisal came in at $1,500,000 as predicted.

This meant they received a mortgage of $1,050,000 (70% of $1,500,000). John and Nancy paid out every expense generated during the renovation period and were rewarded with $120,000 of cash and a property that would provide them with over $60,000 of cash flow annually!

Simply amazing.

The Numbers Part 4 – How the Cookie Crumbled

Appraised Value: $1,500,000

Purchase/Closing/Holding/Renovations: $930,000

Forced Equity (After paid all expenses): $570,000

Refinance Mortgage Amount at 70% Loan to Value: $1,050,000

Income: $167,400 (Rent, Laundry, and Parking)

Property Tax: $ 18,100

Insurance: $3,500

Gas: $4,046

Hydro: $2,009

Water: $3,927

Maintenance/Management/Vacancy (15% of gross rent): $23,265

Laundry Rental: $1,200

Mortgage: $43,785 (25-year amortization at 4.75% interest)

Cash Flow: $67,568 ($5,630 monthly)

A True Homerun

As John and Nancy reflected on the incredible deal over a relaxed dinner and a glass of wine, they recalled a conversation they had with Jaq a long time before.

"Remember when Jaq said the real estate game is won by singles but that home runs come along every now and then?" said Nancy.

"I sure do. I didn't know what a homerun would feel like at the time. Does it ever feel good!" said John.

"It feels incredible, but after hitting one, I have a new respect for homerun hitters and real estate investors. It takes a lot of groundwork, practice, and effort to get good enough to hit a homerun," said Nancy.

"Amen," said John.

The two sat reflectively drifting off into their own thoughts. If their single-family and small multi-family efforts had secured their financial future and brought them a steady supply of investment capital, this first multi-family building put them in rarified company.

With thousands of dollars of cash flow each month they were now in the tiny fraction of people on earth whose wealth would grow significantly each and every month regardless if they never worked another day in their life.

It was a game changing investment and it was only their first big multi-family purchase. The realization of what they'd done slowly settled in, but it didn't come without some question marks, too.

Most people settle themselves to the fact that they'll have to work for a living for the rest of their lives. They're never faced with that question of what else they might do with their lives once they reach a point of not having to work anymore.

"This feels weird," said Nancy.

"I was just thinking the same thing. I mean. I always knew this was theoretically possible, but now it's real. What are we going to do?" said John.

"It's a new challenge. That's for sure, but as for what we're going to do, I don't know. I suggest we take some time to let it settle in before making any decisions," said Nancy.

"I don't think we have any other choice," said John.

The two laughed, toasted their future, and shared enormous pride about what they'd accomplished.

Homerun Hitting to Higher Causes

In this chapter, we saw how an excellent multi-family investment can be a true real estate homerun and how such a homerun can be a life changing investment.

Many BFRR investors start out in the game seeking riches, but very few consider what they will do once they acquire such riches. The next chapter will explore some of the new problems that arise once BFRR success is achieved.

Read on to learn about the new set of challenges faced by John and Nancy as they step into the next phase of their BFRR (and life) journey.

"Be the change you want to see in the world."

_____

Mahatma Gandhi

CHAPTER 13

Paying it Forward

Highest Calling

Have you ever considered what your highest calling is? What would you love to do if money wasn't an obstacle?

A lot of people dream of this scenario, but not everyone has the chance to really find out. This entire book has been dedicated to teaching and demonstrating how to get to riches, but this chapter focuses on the new set of problems that arise when a person is actually faced with the opportunity to do anything.

Although this might seem like a distant problem, this is an important consideration, as understanding your long term vision can be the best driver to get through the difficulties of the journey.

Pride and Giving Back

One chilly February evening, John attended a local Cashflowsville Real Estate Investment Club meeting. Rather than just go to the meeting and head home after, he decided to get together with Jaq after to discuss the future.

After 5 years using the BFRR strategy, John and Nancy had advanced their finances and their lives further than they could have imagined. From being fearful of being able to comfortably retire they now had the option of retiring early.

John was happy continuing to add properties to his portfolio here and there, but he no longer felt like he needed to, which put him at a crossroads. He was wondering if there was another level he should seek as an investor and wanted to hear Jaq's wisdom on the topic.

As the meeting wrapped up, the two went to a local pub to solve all the world's problems. They found a comfortable place to sit, ordered some drinks and food, and started chatting.

"What's on your mind, John?" said Jaq.

"Jaq, you've seen our progress over the last 5 years. You know how far we've come, and we owe a lot of that to you. I'm not one to rest on my laurels, but I feel comfortable calling myself an expert real estate investor now. Heck, by most people's standards, I've been an expert real estate investor for a few years already," said John.

"Your success has been remarkable, but please don't give me too much credit. The hard work was all you. The potential was already within you. I gave you some good information, but you went out and made it happen. Furthermore, you made the decision to work with a coach, which you should be commended for. Most people never take that step and therefore don't reach the success you have," said Jaq.

"Thank you for those kind words. Here's the deal, though. I'm 40 years old, which is far too young to retire and sit on a beach somewhere. Don't get me wrong the beach is great. Nancy and I like to spend at least a month in the Caribbean every year, and we'll continue to do that over time.

However, I need to put my energy into something, and after a month on the beach I'm raring to go again. I could continue to buy properties for the next 20 or 30 years and grow the portfolio indefinitely, or I could spend a few years turning all of our singles and small multi-family properties into larger multi-family properties, or I could do both, but I'm not yet sure if that's what I want to do," said John.

"One thing's for sure, you sure have a better class of problems than you used to. Let me ask you something. How much effort does your portfolio take you now?" said Jaq.

"We've gotten pretty good at property management over the years, and we have an outstanding real estate team. Our multi-family building is professionally managed, but we still manage our single-family and small multi-family properties. It's not too difficult, but I don't think I want to keep managing them forever," said John

"That's probably a good idea. It sounds like you could spend some time converting your entire portfolio into larger multi-family, or you could bring in an in-house property manager for you entire portfolio, or you could hire a third-party property management company to manage your entire portfolio. You have some analysis to do here. I know you don't like selling, so I'm sure the prospect of selling a bunch of properties and turning your portfolio into multi-family buildings isn't too appealing for that reason," said Jaq.

"That's true. The cost of selling and re-buying isn't appealing to me. Like you said, it's a better class of problem these days. The way I see it, my biggest question is how aggressively I should keep expanding. One way or another, management of the whole portfolio will be outsourced soon, whether we keep holding the smaller properties or convert them," said John.

"Well, I'd say only you and Nancy can answer the question of how much more you want to keep expanding. It depends on your goals. What is your gut telling you?" said Jaq.

"I think if we add one multi-family building every year it will be plenty, and that's just for now. We may scale that back in the future, or if the kids show an interest in moving into the business, we may ramp it up. Either way we have the infrastructure in place to continue," said John.

"It sounds like you know exactly what you want to do, John. So, what are we really talking about here?" said Jaq.

"Ha! You're perceptive," said John.

"I hope so. This is what I do," said Jaq.

"It's just... I feel like there's *something else*. Making money is fantastic, and I will cherish all the money we have made and will continue to make for. I always pictured myself working like a dog until the normal retirement at 65 or even later," said John.

"Most can't imagine anything more," said Jaq.

"This is what's messing me up. I haven't given this much serious thought. Sure, I've dreamed, but when it's real, it's different. I want to do something more meaningful, but what?" said John.

"That's natural. It's called coming full circle. You're looking to give back to the world that gave you so much, and now you're in a position to do it," said Jaq.

"That's exactly it. Nancy and I have even had some crazy ideas, like moving overseas and volunteering at an orphanage once the girls grow up," said John.

"That doesn't sound crazy. Only you and Nancy will know what's the right fit for you, but how cool is it that you have the option and that you're looking to give back?" said Jaq.

"It's great, and I'm sure we'll find the right fit, but what about you? I mean, you were in a similar position 5 years ago. Did you have the same feeling? Were you looking to do something different once real estate reached a certain point?" said John.

"You're looking at it. When I met you 5 years ago, I was in a similar position. I was wondering how much I should continue buying, how much I wanted to expand my portfolio, and what I should do with my time. I'm still expanding my portfolio to this day, albeit slowly, and I'll continue to as time goes on, but like you it's more on autopilot than it once was. Mentoring new BFRR investors has been my way to give back over the past few years," said Jaq.

"Well, it's a valuable role. You've helped transform our life and the lives of our investors," said John.

"Listen, you'll figure out what the next phase looks like, but let's not forget how different this conversation is than the conversation you were having with Bill in the Equity Café 5 years ago. At that time you had an attitude of despair rather than confidence. That's the remarkable thing about the BFRR strategy and the power of real estate. Whatever you do from here on will be amazing, since you're in the right state of mind now," said Jaq.

As always, Jaq helped provide John with the clarity he was looking for. As the night went on, they reminisced about John's real estate adventures and how far he'd come. The conversation opened John's eyes further and he left with renewed vigor.

Cleaning Up

John and Nancy decided to spend the next couple years streamlining their business, which for them meant getting all of their units under professional property management rather than doing it themselves.

They were pragmatic about how they should handle their properties going forward. They didn't like selling, so they avoided it as much as they could, but on some occasions it was the best option as their joint venture partner wanted to cash out of the property and a buy-out wasn't possible. They used some of that money to buy-out other JV partners.

They used some of their own cash, but mostly investor cash to purchase multi-family buildings over the next few years while continuing to streamline the business for the future.

In the mean time, John continued to think about how he wanted to give back. Should they just build up wealth and give back monetary gifts to the community? Should he volunteer at the orphanage? Should he start a whole different business and go through the same process again? He was young enough to do anything. His mind was filled with ideas every day.

John's Full Circle Moment

John had a lot more freedom these days. He continued to work at his job but had negotiated a three-day workweek and promotion with his boss a few years prior. He still enjoyed it, but he knew he'd quit once something better came up.

For several years, John used all this spare time on his real estate business. In fact, that was the original reason for asking his boss for a three-day workweek.

However, as he and Nancy were no longer growing their portfolio as aggressively and since things were more streamlined with less daily responsibility on him, John found himself spending more of his afternoons golfing or sitting in the Equity Café reading.

He was sipping on a chai pumpkin spice latte and reading a newspaper one day when he overheard two friends having a serious conversation.

"I don't know, Frank. I've put my heart and soul into this company, but I don't feel I'm any further ahead at the age of 35 than I did when I started there as a fresh-faced recruit," said the first friend.

"I hear you, Tom. I often wonder when I'm going to get off this treadmill. I mean, things are going along well, but it's not like my mutual funds have been setting the world on fire. Retirement is scary, and I don't see any way I can pay for my kids education," said Frank.

John listened as the friends went on about their problems for 45 minutes. His mind went back to that day five years ago, when he sat across from Bill going over an eerily similar set of problems.

John tried not to be obvious, but he listened to everything the two friends were saying, and at times almost stepped in. The answers were so obvious. Then he remembered that they weren't so obvious. They were only obvious to him because he'd been in the trenches, fought the battles, and now he was sitting on the other side.

"I like my real estate. It makes me feel safe knowing it will be there as I retire, and I'd like to buy another property, but with the ongoing repairs it can be a pain in the butt. I'm not a fan of fixing things. Oh well, at least my real estate is better than mutual funds," said Tom

It was as though John was in some strange twilight zone. Here were two friends having the exact same conversation he once had – in the exact same place. The only difference was that the characters had changed. He started to sense that this was a life-changing moment, for both him and Tom.

Something stirred inside him. It was different than the thought of living on the beach, working at an orphanage, or volunteering at a soup kitchen. He knew he could make a big difference here.

He hadn't felt this excited in a long while. In an instant he knew his personal struggle was over. He *needed* to help people like Tom. He was now a holder of the knowledge rather than a fresh-faced recruit. John remembered his own despair so vividly as he listened.

Others needed him.

Success hadn't made him complacent by any means, but it was easy for him to forget the level of despair he felt 5 years earlier before he'd pulled off a complex multi-family deal, before he'd done a bunch of momentum building small multi-family deals, before he'd added over $1 million dollars of assets to his portfolio during the initial 2 years of investing in single family deals, before he even believed he could manage a small renovation on a townhouse.

John was snapped out of his daydream by what he heard next.

"Listen, I have to go. I'll catch you next Sunday for football, right?" said Frank.

"Yep, see you then," said Tom.

Frank walked out the door, but Tom remained sitting alone, looking despondent. Without thought, John put down his newspaper, stood up, and walked over to the table by the window where Tom was sitting.

"Hi. Sorry to bother you, but I couldn't help but overhear your conversation. My name is John. Do you have a few minutes to chat?" said John.

Tom looked stunned, "Um, yeah sure. Have a seat," he said.

Author Biography – Quentin D'Souza

Quentin D'Souza is a highly respected multiple award winning Real Estate Investor in the Ontario Real Estate Investing community. He has appeared in, and been quoted in, many different real estate publications and books.

Quentin is a trusted authority on the Durham Real Estate Market and has worked with and mentored thousands of Real Estate Investors through the Durham Real Estate Investor Club (www.DurhamREI.ca) since 2008.

Quentin is also the author of *The Property Management Toolbox: A How-To Guide for Ontario Real Estate Investors and Landlords"* (www.TheOntarioLandlordToolbox.ca), which is a comprehensive guide for getting a real estate business going.

Quentin manages a large real estate portfolio and works with other investors using joint ventures through his company Appleridge Homes (www.AppleridgeHomes. ca).

Quentin can often be found at one of his two sons' sports events or activities.

To learn more about Quentin go to www. AppleridgeHomes.ca.

Follow Quentin on Twitter @qmanrei

Connect with Quentin on Facebook www.facebook. com/qdsouza

Author Biography – Jeff Woods

 Jeff is an award winning real estate investor, entrepreneur, business owner, real estate based wealth coach, speaker, work shop leader, author, and highly sought after educator. In other words, he's a busy and in demand real estate expert.

However, it was not always that way. Jeff came from humble beginnings and has overcome a great deal of adversity. Using this adversity to fuel passion, Jeff helps others create financial freedom so they gain the power and ability to live life on their own terms.

Today, Jeff owns more than 150 rental units (residential and commercial) throughout Ontario and Central America. Jeff manages many millions worth of real estate and most recently has developed an educational arm of his business.

To learn more about Jeff Woods go to <u>www.wamproperties.com</u> and <u>www.correctactionrealestate.com</u>

Follow Jeff on Twitter @Jwoods18

Connect with Jeff on Facebook www.facebook.com/WAM.Properties

Author Biography – Andrew Brennan

Andrew Brennan is a multiple award winning investor and skilled renovator. He has offered his experience to others through television, radio, public appearances and in print.

Andrew owns a large real estate portfolio in the Barrie, Ontario area. He specializes in working with joint venture partners to offer hands off investment opportunities through his company *Brennan Property Investments*.

To connect with Andrew Brennan visit www. BPIrealestate.ca

CPSIA information can be obtained at www.ICGtesting.com
Printed in the USA
BVOW02s2153230315

392987BV00012B/62/P